What people are saying about …

EMBODIED

"The history has not always been good between people of faith and those who identify as transgender. This history, combined with a desire for much better, is what makes voices like Preston's so essential for the times in which we live. Preston has this wonderful, Jesus-like way of flexing the muscles of conviction and compassion, of truth and grace, of law and love, of empathy and human design, all at the same time. As he does this, he not only finds the way but shows the way to befriend, empathize with, and come alongside those whom Jesus has called us to love. I need this book, and I suspect that you do too."

Scott Sauls, senior pastor of Christ Presbyterian Church in Nashville and author of *Jesus Outside the Line* and *A Gentle Answer*

"There are many good books written on transgender identities, but if you are looking for one book that is scientifically sound, theologically grounded, and gracious in its demeanor, *Embodied* is the book to get. Whether you are a scholar looking to understand the issue more deeply, a parent trying to help his or her transgender child, a friend wanting to better love transgender people, or someone wrestling with your own gender identity, this book will be an indispensable resource. My thanks to Sprinkle for writing and researching such an important and timely book."

> **Sean McDowell**, PhD, associate professor
> at Talbot School of Theology, speaker,
> and author of *Same-Sex Marriage*

"In *Embodied*, my friend Dr. Preston Sprinkle tenderly tackles topics most run from. He hosts the very conversations the church avoids or mishandles. This work is researched the way Preston loves ... deeply. I fought back tears as I read and found myself convicted, challenged, and equipped to love, listen, and learn. Everyone deserves to know that they are intimately woven for the love of God."

> **Lisa Bevere,** *New York Times* bestselling
> author of *Without Rival*

"Dr. Preston Sprinkle has become the go-to voice for a biblical theology of sexuality that is orthodox, intelligent, well-researched, nuanced, open-minded, yet firm in conviction, compassionate, and above all, grounded in reality. This book has more than dry data; it has compelling stories of real flesh-and-blood sexual minorities and their quest to follow Jesus in a cultural moment of ideologies and agendas. This is simply the best book I've found on the subject."

> **John Mark Comer,** pastor for teaching and
> vision at Bridgetown Church and author
> of *The Ruthless Elimination of Hurry*

"In *Embodied*, Preston Sprinkle has done the church a great service by biblically, sensitively, and pastorally navigating the transgender debate. His biblical and exegetical credibility is evident as he handles the Bible with care and precision. And his pastoral sensitivity to transgender people, which comes out of real relationships with them, enables him to provide such wise counsel for the church. Though readers might disagree with Preston in places, his approach is both biblically sound and relationally compassionate. I know of no better work on this complicated issue than *Embodied* and no one better positioned than Preston Sprinkle to write such a book."

Scott B. Rae, dean of faculty, professor
of Christian ethics, Talbot School
of Theology, Biola University

"Preston's *Embodied* is one of the first (and most comprehensive) theological looks into the trans* conversation. As a non-binary Christian I am thankful that he has offered a much-needed voice to this topic. While we do often come to different conclusions, I greatly appreciate his voice in this conversation and his sincere desire to present a holistic approach to better love and understand trans* people in our churches."

Lesli Hudson-Reynolds, gender identity
ministry director of Posture Shift

"I read Embodied in one sitting because I just couldn't put it down. Sprinkle once again handles an important conversation with honesty and authenticity, humility, wisdom, and grace. Sprinkle is careful to make this about more than theological debates. He keeps the focus on the real lives of people who deserve dignity, respect, and love. I am disappointed in myself for not knowing enough about this subject before reading *Embodied*. I am thankful for Sprinkle's extensive study and wise Christian reflections."

Nijay K. Gupta, professor of New
Testament, Northern Seminary

"As someone who follows Christ and also experiences incongruence with my gender, I have been hungry for literature that is well researched, compassionate, and practical. It is no small feat that Preston Sprinkle has achieved all three of these things in his book *Embodied*. For anyone looking to understand trans* people better, or looking for answers for themselves, I would highly recommend this book. At the very least, it serves as a wonderful primer to engage this challenging conversation thoughtfully and carefully."

Benjamin Schulke, MDiv

"In a time of confusion and pain on almost every front, Preston Sprinkle brings light and clarity to the conversation about, and the lived experiences of, trans* persons. Drawing on psychological, physiological, and biblical research, Sprinkle calls us to listen first and lead with love. *Embodied* is a must-read for anyone who wants to understand their neighbors."

Roberta Green Ahmanson, writer,
philanthropist, and art patron

EM
BOD
IED

Preston Sprinkle

EM
BOD
IED

TRANSGENDER IDENTITIES, THE CHURCH

—————— & ——————

WHAT THE BIBLE HAS TO SAY

DAVID **C** COOK

transforming lives together

EMBODIED
Published by David C Cook
4050 Lee Vance Drive
Colorado Springs, CO 80918 USA

Integrity Music Limited, a Division of David C Cook
Brighton, East Sussex BN1 2RE, England

The graphic circle C logo is a registered trademark of David C Cook.

The website addresses recommended throughout this book are offered as a
resource to you. These websites are not intended in any way to be or imply an
endorsement on the part of David C Cook, nor do we vouch for their content.

The author has added italics to Scripture quotations for emphasis.

Library of Congress Control Number 2020937663
ISBN 978-0-8307-8122-5
eISBN 978-0-8307-8123-2

The Team: Michael Covington, Judy Gillispie, James Hershberger, Susan Murdock
Cover Design: Faceout Studio, Tim Green

Printed in the United States of America
First Edition 2021

6 7 8 9 10 11 12 13 14 15

052522

For Lesli,

Mentor, friend,
and faithful servant of Christ and humanity

CONTENTS

PREFACE

The idea for this book was sparked in 2014 on a chilly October evening in East Chicago. I was bundled up outside, smoking cigars with a gay friend named Kevin. He was encouraging me to finish my book on homosexuality.

"But I'm not gay," I said. "We already have too many straight people talking about homosexuality."

"Yes," Kevin responded, "but we don't have many straight Christians talking about us the way you do. You're actually trying to *see* us as you talk *about* us. It feels like you're talking *with* us."

I sat back, choking on my stogie, and mulled over his kind words. But as I was letting those words sink in, he tossed out another, less-encouraging, comment.

"You know, Preston, by the time your book is published, the sexuality conversation will be surpassed by the gender conversation. Your book's going to be dated before it hits the shelves."

Kevin's prophecy proved to be true. In the year between my conversation with Kevin and the publication of my book (*People to Be Loved: Why Homosexuality Is Not Just an Issue*) in November 2015, transgender topics gained significant traction. Caitlyn Jenner's famed transition stirred up international attention. Hit TV shows like *Transparent* and *Orange Is the New Black* showcased transgender people, and the reality show *I Am Jazz* followed the daily life of Jazz Jennings, a well-known transgender child. Popular magazines like *National Geographic* and *Time* ran front-page articles about transgender people. Same-sex marriage was legalized in all fifty US states in June 2015, marking a significant victory for gay activists and making space for transgender rights as the "next civil rights frontier."[1] Trans* issues (I'll explain the asterisk later) have quickly become a focal point in the LGBTQ conversation.

In light of all these events, not long after I finished writing *People to Be Loved*, I turned my attention toward the trans* conversation. And once again, I found myself in over my head. When I had written *People to Be Loved*, my heart was turned inside out at the level of pain many gay people have endured in the pews of our churches. As I researched the book you now hold in your hands, I felt the same pain for trans* people. Millions of gay and trans* people have grown up in our churches, and many of them have left due to shame, ridicule, and dehumanization. "I've never met a Christian who was kind to me," I've heard far too many of them say.

But I'm not trans*, I kept thinking to myself. *What business do I have writing about trans* identities?* I've held that voice close to my heart as I've engaged the trans* conversation. No matter how hard I try to humanize this topic—no matter how many trans* people I befriend, listen to, and learn from—I will never fully understand what it's like to be trans*. There will always be a chasm between me and the people who *are* this topic.

This book is my fragile attempt to help us think more deeply and love more widely through a topic that sometimes lacks both.

Over the years, though, I've also received piles of questions from parents, pastors, Christians, and yes, even trans* people, asking me what the Bible and science say about the topic. They're not asking for me to write a memoir about the trans* experience. But they are asking me to help them think theologically and scientifically about human nature. What does it mean to be male and female? Are these the only two options? Is it okay for a male to act feminine, or a female to act masculine? Could someone be born in the wrong body or have the soul of another sex? What pronouns should I use for my trans* friend? Where should trans* people sleep at summer camp? Or, perhaps more urgently, my child just came out as trans*, and I don't know what this means or what to do, but I want to love them well and honor Jesus through it all—can you help me?

This book is my fragile attempt to help us think more deeply and love more widely through a topic that sometimes lacks both. Even though my primary audience is non-trans* Christians, I hope the book can also help trans* Christians wrestling with the relationship between their faith identity and gender identity. I've tried to create a book informed by the voices, needs, concerns, and wisdom of actual trans* people. Toward that end, I asked several trans* and intersex people to review early drafts of this manuscript. Some of their comments were encouraging; others were scathing. All of them were helpful, shaping this book into its current form. I hope that the people whose experiences I'm writing about will feel honored and seen as they read, even if they (or you, the reader) don't agree with everything I say.

Since this topic required me to study many different scholarly disciplines (neuroscience, theological anthropology, endocrinology, gender theory, and clinical psychology, among others), I had over a dozen scholars in those fields read through earlier drafts. I don't think I've ever put a book through as much scrutiny as I have with this one. Whatever mistakes, offenses, or stupidities remain are, of course, my own responsibility and not those of my readers (or my beleaguered editor).

One reader stands out in particular. This person is a friend—a mentor, really—who has held my hand through this entire conversation. They've helped me understand difficult nuances, kicked my butt when it needed kicking, and modeled for me the love of Jesus. I owe them in more ways than they know. It is to them that I dedicate this book.

Chapter 1

PEOPLE

My friend Lesli was born female. But from the time Lesli was four years old, they experienced life as a boy.[1] Lesli felt like a boy. Thought like a boy. Played like a boy. "When all of the other little girls wanted to play tea or house, I wanted to play football," Lesli told me. "At the age of four I proclaimed that Wonder Woman was going to be my wife and we would have super-powered children. I thought nothing of it."[2]

Lesli also remembers loving Jesus wholeheartedly from a very young age. "My earliest memories are of the church nursery and Sunday school. I have always known that I was a beloved child of God. I cannot remember a time when God's truth was not an integral part of my life."

Lesli's struggle increased with age, making it hard to fit in at youth group. "I started to keenly feel a distance between myself and other girls," Lesli remembers. "I could not relate to their emerging womanhood. They were spending hours putting on makeup, styling their hair, and talking about boys. None of this interested me in the least."

Like most kids wrestling with their gender identity, Lesli was wrestling alone. No one to talk to, no one to listen. Nobody seemed to care. Lesli sank into dark periods of depression. And when isolation met depression, suicidal thoughts quickly followed. "I lived this charade until high school rolled around," Lesli said, "becoming increasingly despondent and suicidal."

Finally, Lesli summoned the courage to go to the pastor for help. Lesli explained their dysphoria to him, hoping for some pastoral guidance. Instead of offering guidance, Lesli recalled, "My pastor escorted me out the back door of his office and told me to never come back again. And I didn't. I didn't step foot in a church for the next eighteen years. I hated Christians, especially pastors, from that point on."

Lesli, desperate to follow Jesus, was ushered out of the church simply for struggling with gender dysphoria.

This book is about people. Beautiful, honest, and courageous people like Lesli. And people like Carol and Stephanie.

Stephanie grew up as a stereotypically feminine girl on the autism spectrum.[3] When she was thirteen years old, she told her mother, Carol, that she was transgender. Stephanie's declaration seemed to come out of nowhere. No prior history of gender dysphoria. No tomboyish interests or behavior. Carol found out that Stephanie had just heard a presentation about being transgender at school—a school where over 5 percent of the student population identified as transgender or nonbinary.

Carol took Stephanie to a gender clinic to seek counsel. The clinician told Carol that

I must refer to my daughter with masculine pronouns, call her by a masculine name, and buy her a binder to flatten her breasts. He recommended no therapy, and there was no consideration of the social factors that obviously affected her thinking. I was directed to put her on puberty-blocking drugs.

Doctors often recommend puberty blocking drugs for pre-pubescent children wrestling with their gender identity. But we don't know a lot about the long-term health risks when kids take these drugs. From what we do know, they may have an adverse effect on a person's bones, heart, and brain.[4] Nevertheless, clinicians told Carol that puberty blockers were the best way to treat her thirteen-year-old daughter. "I was falsely assured that these drugs were well-studied and that they were a perfectly safe way for her to 'explore gender.' I was told that if I did not comply, she would be at higher risk of suicide."

Carol feared that if she pushed back or questioned the medi-calization of her child, she might lose custody of her, since such questioning could be viewed as bigotry and lack of acceptance. In New Jersey, where Carol and Stephanie lived, "the Department of Education officially encourages schools to report such parents." Still, Carol wondered, "Why are physicians medicalizing children in the name of an unproven, malleable gender identity?"

This book is about people. People like Lesli, Stephanie, and Carol. And people like Alan.

Alan grew up as a pastor's kid but couldn't wait to leave the church after he graduated high school.[5] Ever since he could remember, Alan had an unchosen desire to dress, act, and behave like a woman. He had no one to talk to, no one to guide him. And seeing the church's attitude toward LGBTQ people made him feel even more isolated and ashamed. He also grew tired of the hypocrisy in the church: "Despite being a pastor's kid, I'd become upset at the hypocrisy of Christians saying they were full of grace but not putting it into practice (especially concerning LGBTQ+ issues)."

After high school, Alan left the church. But he couldn't get away from Christians. One day, a Christian friend asked to hear Alan's story, so Alan told him everything. His desire to be a woman. His sexual attraction to men. His failures in trying to follow his own convictions about sexual ethics.

Alan expected to be condemned. To his surprise, he was loved. "Instead of the shaming and condemnation I expected, I was told that despite my past and present desires, God didn't hate me and I was lovable by others and by God." These simple words pierced his soul. Alan gave his life to Christ, all because he had the courage to share his story with a friend who received him graciously. "If I never learned about pure, undistilled grace, I would have transitioned to a female and left the church," Alan said.

> The thing that brought me to an acceptance of Biblical masculinity was not a poignantly laid-out exegetical argument against transsexuality nor a fire and brimstone diatribe against homosexuality but *a man who gave me the space to speak about my desires openly and let me know he and God loved me nevertheless.*

Alan's profound point is worth repeating: *"A man who gave me the space to speak about my desires openly and let me know that he and God loved me nevertheless."* It was love, not logic, that changed Alan's heart. People are rarely argued into the kingdom.

This book is about people. People like Lesli, Stephanie, Carol, Alan, and many others you'll meet in the coming pages. It's about Kat and Christian, about my friend Kyla, who transitioned to male eight years ago but encountered Jesus several years later and detransitioned back to female. It's about Benjamin, a pastor who has wrestled with gender dysphoria his whole life. It's about fathers whose daughters are now sons, and sons whose fathers are now mothers. It's about Matt, whose struggles with periodic anxiety only seem to diminish when he wears women's underwear. It's about my dear friend Hannah, who is one of the friendliest, most enjoyable, most biblically astute Christians I know—and who also transitioned from male to female three years ago.

PEOPLE *AND* CONCEPTS

This book is about people. A diverse group of beautiful people created in God's image. People who are often marginalized and mis-understood, shamed and shunned by those who don't share their experiences. People who are infinitely valuable in God's eyes. And it's because of people that we need to understand *concepts*: biblical, theological, scientific, medical, and philosophical concepts about human nature, male and female bodies, and what it means to live according to the image God created us to be.

There are two dangerous trends I sometimes witness in the transgender conversation. The first trend is to become a culture warrior in all things trans*. These soldiers couldn't care less about actual trans* people. Their only interest in the topic is to disprove the transgender ideologies they read about in clickbait headlines. *Women becoming men. Men becoming women. Ten thousand genders! Has everyone gone mad!?* So you read, and only read, certain tirades mocking the views of trans* activists, exposing them for being illogical and unscientific. You feel the satisfying warmth of winning an argument as you live vicariously through your favorite political pundit. Meanwhile, little do you know that the person you sit next to in church every week secretly struggles with his gender identity. It's tearing him up inside, and he has no one to talk to. He experiences church not as a hospital for saints but as a graveyard for the marginalized—and so many Christians are whistling through it.

Jesus is building an upside-down kingdom where outcasts have their feet washed, the marginalized are welcomed, and dehumanized people feel humanized once again. Where truth is upheld, celebrated, and proclaimed. Where those who fall short of that truth are loved.

A second trend is to react against the first trend and become a lover instead of a thinker. *I'm just going to love people—period.* By which some people mean, *I don't need to bother with all the theological and scientific complexities of human nature. All that stuff just callouses over your heart.* I certainly resonate with these concerns. Some theological discussions hiss with hate and pacify our love for actual people—the people who are often the subjects of our debates. But swinging the pendulum too far in the other direction—empathizing *instead of* thinking deeply—can do deep damage as well.[6] Christian economists Steve Corbett and Brian Fikkert prove this quite well in their aptly titled book *When Helping Hurts.*[7] Sometimes compassion without critical thinking can move you to do things that make a person feel good in the short run but cause harm in the long run. If I'm rushed to the ER with a severed limb and blood squirting out of my shoulder, I don't want a surgeon with empathy. I want a surgeon who excelled in medical school.

People *and* concepts. Both are important. Both are necessary. Jesus is building an upside-down kingdom where outcasts have their feet washed, the marginalized are welcomed, and dehumanized people feel humanized once again. Where truth is upheld, celebrated, and proclaimed. Where those who fall short of that truth are loved. We will be better positioned to embody the kingdom and love people well once we've understood some basic (and some quite complex) biblical, theological, and scientific concepts about what it means to be human—sexed and embodied beings who bear God's image.

THE QUESTION OF INCONGRUENCE

It's because of people that we're going to explore various conceptual questions in this book. Are male and female the only options? What about people who are intersex? Can someone be born with a male brain in a female body, or vice versa? Do men have to act masculine and women have to act feminine to be godly? Should a Christian ever transition? And which pronouns should non-transgender people use for transgender people?

We'll get to all these questions and many others. But one foundational question underlies them all. It's a question fundamental to all the others. And it's one we'll keep coming back to in the coming pages. The question is this:

> *If someone experiences incongruence between their biological sex and their internal sense of self, which one determines who they are—and why?*

For example: If a biological male feels or thinks or believes that they are a woman, are they a woman or a man? If they have an internal sense that they are female, and their body says they are male, then which one are they, and why? Is the body or mind more definitive for determining who we are?

Why would the body overrule the mind, if there's incongruence? Or why would the mind overrule the body, if there's incongruence? These aren't abstract intellectual questions akin to "how many angels can stand on the head of a pin?" They are foundational questions central to what discipleship looks like for Christians who experience such incongruence.

The question of incongruence is ultimately a question about human *ontology*. Ontology is a philosophical term that has to do with the nature of being; specifically, what does it mean to be human, especially a sexed embodied human? Ontology isn't just a fancy philosophical concept that should be locked up in the ivory towers of academia. It's fundamental for discipleship—becoming more like Christ. We need to first understand who we *are* (ontology) before we know what it means to become who God wants us to *be* (discipleship). Ontology is integral to discipleship, because discipleship means living as we were designed to live—living as divine images.

Another crucial aspect of living as we were designed to live—an aspect embodied by Jesus and demanded of all who claim to follow him—is that we would be *kind*. Embodying God's kindness (Rom. 2:4) is an essential part of Christian discipleship, especially toward those the church has shamed and shunned. Especially toward people like my friend Lesli.

WE WOULD BE HONORED TO

As you might recall, Lesli was booted out the back door of a pastor's office after going to him for help. But people need love and community. If they can't find it in the church, they'll search for it elsewhere. And that's what Lesli did. They quickly found love and acceptance among LGBTQ people, many of whom had also experienced ridicule from Christians. Lesli also fell in love with a woman named Sue, and they ended up getting married. Sue had a rare disease that caused her hands to shake. One night, she went outside for a smoke, but her hands were shaking so badly that as she was lighting her cigarette, she lit herself on fire. Lesli was inside doing the dishes when they heard Sue screaming. Running outside to see what was happening, Lesli found Sue engulfed in flames. Immediately, Sue was rushed to the hospital, but the burns were too severe. Three days later, Sue died.

The crushing blow of losing a spouse was unbearable. Half-dazed, Lesli scrambled to find a church that might be willing to do Sue's funeral. After not setting foot in a church for eighteen years, Lesli called the only church they were aware of. It was a church Sue had once volunteered at, and it happened to be one of the most conservative churches in the area. The pastor picked up the phone. Stammering, Lesli said, "Hi, my name is Lesli, and my wife just died. We're lesbians, but, um … I want to know if you would do my wife's funeral."

The pastor didn't say, "Let me think about that," or "Maybe, but you have to first know where we stand on the issue of transgenderism and the lesbian lifestyle." With compassion and conviction, the pastor said:

"We would be *honored* to."

"I'm *so sorry* for your loss," the pastor went on to say. "You must be truly grieving right now. I can't imagine what it would be like to lose a loved one. Please, Lesli, let us take care of all the details of the funeral—the cost, the arrangements, whatever you need. Please, Lesli, let us love you through your pain."

The church surrounded Lesli with love—something Lesli had never felt from Christians. Lesli had experienced such love and kindness from LGBTQ people. But not from *Christians*. And it was this simple embodiment of Christlike kindness that reignited Lesli's passion for Jesus and brought Lesli back to faith in Christ. Lesli will be hanging out with us for all eternity in the new creation, all because one pastor had the courage to manifest God's kindness.

Embodying God's kindness is an essential part
of Christian discipleship, especially toward those
the church has shamed and shunned.

Lesli is one of the most beautiful, Christlike, sacrificial people I've ever met. If I need prayer, I turn to Lesli. If I need encouragement, I FaceTime Lesli. If I need a good, solid, spiritual kick in the pants, Lesli will swing their spiritual leg in my direction. Lesli embodies the grace and truth and kindness of God more than most Christians I know. I've seen Lesli stay up until the wee hours of the night talking teenagers down from suicide. Lesli provides a listening ear when these teens have no one else to talk to, when they can find no other space in the church to say, "I feel like I was born in the wrong body, and I don't know what to do with this. I think killing myself is the only answer."

Lesli is not an issue.

Lesli is not a debate.

Lesli is literally saving people's lives.

Lesli is not just *needy,* but *needed.*

Lesli is not some interruption to our nice and easy church services, where people who think they have all their stuff together can sit around and celebrate that they have all their stuff together. Lesli is a *gift* to the church, and the church looks more like Jesus because Lesli is a part of it. Lesli isn't perfect, obviously. (Lesli *really* wanted to make sure I don't make them out to be more saintly than they really are—a concern I don't always witness from non-trans* Christian leaders.) But Lesli embodies the very kindness and truth that they received from Jesus, all because one pastor had the courage to say, *"We would be honored to love you."*

As we continue to think through questions related to trans* identities, just remember: there might be a fourteen-year-old girl in your youth group on the verge of suicide because she doesn't feel like a girl and has no one to talk to. She was created in God's image and is beloved by Jesus.

Will she be loved by you?

Chapter 2

TEN THOUSAND GENDERS

Language is essential to the transgender conversation. But trying to understand the growing number of terms in this conversation can feel like fixing a flat tire on a rolling car. We could discuss literally hundreds of terms, but spending precious mental energy on every single term would send us deep into a linguistic forest.

So we won't cover every term in this book. That's what Google is for. Still, I do want to survey some of the most important terms and phrases in the trans* conversation. And yes, I'll discuss that asterisk (*) anon. We'll spend most of our time (in the last half of this chapter) on the two most important terms in the conversation: sex and gender.

KEY TERMS

Let's start with the term that is the subject of this book: *transgender*. According to Christian psychologist Mark Yarhouse, *transgender* is "an umbrella term for the many ways in which people might experience and/or present and express (or live out) their gender identities differently from people whose sense of gender identity is congruent with their biological sex."[1] I can't stress enough the "umbrella" nature of this term; that is, it covers many different kinds of experiences. Under one corner of the umbrella might sit a male who simply doesn't feel very masculine, and they use *transgender* to describe this tension. At the other corner of the umbrella is someone who has severe gender dysphoria and feels like they've been born in the wrong body. In the next chapter, we'll explore at length the different ways the term *transgender* is used.

Similarly, the term *nonbinary* refers to a wide range of gender identities that are not exclusively male or female, or masculine or feminine. A *binary* is something that has only two options. Think of it as an either/or: black *or* white, good *or* bad, male *or* female. People who identify as nonbinary feel that these binary categories don't reflect their experience of gender. You may have also heard of terms like *genderqueer, genderfluid,* or *pangender.* These are often considered *nonbinary* identities. People use them when they don't resonate with the majority of male and female experiences.

To be clear, all non-intersex persons (and most intersex persons, as we'll see) are biologically male or female, regardless of how they identify. So if someone says they're *nonbinary* or *genderqueer* or any other term with the word *gender* in it, this doesn't typically mean they are neither male nor female biologically. It often means they don't fit into strict categories of masculinity and femininity, or that they experience some level of incongruence between their bodies and their minds. *Transgender* typically refers to a biological female who identifies as a male (or vice versa), while *nonbinary* refers to a person who identifies as neither male nor female. If you're confused, don't worry. You're not alone. It'll make more sense after we unpack sex and gender in the pages ahead.

Since so many gender identity terms can overlap with each other, some people put an asterisk after the word *trans,* stylizing it as *trans*,* when they want to use it as broad umbrella term to include a whole range of identities that aren't strictly *transgender,* such as *nonbinary, genderqueer,* and the like. I'll do the same in this book.

Gender dysphoria is a psychological term for the distress some people feel when their internal sense of self doesn't match their biological sex. It can be used as a general description of how someone feels, or more formally as a psychological diagnosis. As a diagnosis, *Gender Dysphoria* used to be called *Gender Identity Disorder,* but the name was changed to *Gender Dysphoria* in the latest edition of the *Diagnostic and Statistical Manual of Mental Disorders* (5th edition) in 2013.

The experience of dysphoria can range from mild to severe. It can come in waves or buzz steadily in the background of someone's life. It's really tough for nondysphoric people to understand how it feels, which is why it's important to listen to people who experience it. Some describe their dysphoria as:

- "… the-piercing-to-the-heart feeling when you feel like every single person in the room is staring at you. Like your heart is ripped open and they are just picking at the pieces. This may sound pretty harsh to someone who has never experienced gender dysphoria, however for me it happens in some degree almost every time I'm out in public places with people around me. It also happens before I get ready to go out, and this has become such a battle. Fighting just to leave my house and by the time I have fought for hours at a time I'm exhausted and broken.... I feel inadequate, broken, and I just want to disappear."[2]

- "... an electric current through my body that caused my joints to ache, my stomach [to] turn, my hands [to] shake, and nausea in the most severe moments of dysphoria. Laying in bed at night, it almost felt that the electric circuits in my body didn't quite match up, like cramming two wrong puzzle pieces together."[3]

- "... some creepy serum ... injected all over my body to create an odd, numb yet painful feeling coursing through my blood vessels and seeping into my flesh. My torso and limbs feel like static, and not from pins and needles. My stomach is always uneasy and my whole body is slightly tensed up, yet tired as hell from all that time being stiff."[4]

As you can imagine, people who experience gender dysphoria have a hard time hearing statements like "Feelings don't determine who you are," "It's all just in your mind," "Why did you choose to be trans?" or "You're rebelling against God." Better to sit down to listen and love a person before waxing eloquent on the nature of their experience.

Now, not everyone who identifies as transgender experiences gender dysphoria. And not everyone who experiences gender dysphoria identifies as transgender. *Gender dysphoria* and *transgender* aren't synonyms.

Transition is the term most trans* people prefer for what is sometimes called "sex change." *Transition* can include three different levels: social, hormonal, and surgical. A person who transitions socially will typically dress and act like the sex they identify with, and they might take on a new name and pronouns that match their gender identity rather than their biological sex.

Transitioning at the hormonal level means taking high levels of hormones typically produced by the opposite biological sex: those transitioning to male take testosterone, and those transitioning to female take estrogen. This hormonal intervention is called "cross-sex hormone therapy" (CHT) or "hormone replacement therapy" (HRT or HT).

Surgical transition goes by various names: "gender confirmation surgery" (GCS), "sex reassignment surgery" (SRS), and a few others. Each term comes with its own ideological assumptions; no neutral term pleases everyone. I'll use the acronym SRS, which is still quite common in the medical community. SRS might include a double mastectomy, hysterectomy, ovariectomy, and phalloplasty (construction of a penis) for biological females transitioning to male (although not everyone will opt for all of these, and phalloplasty isn't very common). For biological males transitioning to female, SRS might include the construction of a vulva and vagina in the place of a penis and testes, along with breast implants and other cosmetic changes. It's worth keeping in mind, though, that most trans*-identified people have not transitioned surgically and never will.[5]

Transman and *transwoman* are terms used to describe a biological female who identifies as male (transman) and a biological male who identifies as female (transwoman). It can be tough to keep these terms in order if you're not used to them. Just remember—the "woman" or "man" in these terms refers to how a person identifies.

You may also see these terms shortened as FtM (female to male) for transmen and MtF (male to female) for transwomen. Typically, but not always, these abbreviations are used for transgender-identified people who have transitioned on some level.

Cisgender is a recent term that refers to those who identify (and are comfortable) with their biological sex. (*Cis* means "on the side of.") Basically, *cisgender* refers to everyone who doesn't identify as trans*. Since the term sometimes comes with ideological assumptions and connotations, I'll avoid it in this book unless the context or quote demands it. Instead, I'll use the more neutral term *non-trans** to refer to people who don't identify as trans*.

Intersex is a term used to describe the sixteen or so medical conditions where a person is born with one or more atypical features in their sexual anatomy or sex chromosomes. The medical term for intersex conditions is "differences/disorders of sex development," or DSD. Please don't use the term "hermaphrodite" to describe intersex people. It's a potentially offensive term and is quite outdated. It would be like walking into an IT department and asking about the latest advancements in floppy disks. (If you're totally into floppy disks and don't understand the analogy, then I'm excited you're reading this book.)

We'll discuss intersex in much more detail in chapter 7. For now, it's important to know two things: (1) *Intersex* is different from *transgender*. (2) Ninety-nine percent of people with an intersex condition are biologically male or female (and the other 1 percent are both). In other words, *intersex* does not mean "neither male nor female."

But this raises the question: What is *male* and *female*? Are they identities or realities (or both)? That is, do people *identify as* male, female, both, or neither? Or are they born male or female as a biological fact? The answers to these questions depend on how we understand the relationship between sex and gender.

Now we're getting into the heart of the conversation.

SEX AND GENDER

Sex and gender are the two most important concepts in this conversation. Everything else flows from these two terms. Until we understand what sex and gender mean, we'll be hopelessly wandering through a jungle without a compass or a map.

You'd better pour another cup of coffee, because we're going to dive deep into the meaning of these two terms. Let's start with the term that is less contested: sex. (Not *having* sex, but *biological* sex. Sorry to disappoint.)

Sex

Humans, like most species, are sexually dimorphic. Part of being sexually dimorphic means that humans reproduce when the gamete (sperm) of one kind of human is fused with the gamete (egg) of another kind of human to produce a new organism. The categories used to classify the respective roles humans play in reproduction are "male" and "female."

Females are distinguished from males based on their different reproductive structures. Female humans will develop internal (ovaries, uterus, vagina) and external (breasts, vulva) anatomical features that are, in part, designed to contribute to reproduction. Males will also develop anatomical features that contribute to reproduction (penis, testes).

Males and females also have different levels of hormones that contribute to their sexual dimorphism. For instance, females have higher levels of estrogen and males have higher levels of testosterone. These respective "sex" hormones lead to the development of various secondary sex characteristics, such as the development of breasts and wider hips in females and more muscle mass and facial hair in males. Sex hormones might also affect behavior (as when high levels of testosterone make a person physically aggressive), though the extent to which this is true is widely disputed.

If you slept through high school biology, you might be dozing off right now. But please fight the urge. All this stuff about gametes and reproduction is important for our topic. Slap yourself if you need to.

Genetically, the presence of a Y chromosome distinguishes males from females. Most females have XX chromosomes while most males have XY chromosomes. Some males and females might have an extra X chromosome (or two or three extra X chromosomes, or a missing X chromosome), indicating one of several different intersex conditions.

The topic of intersex has its own set of questions and assumptions. It'll be better to discuss intersex head-on, rather than weaving intersex in and out of conversations about non-intersex trans* people. So, for the next several chapters, **I want to focus on humans who don't have an intersex condition.** My motivation for doing so is to honor my intersex friends, not to sideline them. It's common for non-intersex people to invoke "intersex" as some faceless concept in service of an argument. But I find this practice rather dehumanizing to actual intersex people, and many intersex people do as well. I'd much rather talk about (and with) intersex people extensively in a separate chapter before considering how intersex relates to our conversation.

For the first several chapters of this book, we'll focus on humans whose biological sex is unambiguous.

To sum it up, a person is biologically either male or female based on four things:

- Presence or absence of a Y chromosome
- Internal reproductive organs
- External sexual anatomy
- Endocrine systems that produce secondary sex characteristics

Before moving to gender, I want to point out that everything I've said about sex so far is basic science and can be found in any biology textbook.[6] It's therefore widely accepted among scientists and scholars and anyone you'd want operating on you in the ER. And it doesn't matter whether they're conservative or liberal. For instance, Hilary Lips is a renowned psychologist and feminist who wrote one of the leading textbooks on sex and gender. She says that sex refers to "a person's biological maleness or femaleness" and "is reserved for discussions of anatomy and the classification of individuals based on their anatomical category."[7] Feminist philosopher Rebecca Reilly-Cooper describes "female" and "male" as "general biological categories that apply to all species that reproduce sexually."[8] The American Psychological Association says, "Sex refers to a person's biological status and is typically categorized as male, female or intersex. There are a number of indicators of biological sex, including sex chromosomes, gonads, internal reproductive organs and external genitalia."[9]

Sexual dimorphism among non-intersex humans is an established, observable, objective, scientific, the-earth-is-round-and-not-flat sort of fact. "[A]n organism is male or female if it is structured to perform one of the respective roles in reproduction," and "[t]here is no other widely accepted biological classification for the sexes."[10]

This doesn't mean that our femaleness and maleness don't affect other aspects of our lives. Of course they do. Sex hormones, for instance, have at least some effect on our thoughts, emotions, interests, and social interactions as males and females. But we don't determine whether a non-intersex person is male or female based on their emotions, behaviors, or interests—things that belong under the category of gender (see the next section). Male and female are categories of biological sex based on structures of reproduction.

Our interpretations of sex and sexed bodies might be socially constructed, but sex itself is not socially constructed.

Now, the value we assign to being male or female, how we interpret our male and female bodies, and how males and females interact with each other are all loaded with culturally shaped realities that include much more than biological structures of reproduction. For this reason, some scholars will say that biological sex itself is a social construct. (Judith Butler and Anne Fausto-Sterling are leading examples of this view.) One argument for the constructed nature of biological sex has to do with intersex persons and the doctors who "assign" them a particular sex when their sex is ambiguous. In these cases, doctors might be driven by cultural expectations that all humans must be clearly male or female, and so they quite literally construct a biological sex for a child.

In addition to this argument about intersex persons, constructionists will also point out that we can't cleanly separate the physical from the social, nature from nurture, sex from gender. "As we grow and develop," writes Anne Fausto-Sterling, "we literally ... construct our bodies, incorporating experience into our very flesh. To understand this claim, we must erode the distinctions between the physical and the social body."[11] Moreover, it's impossible for us to look at our sexed bodies and not interpret these bodies through cultural and social lenses. Sexed bodies don't exist in a cultural vacuum, as the social constructionists rightly point out.

All of this is true, of course. But exploring the value that we assign to male and female bodies—and to masculinity and femininity—does not negate the cold hard fact *that* sexual dimorphism exists in humans. For instance, I may look at a six-foot-four chiseled male body and make all kinds of assumptions about the person—assumptions shaped and nurtured by my culture. And when I find out that he's a terrible athlete and sings soprano in the local gay men's choir, my cultural assumptions might be challenged. But the bare fact that he is on the "male" side of the sexually dimorphic options remains the same, whether he matches my cultural assumptions or not.

My point is, I don't think that the "sex is a social construct" view alters anything I've said thus far about biological sex. Our interpretations of sex and sexed bodies might be socially constructed, but sex itself is not socially constructed.

Now, understanding sex is easy compared to understanding gender. Conversations about gender are the wild, wild west of scholarly debate.

Gender

What is gender, and how is it related to sex? Sex and gender used to be synonyms. Everything we've said above about sex could also be used to describe gender. Sex was gender and gender was sex. But ever since the late 1960s, the terms *sex* and *gender* have been used to describe different aspects of our male and female experience. (For what it's worth, some people still use *sex* and *gender* interchangeably. Just look at your passport.)

The most basic and widely agreed upon definition of gender is this:

The psychological, social and cultural aspects of being male or female.[12]

We can break this definition down into two different (yet over-lapping) categories. First, *gender identity* describes the psychological aspects associated with being male or female, or "one's internal sense of self as male, female, both, or neither." Second, *gender role* describes the "social and cultural" aspects of being male or female, sometimes shorthanded as "masculinity and femininity."[13]

Let's tease these categories out a bit more, beginning with gender role.

GENDER ROLE

Gender roles have to do with how males and females are expected to act in any given culture. Typically, an "expectation" is formed when the majority of a particular group—males or females, in this case—act a certain way. This subtly plants the idea that *everyone* from each respective group *should* act a certain way. In short, gender roles are largely based on stereotypes. I don't say this negatively. Not all stereotypes are bad. Gender stereotypes, or masculinity and femininity, describe the general or typical ways in which most males and females act. In the West, masculinity is associated with playing sports, being physically aggressive, not crying or being tender, and excelling in STEM fields (science, technology, engineering, and math). Masculine boys prefer blue over pink, jeans instead of dresses, and rough-and-tumble play rather than sitting in a circle chatting with their friends. Feminine women are more nurturing, compassionate, agreeable, and less physically aggressive than men. Women who fit this stereotype prefer pink over blue, talking instead of sports, and working at jobs that involve people rather than blueprints.

Gender roles—or stereotypes—exist. But *why* do they exist? Is it nature or nurture? Are boys typically masculine because society makes them masculine (nurture)? Are girls more nurturing because of biology (nature)? Are *gender roles*—masculinity and femininity—determined by nature or nurture, our biology or our culture?

Certainly, nurture plays some role. Pink and blue are classic examples of this. A hundred years ago, pink was considered a masculine color while blue was feminine. According to the *Ladies Home Journal* in a 1918 article, "[P]ink, being a more decided and stronger color, is more suitable for the boy, while blue, which is more delicate and dainty, is prettier for the girl."[14] (Prior to the twentieth century, all babies were stuffed into white frilly dresses.) And yet today—in the West, at least—boys prefer blue and girls prefer pink. Why? Because we've nurtured girls to like pink and boys to like blue. Nothing in our genes hardwires boys to like blue and girls pink. Pink and blue are cultural constructs.[15]

And yet nature also has a hand in shaping stereotypical male and female behavior. Higher levels of testosterone, for instance, are linked to higher degrees of physical aggression.[16] In utero, most biological males receive a wash of testosterone ("T") during the third trimester that is believed to masculinize the brain. Although the implications of this wash are widely disputed, many believe that a prenatal brain marinated in T predisposes most males to engage in masculine behaviors like rough-and-tumble play.[17] Biological females typically don't receive the same wash of T in utero and thus exhibit less physical aggression even from a young age.[18]

---

*Nothing in our genes hardwires boys to like blue and
girls pink. Pink and blue are cultural constructs.*

Those who argue that masculinity is biologically rooted often appeal to the famous case of David Reimer, who was born in 1965.[19] At seven months old, David was the victim of a botched circumcision that irreparably damaged his penis. Since it's easier to make a hole than a pole, and since—according to John Money (who advised the parents)—gender is a social construct, it seemed easier to surgically transition David to a female and raise him as girl, which is what the parents did. David became Brenda, and she lived happily ever after.

Actually, she didn't. Despite the parents' best efforts, Brenda couldn't be socialized into a girl, despite believing she was one. While scientific journals and the media reported that Brenda was getting along just fine as a girl, he later revealed that he had always felt like a boy trapped in a girl's body. (The pronouns are particularly tough with this story, so I'll keep flip-flopping around.) In fact, this was exactly the case. "She ripped off frilly dresses, rejected dolls in favor of guns, preferred to play with boys, and even insisted on urinating standing up."[20] Finally, at age fourteen, Brenda couldn't take it any longer and said she wanted to transition to a boy. It was then that his parents told him he really was a boy. Brenda took on the name David and lived as a boy.

But the view that masculinity is a social construct is not without support. One study looked at a case very similar to that of David Reimer, where a biological male had his penis severed and was raised as a girl. Only this time the results were opposite: "At ages 16 and 26, the patient was living socially as a woman and denied any uncertainty about being a female."[21]

Nature or nurture? Are gender roles biologically hardwired or socially constructed?

Like many things in life, the answer to this question is probably not an either/or. I'm no sociologist, but from everything I've read, I think a good case can be made for nature *and* nurture both interacting with each other to form our conceptions of masculinity and femininity. But before we get too far down the rabbit hole (is it too late?), I want to point out that those who advocate for nature or nurture both agree on one thing: *gender roles (masculinity and femininity) are based on generalities, not absolutes.* When we say things like "males are more physically aggressive than females," what we mean is that *most* males are more physically aggressive than *most* females. The differences are based on statistical averages, not absolutes. A wide variation exists among males and females within virtually every behavioral trait.

Masculinity and femininity—gender roles—are kind of like height. Males are taller than females. The average height of American males is five feet nine inches tall, while the average height of females is five feet four inches tall. But this doesn't mean *every* male is taller than *every* female. Some women are six feet tall, and yet no one would say they are not female because they fall outside the general pattern. There's a clear difference in average, and yet much variation within each sex.

The same is true of masculinity and femininity. Most males are more physically aggressive than most females. This forms the stereotype that aggression is a masculine trait. On the other hand, some females are more aggressive than some males. This doesn't mean aggressive females aren't females. These behaviors are generalities. We don't determine whether a person is male or female based on whether they match the stereotype of their sex. If you are an aggressive female or a passive male, this doesn't determine *whether* you are a male or a female any more than being five foot two rules you out from being a male. And if you are a male who likes pink and hates blue, this doesn't mean you are female. A hundred years ago, it would have meant you were dripping with masculinity.

Gender role has to do with stereotypical ways males and females act. If someone says their gender is different from their biological sex, and if by "gender" they mean "gender role," then what they mean is that they don't resonate with certain stereotypes. This distinction has many relational and pastoral implications, some of which we'll discuss later in the book.

But what about *gender identity*?

GENDER IDENTITY

Again, gender identity is commonly defined as "one's internal sense of self as male, female, both, or neither."[22] But the precise nature of this "internal sense" isn't often explained very concretely. Is gender identity a state of mind? A metaphysical property? A belief about oneself that may or may not be true? Is it situated in the brain (as in the notion that someone might have a male brain but a female body)? Or does it exist as some other kind of undefined "essence" or spiritual property? We'll explore some of these possibilities in the pages ahead. But based on my own conversations and reading, I'm not sure most people who talk about gender identity could describe what exactly it is beyond just repeating the definition. It does seem to have a rather elusive meaning in popular discourse. In any case, the very concept of gender identity raises at least four questions that are intensely debated.

I want to be careful not to reject a concept simply because I don't know what it's like to experience it.

First, *does gender identity exist?* A bold question, I know, but it's a question sometimes raised in this conversation. Some people assume that gender identity is a distinct ontological essence of a person. There's sex, and there's gender (identity), and both are equally significant aspects of human nature. But others deny that gender identity is any more ontologically significant than a person's other feelings about themselves. Those who call themselves "gender critical feminists" (or sometimes "radical feminists"), for instance, argue that "being a woman is not an 'identity.'"[23] A female body is essential to being a woman. If a person wasn't born with a female body, then they aren't—and never will be—a woman. Certainly, people with gender dysphoria have a real psychological condition which causes them to think and feel like they are a different sex. But this perception doesn't mean they *are* a different sex. "The idea of 'gender identity' disappears biology," writes feminist Sheila Jeffreys, "and all the experiences that those with female biology have of being reared in a caste system based on sex."[24]

I'll admit, the concept of gender identity does feel nebulous. It's not like you can take a blood test to determine your gender identity. But I'm speaking as someone who doesn't experience gender dysphoria. I've never had to think very hard about my internal sense of self. I want to be careful not to reject a concept simply because I don't know what it's like to experience it. Plus, there are some biblical and scientific arguments for gender identity being a more ontologically robust aspect of human nature, which we'll wrestle with throughout this book. Therefore, let's table the "gender identity doesn't exist" perspective until we dive much deeper into our topic.

Second, *how many gender identities are there?* Given the definition of gender identity, this is like asking, "How many internal senses
of selves exist?" Two? Ten? Fifty? At one point, Facebook allowed for
seventy-one gender identities and now has the option of a "custom"
gender.[25] Perhaps there are ten thousand gender identities—or more.

I'm not being smug. This is an actual conversation among
scholars. Psychologists Maggi Price and Avy Skolnik say that "gender
identity can be considered a 'multiverse' wherein there are infinite ways
by which one can identify."[26] Another scholar in psychology, Patrick
Sweeney, says that "gender identity and gender expression have an infinite number of possible variations, and they function as dynamic and
fluid in different social contexts and across the life span."[27]

Now, some people flip out and bark, "There are only two genders!" And this is true, *if* by "gender" they mean *biological sex*. But
that's not the way the word *gender* is typically used today. When two
people use one word in different ways, chaos ensues. It's like the dad
who told his son, "Go put the trunk in the trunk." So the son went
out, hacked off an elephant's nose, and shoved it in the back of the
car. But the dad simply wanted him to put the base of a tree in a
box in the attic. If you learn one thing from this book, let it be this:
when people use the term "gender," make sure you ask them what
they mean.

Third, *how do you determine a person's gender identity?* This question elicits a spectrum of views. One end of the spectrum is called the
"self-ID" view. You are who you say you are. If you say you're trans*,
then you're trans*. If you identify as a woman, then you're a woman.
There are no objective criteria that need to be met.

On the other side of the spectrum is the gender dysphoric view. If a biological male identifies as a female, they must have a medical diagnosis of Gender Dysphoria. A real transgender person is one who has a severe psychological condition where something in their nature got crossed, and their brain doesn't match their sexed body. Their identity can be (and should be) medically determined, not just personally declared.

Fourth, *is gender identity malleable?* Does it change? If someone's gender identity is different from their sex, will it always be this way? Some say gender identity is innate and unchangeable, while others say it's quite malleable. The whole debate has become a hot mess of vitriol and confusion. The fact is—and it is a fact—for some people gender identity changes, and for others it doesn't. This shouldn't be surprising. After all, we're dealing with "one's internal sense of self."

There are other questions about gender identity, but let's not forget our most important question:

> *If someone experiences incongruence between their biological sex and their internal sense of self (gender identity), which one determines who they are—and why?*

All these questions lie at the heart of our conversation, and we'll get to them in due time. But first, let's dive deep into the meaning of *transgender*—because it, too, is a many-layered experience.

Chapter 3

WHAT DOES IT MEAN TO BE TRANS*?

My friend Mark Yarhouse, a psychologist who has studied gender identity extensively, likes to say, "If you've met one transgender person, you've met … one transgender person." Trans* people are about as diverse as non-trans* people. What do Donald Trump, Hillary Clinton, and the Dalai Lama have in common? Not much, other than that they don't identify as trans*. Non-trans* people are diverse, and so are trans* people.

Understanding this diversity has many practical implications. If your girlfriend comes out and tells you they're trans*, this could mean a variety of things. Maybe they believe they were born in the wrong body, or maybe they simply don't resonate with femininity and want to cut their hair short and color it blue. Remember, *transgender* is an umbrella term for the various ways some people experience incongruence between their biological sex and their gender (gender identity or gender role). As an umbrella term, *transgender* can describe many different experiences, identities, and ontological assumptions. Let's survey some different shades of trans* identities.

Keep in mind as we begin that most of these categories are not mutually exclusive. A trans* person might resonate with one, two, or several of these categories at the same time. Each category, however, raises its own set of questions and practical responses.

GENDER DYSPHORIC TRANS*

Gender dysphoria, as you recall from the last chapter, exists on a spectrum from mild to severe. Some trans*-identified people experience gender dysphoria, and some don't. For those who do, there are two broad categories: early-onset gender dysphoria and late/adolescent-onset gender dysphoria. The second of these two categories includes the recently minted subcategory of rapid-onset gender dysphoria, which we'll address in chapter 10.[1]

Those with early-onset gender dysphoria can experience it as young as three years old. For some, it can be utterly debilitating and life-threatening. I've heard of kids as young as six years old attempting suicide because their dysphoria was so aggressive. For others, dysphoria is less severe. It might be a near-constant experience, or it might come in waves.

And for most kids, it goes away. According to all available studies done on the persistence rates of dysphoria in kids, 61 to 88 percent of early-onset dysphoria cases end up desisting; that is, the dysphoria goes away after puberty.[2] Those whose dysphoria doesn't desist after puberty will likely battle dysphoria for the rest of their lives.

NON-GENDER DYSPHORIC TRANS*

Some say you don't need to have gender dysphoria to be trans*. "[M]ore and more people who identify with the label of transgender have also found they haven't ever felt any dysphoria at all," says trans* writer Jessie Earl. "[W]e cannot let dysphoria be the only path, the price of entry, into our community."[3] An extreme example of this perspective comes from Trisha Paytas, a popular YouTuber with five million subscribers, who says, "Do I think I'm transgender? 1,000%. Do I identify as my natural born gender? 1,000%."[4]

This "self-ID" perspective—if you say you're trans*, then you're trans*—has sparked a growing feud within the trans* community. There are those who believe a medical diagnosis of Gender Dysphoria is necessary to truly be trans*, while others think a self-declaration is all you need.[5] Still others argue that acting as a woman (or a man) is enough to be trans*. Two widely popular trans* YouTubers, Blaire White and Natalie Wynn (aka *ContraPoints*), represent different perspectives on this latter issue. Natalie says that if you live like a woman, then you're a woman, while Blaire says you must have a medical diagnosis to truly be trans*.

Which one is right? And *why*? What does it mean to be trans*?

TRANS* EXPERIENCE VERSUS TRANS* ONTOLOGY

Some might use the term *transgender* to describe their experience with dysphoria, while others might mean something more ontologically significant (for example, that a biological male is in fact a woman).[6]

For instance, my friend Kat says she's transgender, and what she means by the term is that she experiences gender dysphoria *as a female*. Kat is a classic tomboy. If you challenged her to a game of basketball, I'm putting my money on Kat. Though she is biologically female, Kat has never resonated with stereotypical femininity. When she says she's transgender, she's not making an ontological statement (that she is in fact a man rather than a woman). She's simply describing her experience of dysphoria as a female.

Just because someone uses the term transgender *or identifies as trans* doesn't necessarily mean they're making an ontological declaration.*

My friend Dan also identifies as transgender (MtF). But Dan uses the term to mean that he—or as Dan prefers, she—is a woman. (We'll talk about the pronoun stuff later.) For Dan, transgender *is* an ontological description: it describes Dan's self-understanding *as* a woman. If someone says, "I don't just *want* to be a woman, I don't just *feel* like a woman, I *am* a woman," that's an ontological declaration that comes with many scientific, philosophical, and theological assumptions.

But again, just because someone uses the term *transgender* or identifies as trans* doesn't necessarily mean they're making an ontological declaration. As Yarhouse reminds us, "If you've met one transgender person, you've met ... one transgender person."

RAPID-ONSET GENDER DYSPHORIC TRANS*

Social networks at school and in online communities can play a role in shaping a person's trans* identity. Some psychologists have named this growing phenomenon Rapid-Onset Gender Dysphoria (ROGD). Others use the term *trans trender* to describe people, typically teenagers, who have been influenced by their social environment to identify as trans*. But *trans trender* can feel like it's invalidating someone's experience, which is never a great way to start a relationship. Whatever term you prefer, there does seem to be a good deal of evidence that social influences are one reason some (perhaps many) teenagers and young adults are identifying as trans*.

Lots of discussions (and heated debates) surround ROGD, which is why we'll spend a whole chapter (chapter 10) discussing it. In any case, this kind of trans* experience might look different than the experience of someone who's had lifelong severe gender dysphoria.

TRANS* DETRANSITIONERS

Detransitioners are another group of (former?) trans* people. Some people were so convinced of their transgender identity that they ended up transitioning (socially, hormonally, or surgically). Then, for whatever reason, they decided that they wanted to live as their biological sex once again. Maybe they weren't satisfied with the operation. Perhaps they thought their depression and anxiety would go away after they transitioned, and when it didn't, they decided to transition back. Or maybe they'd developed ROGD partly because of their social environment, and once they left that environment, the social allure of trans* identity dwindled. Whatever the reason—there could be many—we're witnessing a rapidly growing number of people detransitioning back to their biological sex.

AUTOGYNEPHILIC TRANS*

Another common experience under the trans* umbrella goes by the name *autogynephilia*. This is a largely unfamiliar category, known only in some psychology circles. The term *autogynephilia* is a combination of three Greek terms: *auto* (self), *gyne* (woman), and *philia* (love)—the love of oneself as a woman. Autogynephilia, in others words, describes an experience where a biological male is erotically aroused by the thought of himself as a female. Autogynephilic trans* people are biological males who typically have stereotypically masculine interests and are sexually attracted to women. However, this attraction toward women is directed not so much toward *other* females but toward the thought of themselves *as* females. "I don't wanna be a woman, I just want a woman's body," writes one person about their autogynephilic desires.[7]

Anne Lawrence, herself an autogynephilic transgender (MtF) medical researcher, has done extensive research into this kind of trans* experience,[8] as have Ray Blanchard[9] and J. Michael Bailey,[10] among others. For a punchy review of some of the controversy surrounding autogynephilia, see Alice Dreger's book *Galileo's Middle Finger*.[11] As the book's title suggests, the topic can easily become offensive to a variety of groups. Indeed, the very mention of autogynephilia could get you blasted by others online. It's hotly contested, to say the least. Opinions about autogynephilia range from "it doesn't exist and you're transphobic if you say it does" to "almost all MtF's are autogynephilic." Trans* people themselves hold a wide range of opinions on autogynephilia.[12]

Based on everything I've read and the people I've talked to, I believe without a doubt that some trans* people are autogynephilic. Two friends of mine have struggled with it for years. They both tell me, though, that their experience of autogynephilia is only partially erotic. They say that some descriptions of autogynephilia sound overly sexualized and don't capture the complexity of their experiences. One of my friends says he's just comforted by femininity, which he experiences when he wears soft and silky female clothing. He didn't know there was a name for this experience until I introduced him to the concept of autogynephilia, and he felt like he was looking into a mirror. He feels liberated knowing he's not the only one with these unwanted desires.

Of course, just because this friend finds the category of autogynephilia helpful doesn't mean every person will. If you've met one transgender person, you've met … one transgender person.

MENTAL HEALTH CONCERNS AMONG TRANS*

I said at the beginning of this chapter that the categories we're considering here can overlap with one another, and each category raises its own set of questions and practical responses. This is especially true when it comes to mental health concerns among trans* people, which we'll discuss more thoroughly in chapters 10 and 11. Many trans* people, especially teenagers, have co-occurring mental health concerns, sometimes several, like anxiety, depression, and eating disorders.[13] Trans* people also experience borderline personality disorder, schizophrenia, obsessive compulsive disorder (OCD), attention deficit hyperactive disorder (ADHD), and autism spectrum disorder at a higher rate than the general public.[14] For example, according to one study, people with gender dysphoria are ten times more likely to be on the autism spectrum than non-dysphoric people.[15] Another study shows that 26 percent of trans* teenagers seeking sex reassignment were diagnosed with autism.[16]

Are these mental health issues a cause, a result, or simply correlated with being trans*? Specialists are divided, and I'm not qualified to give an authoritative answer to this complex psychological question. What we can say with confidence is that there *may* be other mental health concerns intertwined with a person's trans* experience. This co-occurrence raises important questions. If a teenager has OCD and is on the autism spectrum, for instance, and if this teen has an ongoing obsession with the idea of becoming the other sex, is this obsession rooted in a trans* identity? Is the obsession shaped by the interaction of their OCD and their autism? Is it a combination of all these things? And should they transition?

Someone who has a one-size-fits-all view of what it means to be trans* might say, "If you're trans* and you want to transition, then you should transition. And anyone who questions this is a nonaffirming, unloving bigot." But this would be an irresponsible and unloving response. Leaving aside the ethical question of transitioning, we need to really get to know someone on a practical level and enter their story before we give an opinion on whether they should make a life-altering decision.

It would also be irresponsible and unloving to assume that every teenager identifying as trans* is a "trender" influenced by their social environment. It would be untruthful to assume that every biological male who identifies as trans* is autogynephilic or on the autism spectrum or has an underlying mental health issue. The point is, a one-size-fits-all understanding of what it means to be trans* needs to be locked in a box and tossed into the sea.

TRANS* AS INTERNAL HOMOPHOBIA OR MISOGYNY

Some trans* people's decision to transition is motivated by an internal, repressed homophobia. Sydney, for instance, was a classic tomboy as a child, and when she became a teenager, she experienced unwanted attractions to other girls. "I knew I was gay—though I was more of a self-loathing gay. The truth is, I didn't like gays, and didn't want to be associated with them. Yet there I was, dating only other girls."[17] Because Sydney hated the fact that she was gay, she became jealous of trans* people who were able to pass as heterosexual. "Here I was getting frowned upon for holding hands with my girlfriend in public, feeling like I'm constantly being judged by everyone, while transgenders could date their same-sex significant other while looking like the opposite sex." Sydney found a therapist who wrote her a prescription for testosterone, so she could begin transitioning to become a guy and, from her perspective, not be gay anymore.

Sydney's story is one story, but her repressed homophobia is more widespread than you might think.[18] Iran, in fact, is among the world's leading countries in performing sex reassignment surgeries.[19] Why? Because being gay is illegal in Iran.[20] Instead of praying the gay away, they transition it away. Turning a gay man into a woman is, in their view, one way to make him not gay anymore.

Some biological females suffer from repressed misogyny.[21] For various reasons, they might view the female sex negatively. Perhaps they associate femininity with weakness or passivity, or maybe they've witnessed a woman being physically abused by a man or been a victim of abuse themselves. Becoming a man, they may believe, will make them strong and protective instead of weak and susceptible to violence. For instance, one four-year-old girl named Rose found her mother lying dead at the bottom of the stairs after being beaten to death by a boyfriend. Rose was adopted at the age of six and started to express a desire to be a boy. "I look like a boy and no one will hurt you," Rose told her adoptive mother. "[B]oys are stronger than girls." Rose revealed to her psychologist that if she had been a boy, she could have saved her mother's life.[22]

If you've met one transgender person, you've met … one transgender person.

LISTENING LOVE

There is no one-size-fits-all category of what it means to be trans*. If someone says they're trans*, all that means is … they just told you they're trans* and an opportunity for a relationship has just plopped into your lap. You are invited to steward this opportunity well.

Part of stewarding this opportunity well is understanding that there are many different kinds of trans* experiences. Being trans* is not one thing. It's not even five things. It's an umbrella identity that captures a wide array of circumstances and assumptions, and it might be intertwined with other challenges lying beneath the surface.

Knowing the diversity of trans* identities opens up fresh opportunities to listen, love, and make a friend. This means that when someone tells you they're trans* and invites you into relationship, the best thing you can do is ask them what they mean by *trans**. Don't interrogate. You may even want to ask if it's okay to inquire about their identity. The point is, don't assume one thing about their identity when they might mean another.

To listen is to love. You can't love without listening. Non-trans* people often have cynical assumptions about what it means to be trans*, sometimes shaped by clickbait media headlines from the left or the right. The best way to smash exaggerated stereotypes is to get to know actual trans* people and become a good listener and friend. Jesus bids us to embody God's kindness and love toward neighbor and enemy alike, and this can't be done if we don't learn how to listen. Truly listen. Listen with the goal of understanding and loving the person who's willing to tell us their story.

The best way to smash exaggerated stereotypes is to get to know actual trans* people and become a good listener and friend.

We're going to spend the next several chapters using the Bible and science to evaluate the central question of this book: *If someone experiences incongruence between their biological sex and their gender, which one determines who they are—and why?*

For those of us who don't live on the spectrum of trans* experiences, it can be easy to adopt a depersonalized posture, one that forgets about the lives of real people. A posture of argumentation instead of listening. A posture of being right instead of being love. This temptation is especially strong if you're an analytical person like me. We "left-brained" people sometimes struggle to listen with love, especially when we're digging into Scripture and analyzing facts and arguments. All this analytic stuff is important and necessary; we're talking about people *and* concepts, not people *instead of* concepts. But we must be rooted in humility even as—*especially* as—we look at what the Bible says about trans* experiences.

My friend Laurie models this humility so well. Laurie is a fellow left-brained, truth-driven, leave-me-in-a-room-with-a-dozen-books-and-I'll-be-fine kind of person. But Laurie has learned to cultivate a humble posture in how she walks with her trans* friends.

Several years ago, God brought Kat into Laurie's life. Kat was raised in the church and experienced gender dysphoria from an early age. "I wasn't very feminine," she recalls. "I loved to play basketball and hated to wear dresses. But I was made to feel like I was being an ungodly woman for not being stereotypically feminine." Kat didn't have dysphoria simply because of stereotypes. Something deep within, something unchosen and seemingly innate, made her feel much more like a boy than a girl. Being surrounded by gender stereotypes only compounded the distress: "The church seemed to reinforce the view that godly women must be stereotypically feminine. But I wasn't. This gave me the impression that I wasn't a godly female."

Kat ended up leaving the church and didn't return until she was twenty-seven. Around the same time she returned to church, Kat went to see a counselor after going through a tough breakup. Since Kat identified as transgender, her counselor was eager to put her on testosterone. But Kat felt like this was only a Band-Aid for the deeper challenges she was wrestling with. Kat recalls, "My counselor didn't ask the deeper questions that I thought were necessary. 'Why do you feel like a man? What is your view of masculinity? Why do you not feel feminine?' She told me that whenever I was ready to transition, she could help get that process started."

One Sunday at church, the worship band played the song "No Longer Slaves," and God met Kat through that song. "I'm no longer a slave to fear," Kat sang, with tears streaming down her face. "I am a child of God."[23] The more she sang those words, the more she believed them. In the midst of her dysphoria, her incongruence, her relationships, her journey, her shame, her fear—she began to recognize that God saw her as his precious child.

Several weeks later, Laurie (who happens to be same-sex attracted, married to a man, and a mother of three—it's a long story) came up to Kat in church and said, "Hey, I've noticed that you sit by yourself. I just want you to know that, if you want, we'd love for you to sit with us."

Initially, Kat was a bit weirded out: "I thought, *This can't be genuine; she must be trying to chalk up extra points in heaven by talking to a trans* person*." But the two struck up a friendship—one that eventually became safe enough for Kat to pour out her heart.

One day when they were deep in conversation, Kat said in frustration, "I'm tired of hearing what everyone else thinks of my gender. I want to know, what does *God* think?"

I love what Laurie said next: "I'm not sure. But I'd love to explore this with you."

And that's what they did. Day after day, week after week, Laurie and Kat kept digging into God's Word and his presence. Through many conversations, nights filled with tears and laughter, Kat and Laurie continued to pursue Jesus together and figure out what it means to be human.

Kat still experiences dysphoria, and sometimes it flares up aggressively. Kat is also one of the most passionate, faithful, authentic, zealous, red-hot worshipers of Jesus I've ever met. She still identifies as transgender, a word she uses to describe her dysphoria. And in all of this, Jesus continues to radiate his compelling presence through Kat's eager desire to make his name known.

I remember talking to Kat about Laurie's response to her question, "What does God think about my gender?" I asked, "What would you have done if Laurie had acted like she had it all figured out, telling you verse by verse exactly what God thinks of your gender?"

Laughing, Kat said, "I would have run the other way. I didn't need a know-it-all Christian. I needed a Christian who desired to know *me*, and who had the humility to admit that they didn't have it all figured out."

Some people might enjoy being instructed by a person who seems to have all the right answers—a two-legged Google with a mouth that never seems to shut. But I think most people are like Kat. They want to know the truth, but they want to find it with a friend.

Let's keep this in mind as we dive into what the Bible says about transgender identities and experiences. Pretend Kat is with you, at your side, ready to ask hard questions and eager to feel a soft heart. Let's study the Bible together in a humble way that helps us become better friends.

Chapter 4

MALE AND FEMALE IN THE IMAGE OF GOD

If someone experiences incongruence between their biological sex and their gender, which one determines who they are—and why? What does the Bible say about this question?

That's the problem. The Bible doesn't directly ask and answer this question. There's no verse in, say, Leviticus 28 that says, "If thy gender identity does not match thy biological sex, then thine body is who you really are." Or whatever. (There is no Leviticus 28, in case you're flipping pages to check.) But the Bible does say quite a few relevant things about human nature and the importance of our biological sex, which will position us to cultivate a theologically informed and biblically rooted answer to our question.

In this chapter, I'm going to explore what the Bible says about biological sex. In chapter 5, I want to look at how the Bible's treatment of sex is related to gender roles, or masculinity and femininity. I'm then going to wrestle with the most important gender-affirming biblical arguments in chapter 6. ("Gender-affirming" simply means that gender identity defines who we are more than biological sex.)

So let's dive in. What does the Bible say about biological sex? I'm going to give eight thesis statements that sum up some of the most important passages and theological themes about our male- and female-sexed bodies.

1. THE BODY IS ESSENTIAL TO OUR IMAGE-BEARING STATUS.

In the Bible's opening moments, Genesis 1 declares the most fundamental truth about human identity: we are created in God's image.

> God created mankind **in his own image**,
> > **in the image of God** he created them;
> > **male and female** he created them.
> > (Gen. 1:27)

Theologians have wrestled for years with what it means to bear "God's image." Is the image of God tied to our rational minds? Our capacity for relationships? Our elevated status? Some combination of these three, or something entirely different?[1] Whatever the image of God points to, one thing is rather clear: our bodies are essential to bearing God's image.

The Hebrew word for "image" is *tselem*, and it almost always refers to "idols" throughout the Old Testament. What are idols? They're visible representations of an invisible deity. The term basically means the physical "carved or hewn statue or copy" of a nonphysical being. In Genesis 1, this "statue or copy" is humanity, and the nonphysical being is Yahweh.[2] "Visibility and bodiliness" are central to the meaning of the phrase "image of God."[3]

I love how theologian Marc Cortez puts it: the image of God is "a declaration that God intended to create human persons to be the physical means through which he would manifest his own divine presence in the world."[4] Or as Old Testament scholars Karl Löning and Erich Zenger write, "According to the meaning of the Hebrew word *tselem,* which stands for 'image,' humans are to be in the world as a kind of living image or statue of God."[5] We are God's idols—visible representations of God on earth.

Now, humans aren't *just* material bodies. Genesis 2:7 says that God "breathed into his nostrils the breath of life, and the man became a living being." God's life-giving spirit is also essential for personhood. But the term *image* precisely highlights human physicality, which means the most fundamental statement about human nature (we bear "God's image [*tselem*]") highlights our embodied nature. And not just embodied nature, but our *sexed* embodied nature. We bear God's image as male and female.[6]

2. MALE AND FEMALE IN GENESIS 1 ARE CATEGORIES OF SEX, NOT GENDER.

The categories of male and female in Genesis 1 describe biological sex, not gender identity or gender role. The biological nature of "male and female" appears clearly in the very next verse, where God commands the male and female to reproduce: "Be fruitful and increase in number" (Gen. 1:28). The command to reproduce wouldn't make as much sense if "male and female" were highlighting social or psychological aspects of being male and female (that is, gender identity or gender roles).

In addition, the Hebrew terms for male (*zakar*) and female (*neqebah*) are also paired up to describe the "male and female" animals who were brought on the ark to repopulate the earth after the flood (6:19; 7:9). *Zakar* and *neqebah* describe the reproductive roles of the animals; these same words are used of humans in Genesis 1:27. Old Testament scholar Phyllis Bird has written extensively on Genesis 1–2, focusing on what it means to be male and female. For what it's worth, Bird isn't a particularly conservative scholar; she's a feminist and an ordained elder in the United Methodist Church. She's probably not going to be invited to speak at the Gospel Coalition's national conference any time soon. Anyway, she argues that the creation accounts of Genesis present the categories of *male and female* as "indispensable to their understanding of humankind by explicit attention to the sexual differentiation of the species." She goes on to say,

> Sex is the constitutive differentiation, observable at birth and encoded in our genes, essential for the survival of the species, and basic to all systems of socialization. It plays a fundamental role in the identity formation of every individual. It must consequently be regarded as an essential datum in any attempt to define the human being and the nature of humankind—and thus provides a primary test for false notions of generic humanity.[7]

Bold words, but I think Bird is right. And she's conveying something that's both biblical and scientific. Biological sex is "an essential datum in any attempt to define the human being." (Of course, this doesn't at all rule out intersex persons. As we'll see in chapter 7, some intersex persons embody both male and female sexes. These intersex people also embody the beautiful truth of Genesis 1:27, that biological sex is an important part of human identity.)

Genesis 1:27 is one of the most powerful, provocative, and even *progressive* statements in all of Scripture. To a world where women are often viewed as lesser beings, God declares that his image is borne not only by males but also by females. The claim is radical precisely because it is a claim about the nature of our sexed embodiment. If sex differentiation is irrelevant here, then the profound elevation of females as distinct from males loses its significance.

3. ADAM AND EVE'S BODIES ARE VIEWED AS SACRED.

Genesis 2 takes a closer, more intimate look at the creation of Adam and Eve. When Eve is described, the author uses a word that implies the sacredness of Adam and Eve's bodies:

> So the LORD God caused the man to fall into a deep sleep;
> and while he was sleeping, he took one of the man's ribs
> and then closed up the place with flesh. Then the LORD
> God made a woman from the rib he had taken out of the
> man, and he brought her to the man. (Gen. 2:21–22)

The word "rib" translates the Hebrew word *tsela*. Despite the familiarity of this translation, *tsela* probably doesn't actually mean "rib" here, since *tsela* occurs more than forty other times in the Old Testament and it *never means "rib."*[8] In almost every other usage, *tsela* refers to the side of a sacred piece of architecture like the tabernacle or the temple.[9] And this meaning informs its usage here in Genesis 2. Adam and Eve's bodies are compared to sacred pieces of architecture, resonating with everything we've seen so far about the image of God. Temples embody God's presence, and so do bodies.

Genesis 1–2 speaks about our sexed embodied nature as something significant for human identity. Our sexed bodies are like sacred pieces of architecture.

4. JESUS VIEWS GENESIS 1-2 AS NORMATIVE.

In a debate with the Pharisees about divorce, Jesus cites Genesis 1:27 and 2:24 to reiterate the creation account's perspective on sexed embodiment:

> "Haven't you read," he replied, "that at the beginning the Creator 'made them male and female,' [Gen. 1:27] and said, 'For this reason a man will leave his father and mother and be united to his wife, and the two will become one flesh' [Gen. 2:24]?" (Matt. 19:4–5)

What can we draw from Jesus' words as they pertain to the trans* conversation? At the very least, it appears that Jesus considers God's original creation of humans as male and female to still be normative thousands of years later. The idea of "male and female" is not just relevant for the beginning of creation. Jesus operates with the conviction that "the created order" as expressed in Genesis 1–2 "is a guide for the moral order."[10]

We need to be careful, however, not to read into Jesus' statement more than he intended to say. He's assuming a rather simple point—taken for granted in Judaism at his time—that marriage is a union between two people of different biological sexes, male and female. Embodied sex difference is assumed, but it's not as if Jesus is directly addressing a question about trans* identities.

5. PAUL SEES THE BODY AS SIGNIFICANT FOR MORAL BEHAVIOR AND CORRELATES THE BODY WITH PERSONHOOD.

Paul seems to agree with Genesis that our bodies are "very good" (Gen. 1:31) and sacred (Gen. 2:21–23). He demonstrates his agreement particularly clearly in 1 Corinthians 6:12–20, referring to the body (*soma* in Greek) eight times and viewing it not only as good but as an essential part of personhood.[11] It's likely that some Corinthians held to a stark dualism between their spirits and their bodies. That is, they believed that the body was not significant for moral behavior. Paul was probably confronting this view when he said:

> Do you not know that your *bodies* are temples of the
> Holy Spirit, who is in *you*, whom you have received
> from God? You are not your own; you were bought
> at a price. Therefore honor God with your bodies.
> (1 Cor. 6:19–20)

Notice how Paul interchanges "you" and "body" in these verses, as he does in several other passages.[12] For instance, in Romans Paul commands believers to "offer *yourselves* to God" (Rom. 6:13, 16) and later says "offer *your bodies* as a living sacrifice, holy and pleasing to God" (Rom. 12:1). For Paul, "your bodies" and "yourselves" are inextricably linked.[13]

We see the same thing in 1 Corinthians 6. Paul interchanges "you" and "your bodies." That's because we can't separate the real you from the embodied you.

Paul is arguing against sexually immoral practices in 1 Corinthians 6. But the principle fueling his argument is anthropological. It's *because* of the sexed body that we should avoid sexual union with another sexed body other than our spouse; the one who does sin in a sexually embodied way "sins against their own body" (v. 18). Paul didn't think that what we do with our bodies is morally neutral. Personhood is a body. We are not souls with bodies, but embodied souls.[14]

We can't separate the real you from the embodied you.

---

6. SCRIPTURE PROHIBITS CROSS-SEX BEHAVIOR.

Scripture doesn't often mention people publicly presenting themselves as the opposite sex. But when it does, it always prohibits such behavior.

Now, these passages are shrouded in interpretive questions, which I've tried to work through in the endnotes. But the point still stands: *whenever* cross-sex self-presentation is mentioned, it's always prohibited.

For instance, Deuteronomy 22:5 prohibits cross-dressing: "A woman must not wear men's clothing, nor a man wear women's clothing, for the LORD your God detests anyone who does this." A few interpretive difficulties surround this command. The most important one is whether this command applies to Christians or whether it's only part of the old covenant law that's no longer applicable to Christians. For reasons stated in the endnote, I see more evidence in favor of this command carrying lasting relevance for followers of Jesus.[15]

First Corinthians 6:9 includes the term *malak* ("soft, effeminate") in a list of those who will not inherit the kingdom of heaven. Most scholars recognize that the term primarily describes men who act like or identify as women. And by "act like," I don't mean they couldn't throw a football. One of the most common ways that *malakoi* would "act like women" was by engaging in same-sex sexual activity with men. This sexual role is probably what Paul has in mind here.[16]

Paul also highlights sex and gender distinctions in 1 Corinthians 11:2–16. Now, this passage has more interpretive difficulties than Donald Trump has Twitter typos, so we have to tread cautiously. From head coverings to prophecies to strict dress codes for men and women, this passage has given rise to all kinds of interesting church practices. Some parts of the passage look like they were borrowed from *The Handmaid's Tale* (1 Cor. 11:7–9), while others appear to come from the Women's Liberation Front (1 Cor. 11:11–12). This passage isn't for the fainthearted interpreter.

Whether you read the passage as complimentarian or egalitarian, almost all interpreters agree on two things. First, Paul maintains sex differences—even emphasizes them—as something that should be upheld and celebrated in public worship. And second, he appeals to creation (Gen. 1–2) to do so.[17] Most interpreters recognize that head coverings and hairstyles had distinct meaning in their first-century context and don't carry the same meaning for every culture. But the principle driving these culturally bound commands is that men and women are different.

Romans 1:26–27 also speaks negatively about same-sex sexual relationships, and Paul's logic is rooted in God's creational intent for males and females. That is, sexual differentiation in Genesis 1:27 (and Genesis 1 as a whole) shapes Paul's logic for the same-sex prohibition. (The same is less explicit but still apparent in Leviticus 18:22.) One reason why same-sex sexual relations are wrong is because they transgress sex distinctions.[18]

I hesitate even mentioning the above passages, since people sometimes quote them thoughtlessly, with no attention to their context or the various interpretive difficulties that surround them. I can't emphasize enough that we shouldn't assume each of these passages speaks directly or definitively to modern questions about transgender identities. And yet these passages do seem to agree with Genesis 1–2 that our sexed bodies are sacred. Whatever interpretive hurdles exist, they all—on some level and to varying degrees—affirm that male and female sex distinctions are a creational good that should be honored. (We'll address Galatians 3:28 in chapter 6 and intersex in chapter 7.)

7. THE INCARNATION OF CHRIST AFFIRMS THE GOODNESS OF OUR SEXED EMBODIMENT.

Genesis says that all humans bear God's image. But the New Testament adds a significant climax to this truth: Jesus is *the* image of God. He is "the image of the invisible God" (Col. 1:15; cf. 2 Cor. 4:4), "the exact representation" of God's nature (Heb 1:3), and we are being "transformed into his image" (2 Cor. 3:18). If you want to know what God is like, look at Jesus. If you want to know what we are like and what we should become, look at Jesus. The image of God is a "Christological reality in which we have been invited to participate."[19]

Just as humanity in Genesis 1 is described as the "image" (*tselem*) of God, so Jesus is described as the most complete "image" (*eikon*) of all. The Greek word *eikon* means physicality, embodiment: "the whole fullness of deity dwells *bodily*" in Jesus (Col. 2:9 ESV; cf. 1:19). As theologian Marc Cortez observes, "To be an image bearer, Jesus must be an embodied being."[20] If Jesus didn't have a body—a sexed body—he wouldn't have borne God's image. And if we want to find out what it means to be human, what it means to bear God's image, then we must look at Jesus as the ultimate expression of this.

Jesus' sexed embodiment challenges the notion that biology is irrelevant to identity.[21]

If you want to know what God is like, look at Jesus. If you want to know what we are like and what we should become, look at Jesus.

---

8. SEX DIFFERENCE PROBABLY REMAINS AFTER THE RESURRECTION.

Resurrection is fundamental to Christian ethics. That's why we often see biblical writers refer to our future existence as the basis for current living. What we will be like *then* provides a moral basis for how we should live *now*. We see this principle at play in the 1 Corinthians 6 passage we just examined: "By his power God raised the Lord from the dead, and he will raise us also. Do you not know that your bodies are members of Christ himself? Shall I then take the members of Christ and unite them with a prostitute? Never!" (vv. 14–15). The moral emphasis on our bodies is rooted in Christ's resurrection. *Since* Christ has been raised from the dead, Paul argues, therefore you should live in a certain way (see also 1 Cor. 15 as a whole). "Christian ethics depends upon the resurrection of Jesus Christ from the dead," writes British scholar Oliver O'Donovan.[22] "In proclaiming the resurrection of Christ, the apostles proclaimed also the resurrection of mankind in Christ, and in proclaiming the resurrection of mankind, they proclaimed the renewal of all creation with him."[23] Christian ethics is rooted in bodily resurrection; no serious theologian disagrees with this.[24]

But—and here's where there is some disagreement—will our resurrection bodies be sexed?[25] There are a couple different passages (Gal. 3:28 and Matt. 22:30) that seem to say no, and we'll look at these passages in chapter 6. But other passages and theological themes appear to say that our resurrection bodies will be sexed as male and female.

I want to be very cautious here. I think there's a good deal of ambiguity in what exactly our resurrected bodies will be like. We *don't* know far more than we *do* know. Still, with much caution and openness to being wrong, I think there are some good biblical and theological reasons for believing that our sexed embodiment will continue to be part of our eternal identity. If this is true, it carries ethical significance for how we view and live in our sexed bodies on this side of resurrection.

Here are four reasons why I think it's more likely that our bodies will be sexed in the resurrection:

First, not only is sex difference part of God's pre-fall creation (Gen. 1:27; 2:18–24), it's a central part of human personhood and integral to how we mirror God's image (as we saw above). Unless Scripture explicitly says that sex difference will be done away with in the resurrection, it makes more sense that sex differences will be part of our resurrection bodies.

Second, since Jesus was male before his resurrection, and since the sexed body is a significant part of personhood, we would expect such embodied personhood to remain in the resurrection—unless, of course, there's explicit evidence to the contrary, which there is not.

Third, Jesus' resurrection is a model for our own resurrection. "When Christ appears," John says, "we shall be like him" (1 John 3:2). Not that we will be *just* like him: male, Jewish, brown hair, and brown eyes, or whatever. But "like him" in the sense that our current bodies also will be given life. Or as Paul writes elsewhere, "he who raised Christ from the dead will also give life to *your mortal bodies*" (Rom. 8:11). Our "mortal bodies"—the bodies we have *now*—are not sexless (even if they're intersex), but male and female. Paul's statement here suggests some level of continuity between our mortal bodies of today and our immortal bodies of the resurrection.

Fourth, Paul's most detailed description of our resurrected bodies (1 Cor. 15:35–58) draws extensively on Genesis 1–3, affirming the goodness of our bodies.[26] Paul does talk about some differences between our earthly bodies and our future resurrection bodies. The difference, though, is not between sexed earthly bodies and sexless resurrected bodies but between our corruptible earthly bodies and our incorruptible resurrected bodies (see especially 1 Cor. 15:50, 52–54).[27] The fact that our sexed bodies are significant to our embodied existence and our personhood (according to Genesis 1–3) suggests that sex difference will be part of our resurrected state.

Again, I want to hold these four points with an open hand, and I recommend that you do too. We're trying to fill several silent gaps with assumptions—theologically informed assumptions, but assumptions nonetheless. And yet, it does appear *more* likely that our future resurrection bodies will be sexed and *less* likely that we'll be given androgynous bodies in the resurrection. If our future glorified existence will be in a sexed body, then it would seem reasonably consistent that we should honor our embodied sex now. This approach does at least resonate with the dominant way in which Scripture values our sexed embodiment as integral to our humanity.

SUMMARY

Our sexed bodies play an essential, though not exhaustive, role in determining who we are. Male and female sexed bodies do not linger on the fringes of Christian theological anthropology. "[W]e are made in God's image as persons who are not completely defined by their sex, but who cannot be defined apart from their embodied sex."[28] Scripturally, biological sex is a significant aspect of human identity.

Showing that biological sex matters to our identity is important, but this alone doesn't answer the question of how we should think about gender. We need to hit the brakes if you think we're ready to say that biological sex *and not* gender (identity or role) defines who we are. Again, it's not as if the Bible directly addresses a case where someone's gender identity is at odds with their biological sex. We've got a lot more questions and arguments to wrestle with before we reach an answer about how to respond to incongruities between biological sex and internal gender identity. Let's make sure we're being both thorough and cautious, humbly considering all angles in the discussion. For now, we can safely say that the Bible has a very high view of our sexed embodiment and considers our male and female biology to be a significant part of human identity.

But what about masculinity and femininity? Do males have to be masculine, and females feminine, to be godly?

No. Let's talk about why not.

Chapter 5

GENDER STEREOTYPES

K.D. grew up as the youngest of several brothers in a context where men were expected to be masculine and women to be feminine. "Real men" served in the military, and women typically stayed home and made babies. K.D.'s brothers naturally joined the military and went off to war. They were the epitome of masculinity. K.D., on the other hand, had another sort of gift: he loved to write poetry.

K.D. struggled with many emotions throughout his life: doubt, depression, anxiety. He also had times when he was so filled with joy he could hardly contain himself. Often, he would grab a pen and bleed his emotions onto paper.

Like many poets, K.D. also had a talent for writing and playing music. While his brothers were off at war, K.D. stayed home and wrote poetry and music, singing songs about nature, beauty, depression, God, and his best friend, John.

John and K.D. were inseparable. They spent loads of time together and desperately missed each other when they were apart. K.D. vowed that he would spend the rest of his life with John, and John felt the same. They weren't sexual with each other. But they were more than your typical American male friends. When they were together, they would laugh, they would cry, they would talk, and they would hug. Sometimes they would even kiss—in a friendship sort of way.

A few years later, John enlisted in the military and went off to war. He rose through the ranks and was a skilled fighter. But, one day, John was killed in battle.

When the news reached K.D.'s ears, he was devastated. He fell into a depression. He refused to eat, and he wept profusely. Once the tears dried up enough for him to see, K.D. did the only thing that could soothe his pain. He took his pen and poured out his heart in a poem, describing John's love as better than the love he felt toward women. After K.D.'s own death, the poem would be published and read by millions. So moving, so intimate, so loving were the words of that poem that some people to this day believe that K.D. and John were gay.

If you haven't caught it by now, K.D. stands for King David.

Though the Bible gives no evidence that David and Jonathan were in a sexual relationship, it's true that David's intimate words toward Jonathan have led some readers to say they were.[1] And of course, David manifested many masculine traits like chopping off the head of a giant and killing a lion with his bare hands. But David also sat on a hilltop, wrote poetry, played the harp, and hugged and kissed his best friend and said, "Your love for me was wonderful, more wonderful than that of women" (2 Sam. 1:26).

By most American standards, David did some feminine things as well as a bunch of masculine ones. But what is "biblical" masculinity and femininity? Was David in sin when he was crying or playing his harp? Unfortunately, many of our beliefs about masculinity and femininity come from culture rather than the Bible, even though we sometimes rubber stamp these cultural norms with the label "biblical." If something is truly "biblical," it needs to actually come from the Bible.

In the Bible, men often kiss other men (1 Sam. 10:1) and cry (Gen. 33:4). They are tender and called to be tenderhearted (Eph. 4:32). They are profoundly emotional (the Psalms) and relational (1 Sam. 18:1–5). They are called to turn the other cheek (Matt. 5:39), to love—not kill—their enemies (Matt. 5:44), to weep with those who weep (Rom. 12:15), to raise up and teach children (Eph. 6:4), to be sensitive (Eph. 4:2), to be kind (Prov. 11:17), and to be peacemakers (Matt. 5:9), if they want to truly be men.

Biblical women also defy current stereotypes. Sure, the Proverbs 31 woman is an "excellent wife" (v. 10 ESV) who rises up early and "provides food for her household" (v. 15 ESV), who makes "bed coverings" and "linen garments" (vv. 22, 24 ESV). But then she taps into her entrepreneurial skills and sells those linen garments for a profit after she "considers a field and buys it" (vv. 24, 16). She's wise, hardworking, has strong arms, and engages in social justice in her spare time (v. 20). *Fortune* 500 companies long for a CEO as qualified as the Proverbs 31 woman.

Women in the Bible do all sorts of things that weren't considered "feminine." They fight in battles and win wars, sometimes by smashing tent pegs through the skulls of men (Judg. 4:21). They are unmarried businesswomen like Lydia (Acts 16:14–15). They are fearless, like the three women named Mary who stood by Jesus at the cross after most of the men had scattered (John 19:25). Many wealthy women followed Jesus and even funded his ministry (Luke 8:1–3)—quite a challenge for those who think males must always be the breadwinners. And what a sight that must have been: when Jesus wasn't pulling loaves and fish out of thin air, he was waiting for his female disciples to pick up the tab at the local falafel shop.

Most gender stereotypes come from culture, not the Bible.

Gender stereotypes were around in biblical times. The Jewish and Greco-Roman cultures of biblical times were saturated with expectations about how women and men should act. Some of these stereotypes are very similar to the ones we have today (at least in the West). Men were expected to be hairy-chested, sexually charged, domineering men. And real men were military men. Joining the military and becoming a soldier "was the only way many Roman males could lay claim to being a man."[2] Any male who cried in public, showed affection (not just lust) toward women, abstained from sex outside of marriage, or honored lower-class people—the poor, the marginalized, and children—was not considered a *real* masculine man.[3] A real man would never have washed another man's feet.

Enter Jesus.

Jesus not only turned over tables in the temple but also overturned social views about masculinity and femininity. In addition to his "masculine" table-flipping, Jesus also wept over Jerusalem and longed to "gather your children together, as a hen gathers her chicks under her wings" (Luke 13:34). Onlookers might have considered Jesus masculine when he chewed out the religious leaders in Matthew 23. (Or is that a feminine trait?) But he also let others slap him in the face and smack him on the head, and he rarely stood up for his personal rights. Jesus comes to us as one who "challenges cultural notions of masculinity. He washes feet, touches sick people, shows compassion to sinful women, loves children, and more."[4] Jesus, in other words, supplies us with a countercultural view of masculinity.

There's nothing wrong with being a man who loves sports and rough-and-tumble play. Many men do. And there's nothing wrong with being a woman who desires to stay at home and raise eight kids while making homemade clothes. Many women … well, okay, most women still don't want that many kids and would rather buy fifteen-dollar shirts from Target instead of spinning them on a wheel. My point is, stereotypes might fit the natural desires and experiences of *many* or even *most* males and females, but not all. Stereotypes are *descriptions* of how many men and women behave, but they aren't biblical *prescriptions* for all.

Many of our beliefs about masculinity and femininity come from culture rather than the Bible, even though we sometimes rubber stamp these cultural norms with the label "biblical."

The Bible is profoundly liberating when it comes to how males and females are expected to act. This is why almost every command in the Bible isn't tailored to a certain sex. Men aren't commanded to be masculine, and women aren't commanded to be feminine. They're both just commanded to be *godly*.

The fruit of the Spirit (Gal. 5:22–23), for instance, doesn't have male and female fruit. It's just fruit. "Love, joy, peace, forbearance, kindness, goodness, faithfulness, gentleness and self-control" are what springs from *both* men and women who are walking in the Spirit. Paul never said that only women were to "love one another," "rejoice with those who rejoice," and "weep with those who weep," while men are to "do what is honorable in the sight of all" (Rom. 12:10, 15, 17 ESV). Almost every command in the New Testament is given to all believers irrespective of sex.

The Bible is much more concerned that we be godly, not stereotypically masculine or feminine. While our culture reinforces narrow stereotypes of masculinity and femininity, the Bible doesn't give us narrow mandates for how all men and women must behave. We are all called to be virtuous. While the Bible celebrates our sex differences as male and female, it gives us tremendous freedom in how we live within our sexed bodies.[5]

Unfortunately, the church doesn't always celebrate this freedom. I know, because I've been to men's retreats.

Men's retreats don't tend to be very inclusive of all men; they are geared much more toward "masculine" men. We don't often say it, but men's retreats—and, I assume, women's retreats as well—prioritize gender roles over biological sex. They typically appeal to males and females who fit the stereotypes, who conform to the majority. They are designed for men who love pick-up football games and women who love to pick up some thread and start knitting. Men's retreats serve ribs and women's retreats serve salad, even though the men could probably use a bit more salad and plenty of women crave the sweet smell of hickory smoke wafting off a grill.

None of this is bad or immoral. Stereotypes often become stereotypes because they resonate with the majority. And although I haven't said it yet, *I'm the stereotype.* I love sports, ribs, large trucks, and road maps. All the more reason for me to be aware of how stereotypical categories reinforced by the majority can, unintentionally, exclude the minority—those whose biological sex qualifies them to attend the men's retreat, but whose vegan diet and love for poetry will probably prompt them to stay home.

What does all this have to do with the trans* conversation? Quite a bit, actually.

STEREOTYPES AND TRANS* EXPERIENCES

Gender stereotypes are an important part of the transgender conversation. Women have been particularly affected by these stereotypes. After all, most women know what it's like to be stuffed into narrow boxes of femininity. Sensual makeup, pink dresses, sexy high heels, and expecting to grow up to become a helpless princess at the top of a tower waiting for her masculine hero to sweep her away. Images like these are often associated with being a woman. But what if you don't want to wear painful high heels so that your legs will look sexier for men? What if you're not helpless and don't need a man to rescue you? Are you still a woman?

Of course you are. And yet some people say that if you are drawn to these stereotypes—pink dresses, high heels, fantasies about being a princess—this means that you might be a girl. We see this especially in how some experts advise parents to determine whether their kid is trans*.

"I was into sports and skateboards, but never into girls' toys, dolls, princesses or anything pink," says Alfie, a transman describing childhood. "My mum would say it was just a phase: 'You won't always be like this. When you get to secondary school, you'll like makeup and boys and all this other stuff.' And in my head it was so

strong, the feelings, that I could never see myself being like that.…
In my head, I felt like a boy."[6]

My heart goes out to people like Alfie who from a young age
felt like they were trapped in the wrong body. Gender dysphoria can
be utterly debilitating—like a creepy serum coursing through your
veins. I do wonder whether gender stereotypes are only exacerbating
the problem. Alfie, born female, was "into sports and skateboards,
but never into *girls' toys, dolls, princesses or anything pink.*" Does this
mean that Alfie wasn't actually a girl? Can't girls play sports, ride
skateboards, and abhor the color pink?

Similarly, one parent of a trans* child named Eva says:

> When Eva was about 2 years old and people said, "What
> a cute little boy," she would respond emphatically, "I'm
> not a boy. I'm a girl!" She showed a strong preference for
> female playmates, dolls, and anything pink. At daycare
> and at home, she always wore a towel or T-shirt on her
> head, which represented "long hair," as she called it.[7]

Dolls, long hair, and anything pink are all feminine stereotypes
reinforced by culture. (Remember, one hundred years ago, pink
was considered quite masculine.) Do these things make Eva female?
Certainly, when a two-year-old biological male declares they are a
girl, there's a good chance this child will wrestle with gender dysphoria at least until adolescence. But I don't think it's helpful to take the
child's preference for dolls, pink, and long hair as evidence that they
really are a girl, since it relies on stereotypes to define what it means
to be a girl.

Another parent describes their male-born child, Warner (age nine), as having "preferences for pink, sparkles, even her physical mannerism with her hands were very flamboyant, wanting to be a princess. You know, if you took her shopping, she'd go right for dresses." In Warner's own words: "I never actually, like, fitted in with being a boy. I don't like the games, the hairstyles, the clothes ... and I always thought from the very beginning that I was a little bit feminine."[8] But it's our culture, not science—and certainly not the Bible—that says boys aren't allowed to be "a little bit feminine."

One dad was so relieved when his stereotypically feminine son had transitioned to female. He recalls his relief: "I saw her run off to camp after she transitioned. I said, 'Ah, that's just like a girl running!'" The dad was elated that he wouldn't have to say, "Look at my son, he runs like a girl."[9]

I don't think it's helpful to take the child's preference for dolls, pink, and long hair as evidence that they really are a girl, since it relies on stereotypes to define what it means to be a girl.

It's certainly possible that a child born biologically male who "runs like a girl" might also experience gender dysphoria or perceive themselves as female. For many children with dysphoria, latching onto stereotypically masculine or stereotypically feminine things can serve as a kind of coping mechanism. My fear, though, is that parents and medical professionals are only reinforcing these stereotypes when they use a preference for pink, disinterest in sports, or "running like a girl" as the basis for determining whether that child is a boy or a girl.

Some trans* adults also seem to reinforce gender stereotypes. One transwoman says she dresses "as a *normal* woman: lingerie, nylons, dresses, shoes, etc., and applying full makeup and perfume."[10] If being a "normal" woman means wearing lingerie, nylons, and full makeup, then I don't know if my wife is a normal woman. I know hardly any women who actually like these things. Another transwoman says:

> I had very strong desires to dress as a female on a full-time basis and to attract attention as a sexy, feminine woman. I have worn sexy feminine fashions, especially bras, lingerie, pantyhose, short dresses, lace fashions, mini-skirts, high heels, etc., at home since my mid-20's.[11]

It seems like cultural stereotypes are being used to define the essence of what it means to be a woman. Lingerie, pantyhose, short dresses, mini-skirts—these are all cultural constructs of one version of femininity. But they aren't the essence of womanhood. In fact, they might be projections of a male gaze.

This is why some women were upset when Caitlyn Jenner posed on the cover of *Vanity Fair* magazine in seductive apparel. Caitlyn seemed to embody the cultural stereotypes of femininity forged in the lustful minds of men. Miranda Yardley, who is also a transwoman, expressed her concern this way:

> [T]his image of Jenner as being not "a man becoming a woman" but … "a man becoming a man's idea of

what a woman should be"… an idealised body is presented clothed only in lingerie, the makeup is done to
perfection, and every flaw is magically photoshopped
out of existence. Pandering to the male gaze, the body
language is coy, seductive, submissive. This is not liberation, this is not revolution, this is not life-affirming;
this is the crass stereotyping of what it means to be
a woman, meeting every reactionary, culturally conservative ideal of what a woman should be; passive,
objectified, dehumanised.[12]

As Yardley demonstrates, trans* people are by no means in agreement about gender stereotypes. Some seem eager to resurrect them,
while others (like Yardley) are adamantly opposed.

When it comes to stereotypes and dysphoria, it's tough to sort
out causation from correlation: Are stereotypes *causing* dysphoria, or
is dysphoria *causing* people to feel drawn toward stereotypes, or are
the two simply correlated? For some trans* people I know, stereotypes
aren't necessarily the root cause of their dysphoria, but stereotypes
certainly play a role in exacerbating the pain. This is one reason why
Christians with gender dysphoria usually avoid men's and women's
retreats—or other sex-specific church venues. These events tend to
reinforce the view that to be a godly woman is to be feminine, and to
be a godly man is to be masculine.

I'll never forget getting a call from one of my friends with gender
dysphoria. Their voice was trembling—they sounded on the verge of
a breakdown. The reason? They had agreed to host a women's Bible
study at their house. At any moment, they were expecting oodles of

femininity to come pouring through their door. Just the thought of pink dresses, gabby women, and tiny little teacups was enough to make them want to scream.

As it turns out, the women who showed up were less stereotypical than my friend feared. They weren't wearing pink dresses or high heels, and several preferred their coffee black with no sugar and drank it from large mugs. Because you can be a *woman* without being a stereotypically *feminine* woman. And my friend is no less qualified to host a women's Bible study—and no less obedient to the Bible—simply because they reject the sex-specific demands placed on them by society.

But—my trans* friends often ask me—*are there any sex-specific moral demands in the Bible?*

ARE THERE *ANY* SEX-SPECIFIC MORAL PRESCRIPTIONS?

What does it mean to live in a manner consistent with your sexed identity? Is there anything that men *shouldn't* (morally) do that women *must* do (and vice versa)?

Scripture contains hardly any sex-specific commands. Even the passages that do single out a specific sex often give commands that equally apply to the other sex elsewhere in Scripture. Take Titus 2, for instance. Paul instructs Titus to

teach the older women to be reverent in the way they live, not to be slanderers or addicted to much wine, but to teach what is good. Then they can urge the younger women to love their husbands and children, to be self-controlled and pure, **to be busy at home**, to be kind, and **to be subject to their husbands**, so that no one will malign the word of God. (v. 3–5)

Paul gives ten commands to women here. But at least eight of the ten are elsewhere expected of men: to be reverent, not to be slanderers or addicted to much wine, to teach what is good, to love their spouses and children, to be self-controlled and pure, and to be kind. These things are commanded to women here, but they are not female-only commands. Being "self-controlled and pure … [and] kind" are not feminine virtues; they're godly virtues.

The only two commands that *might* only apply to women here are "to be subject to their husbands" and "to be busy at home." The meaning of these commands is highly disputed in Christian circles today. "Busy at home" doesn't mean that women can't work or that they're not allowed to leave the house. It probably has more to do with a specific situation in Ephesus (where Titus pastored) where Christian women were being lazy *while at* home. Paul is not saying that women need to stay at home around the clock.[13]

As far as wives submitting to husbands, we see this elsewhere in the New Testament (Eph. 5:22; Titus 2:5; 1 Pet. 3:1). For what it's worth, all people—men included—are commanded to "submit to one another" in Ephesians 5:21. Submission is a Christian virtue, not a feminine one. And yet we never see the command, "Husbands, submit to your wives."

We've got enough controversy on our plate, so let's not open up a second can of snakes about male headship in the home. Even if you take a more conservative reading of these passages, they still refer to married women, not all women.

In addition to the directives given in Titus 2, we also see the command that women aren't supposed to "teach or to exercise authority over a man" (1 Tim. 2:12 ESV; cf. 1 Cor. 14:34–35), whereas men aren't ever told not to teach or exercise authority over women. This topic is even *more* disputed than the male headship one. Depending on how we interpret these passages, we may conclude that they constitute commands still applicable to present-day women (and not to men). But even if we did reach this debated conclusion, the instructions would still only apply to women's roles within the church context, not to female behavior categorically.

What about the day-to-day lives of Christians, especially those not engaged in ministry leadership? Are any other biblical commands male- or female-specific?

Maybe. I'm thinking of passages like Deuteronomy 22:5 and 1 Corinthians 11:2–16, which tell us to maintain male and female distinctions in how we dress (clothing and hairstyles, in particular).[14] Most readers, including me, would say that head coverings (1 Cor. 11) are necessary for the culture of Paul's first-century Corinthian readers and not for every culture. But biblical scholars across the conservative-liberal spectrum agree almost unanimously that Paul is establishing a principle that men and women should maintain distinctions in how they present themselves.[15]

If this principle about maintaining male and female distinctions still applies to Christians today, then what does it mean to present oneself as a man or woman? Here are four considerations to keep in mind as we grapple with this complex question.

First, the meaning of clothing is culturally bound. What some cultures consider masculine, other cultures consider feminine, and vice versa. When I visited Samoa several years ago, I wore a lavalava, which is a skirtlike wraparound. It's what men wear in the Polynesian islands. But in America, things are different. We have our own cultural codes of distinguishing men from women, but the lines between the two are much blurrier in the West. Sex-appropriate clothing is culturally determined.

The Bible's primary invitation to every Christian is not to act more like a man or to act more like a woman, but to act more like Jesus.

Second, some cultures have clearer distinctions than others when it comes to male- and female-specific clothing. In most ancient cultures—including the biblical world—the line between women's and men's clothing (and hairstyle) was much more black and white. Women wore one thing, and men wore another. But in the modern West, there's quite a bit of crossover. Men can wear jeans, and women can wear jeans. Men can even wear super-tight skinny jeans that used to be considered more feminine ten years ago. Women wear suits. Men wear suits. Women wear long hair. Men wear long hair. The lines between male and female clothing are much grayer in the West, thanks in part to 1980s glamor rock icons and third-wave feminism.

And yet, third, some things even in the West are currently culturally reserved for one sex and not the other. Dresses, high heels, two-piece bathing suits—these are (right now) clearly female attire. *Not* that wearing them makes you female, or that all females must dress like this. But the clothing itself is culturally reserved for women. If a biological male donned a bikini, they would be presenting as a woman, whether in earnest or in jest. And yet, we have to acknowledge again that what constitutes male and female clothing changes over time. It's theoretically possible that today's female attire will tomorrow be considered male attire. Remember the history of pink and blue.

Fourth, presenting oneself as male or female isn't so much about the fabric or shape of clothing but about the purpose behind it. If a biological male wears culturally female clothing as part of a joke or as a costume in a theatrical performance, that clothing means something different than it would when worn by a biological male expressing a female gender identity. In sorting through what the Bible's guidelines about male and female distinctions mean for Christians today, we need to remember that God is far more interested in people's hearts than he is in outward appearances.

Most of all, as we consider what the Bible has to say to people who experience gender dysphoria, we need to make sure we're not arbitrarily creating sex-specific rules and forcing them onto others—especially not rules rooted in unbiblical stereotypes. As we've just seen, while there may be some sex-specific biblical commands, the vast majority of God's commands are given to men and women alike. The Bible's primary invitation to every Christian is not to act more like a man or to act more like a woman, but to act more like Jesus.

Chapter 6

BUT WHAT ABOUT THE EUNUCH? AND OTHER QUESTIONS ...

I want to circle back to our discussion in chapter 4. As you recall, the Bible presents biological sex as a significant aspect of human identity. Now, some agree with this claim but say that it tells only one side of the story, that it neglects other passages and themes that give a more nuanced perspective. Sure, the Bible has a high view of the body. But it also makes room for those who are "gender variant" or experience incongruence between their biological sex and their gender (identity or role). In these cases, their gender—not their sex—determines who they are.

In this chapter, I'm going to wrestle with the biblical reasons why some Christians argue along these lines (that gender should supersede sex when there's incongruence). In no particular order, I'll summarize and respond to each of these arguments.

GENESIS 1 ASSUMES NONBINARY ASPECTS OF CREATION

Some say that the binaries of Genesis 1 are polar ends of a spectrum, allowing for hybrids and variations in between.[1] For instance, Genesis 1 talks about day and night, but dusk and dawn also exist in between day and night. Genesis 1 talks about land and sea creatures, but we can also assume that frogs and other amphibians—creatures of both land and sea (or water)—were part of God's good creation. Therefore, when Genesis 1 talks about the binary of "male and female," these categories are simply the opposite ends of a spectrum of identities, not the only absolute ones. The text assumes variations in between male and female—intersex and transgender being the most obvious examples.

It's true that some statements like "day and night," "land and sea," or even "alpha and omega" bear the sense of *these two opposites and everything in between.* But as we saw in chapter 4, the phrase "male and female" in Genesis 1:27 refers to biological sex, not gender roles or identities.[2] No doubt, there are many variations among females and males. Tall, short, strong, weak, hairy, hairless, Enneagram 3 wing 4 or 2 wing 3. But the beautiful variations among males and among females do not mean that "male and female" are only two of many options. Non-intersex humans are sexually dimorphic. Some intersex persons might combine both biological categories of male and female, but this doesn't mean they constitute something other than male and female. Variations within two categories, or even a blend of two categories, doesn't mean more than two categories exist.

Plus, a quick scan of the Bible shows that rivers and marshes (Ex. 7:19; Ezek. 47:11), dusk and dawn (Gen. 15:17; Deut. 16:6), and frogs and other amphibians (Ex. 8:2; Lev. 11:30) are part of creation. Genesis 1 certainly doesn't cover every asteroid and amphibian in the universe. But whenever Scripture mentions sexed categories of *humanity*, it only names male and female.[3] We simply don't encounter humans identified as something other than male or female in Scripture. (We'll address eunuchs below.)

Therefore, while Genesis 1 certainly assumes various hybrids or shades of "in-betweenness" in many aspects of creation, male and female are still the only categories of embodied sex among humans. Humans differ in *how* they are male and female, but this doesn't mean sex categories exist *in addition* to male and female.

Many scholars who make the "Genesis 1 is not a binary" argument use the term *gender* to make their point—often without defining what they mean by the term. They point out that Scripture assumes nonbinary features (like rivers and marshes, dusk and dawn), then say that the apparent *gender* binary—male and female—of Genesis 1:27 doesn't rule out trans* identities that are neither strictly male nor strictly female. Linda Tatro Herzer, for instance, says:

> *[T]he male or female gender binary* classification system suggested by Genesis 1:27 is ... inadequate to describe the reality of those born with the innate knowledge that their *internal gender identity* does not match their external genitals.[4]

But there's no textual evidence that Genesis 1:27 is talking about a person's internal sense of who they are (gender identity) or whether a male is masculine or a female is feminine (gender role). A male with gender dysphoria, or a female who's not particularly feminine, is very much included in the male/female *sex* binary of Genesis 1:27.

Humans differ in **how** *they are male and female, but this doesn't mean sex categories exist* **in addition** *to male and female.*

In any case, Herzer goes on to apply her nonbinary argument to various biblical characters who don't fit masculine and feminine stereotypes. Like Jacob, who "was definitely gender variant ... given his preference for women's work and for spending his days among the women of his tribe."[5] Or Joseph, because he wore a "girly garment gladly."[6] Or Deborah, who was "settling disputes, speaking on God's behalf, leading an army"—things that "were all strictly men's work."[7]

I appreciate how Herzer shows that various biblical characters didn't fit the masculine and feminine stereotypes of the day. But phrases like "women's work" and "girly garment" end up affirming the very stereotypes that are so problematic in this conversation. Is there a thing called "women's work"? If a female doesn't particularly like "women's work," is she not a woman? When Joseph donned his colorful coat, was it because he was trans*? Or just a man with fabulous taste?[8]

Genesis 1 is talking about biological sex—male and female—not what we have labeled *gender identity* or *gender role*. And it's perfectly fine for males and females to resist cultural stereotypes *as* males and females.

JESUS' ACCEPTANCE OF THE EUNUCH

At the tail end of a conversation about marriage and divorce, Jesus makes a statement about three different kinds of eunuchs:

> For there are eunuchs who were born that way, and there are eunuchs who have been made eunuchs by others—and there are those who choose to live like eunuchs for the sake of the kingdom of heaven. The one who can accept this should accept it. (Matt. 19:12)

Some say that eunuchs "are the closest biblical analogy that we have for transgendered people"[9] and use this passage to make an argument about present-day trans* identities. Before we look closely at this argument, let's first wrap our minds around what Jesus is saying here. Jesus mentions three kinds of eunuchs: (1) those who were *born* eunuchs, (2) those who were *made* eunuchs by others, and (3) those who *choose* to live like eunuchs.

The Greek term *eunouchos* (and its Hebrew and Latin equivalents) is used in Jewish and Greco-Roman literature to cover a broad range of individuals.[10] Some were asexual (having no sexual desire)[11] and therefore served as reliable guardians of the king's harem (or daughters)[12] or as focused military leaders unhindered by sexual distractions.[13] Others were men who lacked secondary male sex characteristics (such as facial hair and deep voice), typically because they had been castrated before puberty. Still others were viewed as sexually charged men who were infertile but not impotent—capable of sexually servicing wealthy women (and, in some cases, their husbands as well) without the risk of pregnancy.[14] In some cases, eunuchs were considered neither masculine enough to be real men nor feminine enough to be real women—an accusation that stems from cultural stereotypes projected upon eunuchs. We don't know anything about the internal psychology, or what we might now call the gender identity, of eunuchs themselves.[15]

The common denominator among all eunuchs is that they were biological males[16] who were *infertile*,[17] most often as a result of some impairment in their sexual anatomy from birth or through castration.[18] As far as I can tell from the literature, eunuchs were never females. They were males deemed unmasculine by culture. Any ambiguity over who eunuchs were had to do with cultural standards of masculinity.

What do we know about the three different types of eunuchs Jesus mentions? In the context of Matthew 19, the eunuch is primarily a symbol of singleness. Remember the situation. Jesus has just given a hardcore statement against divorce, and the Pharisees point out that Moses permitted divorce (Deut. 24). Jesus responds that Moses allowed divorce because the Israelites' hearts were hard; "it was not this way from the beginning" (Matt. 19:8). He then reiterates his divorce prohibition (v. 9). Notice, Jesus is always bringing us back to creation, just as he did earlier (vv. 3–5). Creation and resurrection are the twin pillars of Jesus' ethic.

At this point the disciples jump in and say, "If this is the situation between a husband and wife, it is better not to marry" (v. 10). It's this declaration about not marrying which leads to Jesus' statements about the eunuch (v. 12). In other words, the eunuch exemplifies Jesus' high view of singleness. Is it "better not to marry"? In some cases, yes; just look at the eunuch.

What can we draw from this passage that's relevant to our topic? I think it's fair to say that Jesus' first category of eunuch (the one born a eunuch) is similar to what we call intersex: someone born with some atypical feature in their sexual anatomy. The main difference is that some intersex people are fertile, get married, and have kids, whereas eunuchs are by definition infertile; and, moreover, Jesus' main point is that all three eunuchs in the passage illustrate the point that "it is better not to marry."

We can also say that Jesus' eunuch statements are a slap in the face to the rigid cultural stereotypes of masculinity in both the Jewish and Roman culture. Men who were castrated, infertile, or not well endowed below the belt by Roman standards were considered not "real" men. Size really did matter in ancient Rome. Just Google "Priapus" and see. (Actually, don't Google that.) And in Jewish culture, nearly all men wanted to get married and father many children. Jesus uses the eunuch to show that faithfulness is more important than machismo.

Now, some gender-affirming writers like Linda Tatro Herzer have used the eunuch to argue that "along with the genders of male and female, Jesus also recognized that there actually *is* gender variance."[19] Herzer goes on to propose that "God may also have an accepting, affirming, and inclusive attitude towards the gender variant people of our day."[20] Similarly, Austen Hartke says that Jesus' teaching about eunuchs applies to those who feel "the call to a life outside the gender and sex norms of their time," including transgender Christians.[21]

I think some of the language here is confusing and unhelpful. The terms "male and female," when used in the Bible, refer to sex rather than gender. "Gender variance," "life outside the gender … norms," and "gender variant people" are ambiguous phrases at best. Does Jesus accept, affirm, and celebrate godly men who can't throw a football and who cry while watching *Downton Abbey*? Absolutely. Jesus values godliness, not gender stereotypes. But does Jesus use the eunuch to show that a person's internal sense of self is more definitive than their biological sex when there is incongruence between the two? I think this is a bit of a stretch.

We know nothing about first-century eunuchs' internal sense of self (gender identity). But we do know that, just a few verses earlier, Jesus affirmed about all humanity "at the beginning the Creator 'made them male and female,'" citing Genesis 1:27 (Matt. 19:4). Eunuchs were biologically male, and it seems likely that Jesus regarded them as part of the "male" category in God's good creation even if others considered them to be unmasculine.[22]

Jesus' eunuch statement has a lot to teach us about gender and gender roles. It not only challenges the low view of singleness in our American church culture, but it also deconstructs the gender stereotypes we often promote. The eunuch passage calls us to a broader biblical vision of what it means to be a man or a woman, reminding us that we don't need to mimic the cultural scripts of masculinity and femininity.

Being a man is not about being masculine. It's about being godly. Nonfeminine women are still women. And if these women feel uncomfortable at our women's retreats, then that's the church's problem, not theirs.

"NOR IS THERE MALE AND FEMALE"— GALATIANS 3:28

At the end of a lengthy argument about God's mission to include Gentiles, Paul writes,

> There is neither Jew nor Gentile, neither slave nor free, *nor is there male and female,* for you are all one in Christ Jesus. (Gal. 3:28)

Some people quote this verse (the part about "nor is there male and female") to show that Paul downplayed sex difference and was seeking to move beyond the created order of Genesis 1–2. Paul anticipates that in the resurrection, sex difference will be done away with altogether. When we're resurrected, we'll live forever not as males and females, but as androgynous, nonsexed people.

This interpretation doesn't necessarily affirm that gender identity overrules biological sex when there's incongruence, but it does play a supporting role. If Galatians 3:28 downplays sex difference, then we too shouldn't make a big deal out of it. It's all going to pass away in the end.

Despite some evidence for this interpretation,[23] I find it problematic for at least two reasons. First, nothing in the context of Galatians 3:28, nor in the letter as a whole, nor in any of Paul's letters, suggests that sex difference is no longer important. We would be hard pressed, in fact, to find any other reference to sex difference being a bad thing, or an old thing done away with in Christ, in the entire New Testament. (Later in this chapter, we'll address the statement in Matthew 22 about believers being like the angels of heaven.) It's unlikely that Paul would randomly drop a bomb here in passing—one that conflicts with his own statements upholding sex differences between men and women (1 Cor. 11:2–16; Rom. 1:26–27)—without further comment. Paul is most certainly deconstructing social hierarchies associated with sex difference. But it's unlikely that he's doing away with sex difference itself.

Second, the phrase "male and female" should be understood in light of the other two preceding pairs: "neither Jew nor Gentile, neither slave nor free" (Gal. 3:28). If sex differences are being done away with, then we'd almost have to conclude that the other differences—Jew and Gentile, slave and free—are also erased. But the fact is, after becoming Christians, Jews remain Jews, Gentiles are still Gentiles, slaves are (unfortunately) still slaves, and free people are very much free. Paul's entire argument in Galatians 3 is that Gentiles can become Christians *as Gentiles*. They don't need to become Jews in order to be saved. Paul is challenging hierarchies based on ethnic differences, not challenging the existence of ethnic differences themselves.[24]

Paul is most certainly deconstructing social hierarchies associated with sex difference. But it's unlikely that he's doing away with sex difference itself.

Most likely, then, Paul is using the male/female pair in the same way he's using slave/free and Jew/Gentile. Paul is boldly declaring that women (who were usually treated very poorly in the first century) are given status equal to men in God's kingdom—a beautiful statement that only makes sense if sex differences are real.[25]

NO MARRIAGE IN THE RESURRECTION—
MATTHEW 22:30

In Matthew 22, Jesus makes a statement that is sometimes interpreted to mean sex difference will be erased in the resurrection:

> At the resurrection people will neither marry nor be given in marriage; they will be like the angels in heaven. (Matt. 22:30)

Luke's version of this statement contains some additional words:

> But those who are considered worthy of taking part in the age to come and in the resurrection from the dead will neither marry nor be given in marriage, and they can no longer die; for they are like the angels. (Luke 20:35–36)

Is Jesus saying we'll be resurrected as sexless, androgynous beings? Some say yes, but Jesus doesn't actually say this. He only says we won't *marry*, not become sexless. Obviously, people can still be male or female even if they never marry. Just look at Jesus. While marriage assumes sex difference, sex difference exists apart from marriage. Plus, as we've seen, there's evidence elsewhere in Scripture that our resurrection bodies will reflect our earthly (sexed) bodies.

The mention of being "like the angels" is startling, for sure. But it doesn't have to mean we'll be sexless in the resurrection. Whenever angels appear in the Bible, they always appear as men. When Jesus' audience heard that we'll be "like the angels," they'd have no reason to think "sexless." In fact, a widespread belief in Judaism at that time held that angels had sex with humans back in Genesis 6 and produced gigantic offspring called the *nephilim*. I'm surprised Stephen King hasn't written a book about this yet.

While angels may not be married, this doesn't demand that they are sexless. Even if they were sexless, the point in comparing us to angels is that we won't be married, or, as Luke's gospel emphasizes, that we will never die. It's certainly not clear that when Jesus says "like the angels," he means "sexless."

THE BIBLE IS TOO OUTDATED TO ADDRESS MODERN QUESTIONS ABOUT TRANS* IDENTITIES

People who use this argument might agree that the Bible only talks about humans as male and female. But, they say, that's because its writers weren't aware of all the things we now know about gender dysphoria, gender identity, and trans* identities and experiences.

One thing is for sure: we know *a lot* more about the science and sociology of sex and gender than first-century writers. In the last hundred years alone, we've made monumental advancements in our understanding of biology, psychology, DNA research, neurology, and how society influences our view of ourselves and others. And yet, we also have a long way to go. Science is always advancing and changing and correcting itself and giving us new knowledge previously unknown. No matter what year it is, we still haven't arrived. It's important to keep our fallibility in mind whenever we're tempted to overturn a biblical truth because it seems to clash with some settled perspective in science. Science is rarely settled. Plus, it's not as if the latest science has proven that gender identity overrules biological sex when there's incongruence. One might say it's the other way around: an appeal to science creates more problems than possibilities for the gender-affirming view.

At any rate, while the Bible doesn't tell us everything we need to know about sex and gender, I think it's foolhardy to assume that it has little or nothing to say about human nature or about what it means to be male and female. Every scientist worth her salt knows that science can give us the "is" but it can't tell us the "ought." That is, science can help us make observations about life, but it can't tell us how to live. "Scientific statements of facts and relations," says Albert Einstein, "cannot produce ethical directives."[26] Sound words from a sound mind.

Scientific views about sex, gender, gender dysphoria, gender identity, and many other aspects of this conversation are also widely disputed. Scientists don't agree on any settled conclusions when it comes to, say, gender identity. The only "earth-is-round-and-not-flat" sort of scientific conclusion is that humanity is a sexually dimorphic species. (Actually, I do get some weird emails from the Flat Earth Society, so I guess even that is disputed by some people.) When it comes to questions about the soul, the mind, and other immaterial aspects of human nature, we're dealing more with philosophy and theology than we are with science. You can't determine via CAT scan whether someone has a female soul trapped in a male body.

Now, we do have to be extra cautious about making the biblical writers speak more directly to our current conversation than they intended. We have to understand what the Bible says on its own terms, in its own context, as it addresses its own situations. And yet, when we do this, we see that there might be aspects of continuity between their day and ours when it comes to questions about trans* identities and experiences.

At the time the Bible was written, some well-known and very public figures were biologically male yet expressed themselves as female (or vice versa). For instance, we know that in ancient Mesopotamia there were cult functionaries known as the *assinnu, kurgarrû*, and *kulu'u* who blurred male/female distinctions. They were "men ... by birth as regards their physiology, but their appearance either was feminine or had both male and female characteristics."[27] Their appearance corresponded to the god(dess) of their worship, Ishtar, who was known for "transgressing conventional gender boundaries."[28] Around the time of the New Testament, we see similar cult functionaries in Phrygia known as *galli*, who served the goddesses Atargatis and Cybele. *Galli* were castrated men who dressed up as women and basically took on a feminine role in society.[29]

But crossing gender boundaries was not limited to cultic practices. We see evidence in popular literature of stories that resemble to some extent modern trans* experiences. Writing just prior to the birth of Christ, Ovid tells a tale about a biological girl, Iphis, who was raised as a boy by her mother.[30] (Somehow, the mother kept the secret from her husband, who desperately wanted a boy.) As she grew older, Iphis found herself sexually attracted to Ianthe, a female—and her future bride. Iphis found her same-sex attraction to be unnatural and therefore prayed that the gods would transform her into a boy—a wish that was granted just prior to her wedding: "[U]ntil this very moment, you *were* a female, and now you're a boy."[31]

As far as we can tell, the Roman emperor Elagabalus (reign: AD 218–222) wanted to be, or believed he was, a woman. The Roman author Dio Cassius tells us that Elagabalus had sex with women so he could learn how to act like a woman in bed. He would go to the taverns and dress as a barmaid to pick up men. He would also work the brothels and service men *as a woman*. When he married Hierocles, a male Carian slave, Elagabalus dressed as a bride and gave himself away as a wife. He continued to live out his identity as a woman.[32]

We could explore other examples,[33] but suffice it to say, the biblical authors were probably aware of biological males identifying as or expressing themselves as female (or vice versa). While we shouldn't flippantly map modern-day experiences and questions directly onto biblical material, we also shouldn't assume that the biblical authors' context was completely different than ours. A quick look at the biblical world reveals some relevant parallels to our current conversation about transgender identities.

In short, I don't think the Bible is too out of touch and outdated to speak into our topic with authority.

SHOULD THE CHURCH ACCEPT TRANS* PEOPLE?

I want to close with a pastoral question that's intermixed with some of the biblical questions we've been wrestling with. *Does God accept trans* people as they are?* Transgender scholar Justin Sabia-Tanis draws upon the Ethiopian eunuch of Acts 8 to address this question:

> Philip's ready acceptance of the eunuch as a candidate for baptism proclaims a message of *inclusion for the gender variant* ... we see an affirmation in Scripture that neither *the gender* of the eunuch nor his *gender variance* is

pivotal to his *inclusion* or *exclusion* in the community of
faith.... He brings the particularity of his gender to his
encounter with Philip and ultimately to his relationship
with God ... [who] does not ask us to put aside who we
are in order to be a part of the community of faith.[34]

Look, if a man who's single, castrated, or has atypical features
in his sexual anatomy (in other words, a eunuch) shows up at your
church and is not accepted, then your church has some serious
issues it needs to sort out with Jesus. Or if a woman who doesn't
fit feminine stereotypes (a gender variant) is not accepted at your
church—or feels unwelcomed and out of place at your women's
retreat—then your church might be legalistically promoting human-
made stereotypes in the place of Scripture. And if a trans* person
comes to your church, they should be welcomed with open arms and
accepted. Not just accepted, but embraced, delighted in, listened
to, learned from, honored, loved, cared for, and shown the heavenly
kindness saturated with compassion.

The church hasn't done this very well with trans* people.
Sometimes our stereotypes or ignorance or fear prevent us from
embodying the love of Christ toward the marginalized and those
with minority experiences. There's much about Sabia-Tanis's discussion of the eunuch in Acts 8 that I really love.

And yet, accepting people doesn't mean believing that such people have a flawless view of God, the world, humanity, or themselves.
Christian acceptance is always acceptance into a flawed community
seeking holiness and repentance. It's acceptance into a countercultural family with a different pattern of life, a fresh way to be human,

an otherworldly ethic rooted in creation and longing for resurrection. Acceptance is the first step of discipleship. And Christian discipleship is about pursuing the image God created us to be.

Christian acceptance is always acceptance into a flawed community seeking holiness and repentance.

If our internal sense of self is more definitive of who we are than our bodies, then we should embrace that identity. But if our bodies are more definitive, then Christian discipleship means moving toward embracing our embodied identities. Discipleship includes inviting God to tell us who we are and who he wants us to become.

Should the church accept trans* people? Absolutely. We should even accept non-trans* people. But what is the ethic of being human that we're accepting people into? That's a different question.

Chapter 7

WHAT ABOUT INTERSEX?

In March 2019, I had a public dialogue with author Justin Lee about sexuality in front of nine hundred people.[1] At the end of the talk, the audience texted in a bunch of questions for Justin and me to respond to. I think we received over one hundred questions in the first few minutes, and the questions were ranked in order from "most popular" to "least popular." What was the most popular question?

"What do you guys think about intersex?"

Whenever I give talks about the LGBTQ conversation, I often get questions about the topic of intersex and how this affects, or effects, a theology of gender and sexuality. The questions are usually quite broad and open-ended: "What about intersex?" Sometimes they're asked in a "gotcha" sort of way: "Yeah, but what about intersex? Ha!"

When I get these questions, I typically ask for more specificity: "Which intersex condition are you asking about? Vaginal Agenesis? Androgen Insensitivity Syndrome (AIS)? Klinefelter's? Late Onset Congenital Adrenal Hyperplasia? Some of these? All of these?

Which ones? And what specific question do you have about these conditions? Are you wanting to know what causes AIS? Or about the various of symptoms of Klinefelter's? Or about certain troubling medical practices that have given rise to intersex activism?"[2]

What about intersex? is a vague question. But typically, people want to know two things:

- Does the existence of intersex persons support the idea that a person's internal sense of self determines whether they are male or female?
- Do intersex conditions invalidate the male/female binary (the idea that there are only two sexes)?

Before we dive into these questions, I want to make sure we don't employ "intersex" as some faceless concept in service of an argument or ideology. I fear that progressives and conservatives alike are often guilty of this. Some progressives want to use "intersex" as a trump card against traditional views about marriage, sex, and gender. They often cite the famous (and misleading) statistic that 1.7 percent of people—roughly the same as the number of people with red hair—are neither male nor female.

Some conservatives respond in kind. They point out that intersex persons constitute a low percentage of the population, implying that "intersex" is not worth thinking about. They often engage intersex-related conversations only inasmuch as they seek to refute progressives. Once they believe they've won (or at least addressed) the intellectual argument, they wipe their hands clean of intersex people, never to be thought of again, until another person brings up the intersex argument.

All of this is dehumanizing. We can't just care about "intersex" when it comes up in an argument. Intersex people are *people*—image bearers of the divine and gifts to the church. I've fallen prey to treating such beautiful people as mere concepts, and I'm in a process of repenting from it, largely because I've gotten to know intersex persons and heard their stories and learned from their experiences.[3]

With people in mind, let's look at how intersex conditions often get tangled up in arguments about transgender identities.

Intersex people are **people**—*image bearers of the divine and gifts to the church.*

SINCE INTERSEX, THEREFORE TRANSGENDER

People often appeal to intersex when they argue that gender identity overrules biological sex in cases of incongruence. For instance, theologian Megan DeFranza argues that a transgender person's gender identity is a more accurate expression of their authentic self than their biological sex. She credits this view, in part, to her discovery that some people are born intersex:

> I didn't reconsider transgender experiences until I learned about the complexity of human biology.... I needed a scientist to prove to me that bodies come in more varieties than the simple categories of male (XY chromosomes) or female (XX chromosomes) that I learned in eighth-grade health class.[4]

Linda Tatro Herzer likewise says:

We can no longer argue that being any of the gender variant expressions under the transgender umbrella is "a sin" based on the notion that God creates only male and female, because we now know that God creates at least four different categories of intersex conditions, resulting in approximately one in every one hundred persons being born intersex.[5]

In other words, intersex is the reason why gender identity is more definitive for personhood than biological sex when there's incongruence. Virtually every gender-affirming writer argues along similar lines.[6] The logic almost always proceeds as follows:

- I used to think everyone was male or female
- But then I learned about intersex
- I now know that there aren't only two genders (there's almost always a subtle shift from *sex* to *gender*)
- Therefore, a person's gender identity is a more accurate description of their authentic self than their body
- Because we know intersex persons exist

For what it's worth, some intersex people don't appreciate being included in this kind of argument. "Stop using me as a weapon in your pursuit of a political, not scientific, ideology," writes intersex activist

Claire Graham in response to one such argument. "You are not help-ing the intersex community. You do us more harm than good."[7]

Despite the objection of people like Graham, gender-affirming writers almost always use the "since intersex, therefore transgender" argument. So let's take a closer look at this argument. The specific question we'll wrestle with is this:

> *Does the existence of intersex persons validate the onto-logical claim (or assumption) that a non-intersex person's gender identity is a more accurate indicator of who they really are than their body?*

Or, more simply put:

> *Does intersex prove that a biological female can actually be a man (or vice versa)?*

Our answer to this question partially depends on what we mean by "intersex."

WHAT IS INTERSEX?

"Intersex" does not mean "neither male nor female." More than sixteen different conditions are classified as intersex, also called "differences of sex development" (DSD) or "disorders of sex develop-ment."[8] These conditions include atypical features in a person's sex chromosomes, reproductive organs, or anatomical sex (or two of the three, or all three).

Depending on which conditions are being considered, the prevalence of intersex conditions ranges anywhere from 0.022 percent of the population to 1.7 percent.[9] Not all intersex conditions are the same.

Biologist Anne Fausto-Sterling is well known for saying that 1.7 percent of all human births are intersex. Many people have reiterated this statistic and concluded—wrongly—that 1.7 percent of humans are *neither male nor female*.[10] In defining intersex (and arriving at her 1.7 percent statistic), Fausto-Sterling includes various conditions where there is little to no difficulty in identifying a person as male or female by any standard of biology. Here are a few of the more common intersex conditions, which rarely lead to an ambiguously sexed person:

- Late Onset Congenital Adrenal Hyperplasia (LOCAH)—1.5 in every 100 births.[11]
- Klinefelter Syndrome—1 in every 1,000 births.[12]
- Turner Syndrome—1 in every 2,700 births.[13]
- Vaginal Agenesis—1 in every 6,000 births.[14]

Most people with these conditions present little to no ambiguity in their biological sex. One of my friends in her late thirties found out just three years ago that she has an intersex condition. Some people go through their entire lives without knowing they are intersex, never questioning whether they are male or female. *You* might be intersex and not know it.

People with LOCAH, for instance, usually have typical genitalia that match their chromosomes—XY babies have male genitalia, XX babies have female genitalia. The most common symptom in males (and they are classified as males) is a thinning scalp, which appears in 50 percent of males with this condition. Some females with LOCAH (about 10 percent) have a larger clitoris than females without this condition. Infertility in both males and females is another possible symptom. In short, there is little to no ambiguity in identifying whether a person with LOCAH is either male or female by any basic definition of biological sex. Having a large clitoris doesn't mean you're not female. And yet, people with LOCAH account for 88 percent of all intersex people that constitute Fausto-Sterling's 1.7 percent statistic.[15]

Klinefelter Syndrome is another common intersex condition. Males with Klinefelter's have XXY sex chromosomes (or, more rarely, XXXY or XXXXY) and normal genitalia, though their testicles are typically small. They can achieve an erection and ejaculate, though most males with Klinefelter's are infertile. Some males with Klinefelter's may see an increase in tissue in their chests (called gynecomastia) due to lower levels of testosterone and/or higher levels of estrogen than those of typical males.[16] Fertile males typically go completely undetected.

Since males are classified by the presence of a Y chromosome, systems of reproduction (whether they function or not), and external genitalia, those with Klinefelter's are usually unambiguously male.[17] They simply might not fit the cultural stereotype of what constitutes a masculine man (chiseled chest, raging testosterone, and so on).

In no way should we minimize the psychological difficulties that a person with one of these conditions might experience. These are ripe pastoral opportunities to embody the love and life of Jesus toward people who, for whatever reason, might feel "othered" by society (intentionally or unintentionally) or by their own self-perception of what it means to be a "real" man or woman.

We need to make sure we're talking with *people, not just* about *people.*

The conceptual point I want to make, though, is that most people with an intersex condition are unambiguously male or female in their chromosomes and external genitalia. In fact, it's been estimated that as many as 99 percent of people who have an intersex condition are unambiguously male or female.[18] Intersex people like Claire Graham take issue with non-intersex people arguing that "our bodies make us 'not wholly male or female' for not fitting into your platonic ideal of the perfect body."[19] We need to make sure we're talking *with* people, not just *about* people. Emi Koyama, founder of the Portland-based Intersex Initiative, agrees. In response to the claim that "Intersex people are neither male nor female," Koyama writes: "[M]ost people born with intersex conditions do view themselves as belonging to one binary sex or another. They simply see themselves as a man (or a woman) with a birth condition like any other."[20]

BYE-BYE BINARY?

But what about the 1 percent of intersex persons whose biological sex actually is ambiguous? Are they a third sex, neither male nor female? Here are some of the intersex conditions that can lead to ambiguity in sex:

- Congenital Adrenal Hyperplasia (CAH)—1 in 13,000 births[21]
- Complete Androgen Insensitivity Syndrome (CAIS)—1 in 13,000 births
- Partial Androgen Insensitivity Syndrome (PAIS)—1 in 131,000 births[22]
- Ovotestes—1 in 80,000 births[23]

Complete Androgen Insensitivity Syndrome, for instance, is where a person with a Y chromosome has a defect in the androgen receptor, and therefore the person's cells don't respond to testosterone. Though genetically male, the person typically has female external genitalia, though no uterus or ovaries. Thus, a child with CAIS will typically look unambiguously female, even though she has a Y chromosome.

Such people—beautiful people created in God's image and worthy of respect, value, and admiration— are a blend of the two biological sexes.

My friend Christian was born with a rare intersex condition where they have both XX and XY chromosomes, full male anatomy, and full female anatomy. And, of course, a nice gender-ambiguous name like Christian. If you hung out with Christian, you wouldn't really be sure whether they are male or female. That's because they're *both*. However you slice it, Christian is both male and female.

But more importantly, Christian is one of the most enjoyable, hilarious, and Christlike persons I've ever been around. We were hanging out one night at a sports bar, and I asked Christian, "Are you heading to bed after this?" Christian said they were tired, but they planned to go to the hospital where a friend of theirs was sick. Christian chose to spend the night in a hospital room chair, praying and being present for their friend.

I wish I had more friends like Christian. Christian is a full-time missionary. They travel the world telling people about Jesus while training church leaders, reminding them that Jesus left the ninety-nine to pursue the one.

Does this mean that people with CAIS or my friend Christian are neither male nor female, or a kind of third sex?

I find it more helpful to say that such people—beautiful people created in God's image and worthy of respect, value, and admiration—are a blend of the two biological sexes rather than a third sex. It may sound like I'm splitting hairs, but I think this is more than semantics. When the Bible and science talk about humans as sexed creatures, they recognize two categories of sex: male and female. Though some intersex people embody traits from both categories, there are still only two categories of sex.

For example, non-intersex males have a penis and non-intersex females have a vagina. Most males and females with an intersex condition also have a penis or a vagina, while some intersex persons have both a penis and a vagina. But no intersex person has an innovative new sex organ called a "plankerton" (or whatever) that's neither penis nor vagina, neither male nor female. They may have atypical features in their male or female anatomy, or they might have a blend of male and female parts. But this doesn't mean there are more than two biological sexes. It seems more accurate to say that some people exhibit a combination of both—the only two—biological sexes.

Some things are black and white. Some things are gray. Most people are male or female. Some people are both.

BACK TO THE TRANS* QUESTION

Does the existence of certain types of intersex persons support the idea that a person's internal sense of self is more indicative of who they really are than their bodies?

Before I respond to this question, I want to note that several trans* people I know have found great comfort in the existence of intersex people. Intersex experiences of feeling "in between" can be validating for trans* people, who sometimes also feel "in between" because their bodies don't seem to match their minds. One of my trans* friends told me this:

> When I heard the definition of *intersex* … it made me feel at peace. It made me feel better that there was a physical condition that existed that may point to some validation of my psychological disconnection of internal self and physical body. In listening to other intersex individuals, the language and articulation was bonding to me. I felt as if somebody was describing my childhood feeling akin to the opposite sex rather than just desiring to like boy things.

I think it's helpful for non-trans* people like myself to try to understand the connection that some trans* people feel to intersex experiences. If I put myself in my friend's shoes (which I will never be able to fully do), I can see how discovering the stories of intersex people could help a person feel that they are not crazy. We should keep all this in mind as we address the conceptual argument about intersex, trans*, and human nature.

On a conceptual level, I don't think the existence of intersex persons supports the idea that a person's internal sense of self is more indicative of who they really are than their bodies. We're dealing with two different ontological realities here that shouldn't be quickly mapped onto each other. There's no question about whether intersex persons have an intersex condition. They factually *are* intersex. The same is not true for someone whose internal sense of self differs from their sexed body. The claim that a person's gender identity is more indicative of who they are than their body relies on several questionable assumptions about human nature, the relationship between the body and God's image, and the role that biological sex plays in determining identity.

But the ontological reality of intersex persons whose biological sex might be ambiguous doesn't have any of these evidential challenges. The claims of their ontological reality—*that* their biological sex is ambiguous or blended—is indisputable and objectively verifiable. Claims about gender identity, in contrast, carry a whole different set of ontological assumptions about human nature.

Both sets of claims (verifying the ontology of intersex and transgender) come with their own scientific, theological, ethical, and pastoral questions, most of which are beautifully complex. But these questions are quite different, and I think it's unhelpful to map one upon the other or to use one to justify the other.

IS INTERSEX CAUSED BY THE FALL?

Some say that intersex conditions are caused by "the fall." Others think they were part of God's original pre-fall design. I used to punt to the fall whenever intersex conditions came up in conversation, but I've become a bit more cautious about doing this. Maybe it's theologically true, maybe it's not. I wasn't in the garden before Adam and Eve sinned. And if I'm honest, I know less about the fall and its impact on humanity than I thought I did. Maybe the fall caused a defect in an enzyme that leads to an excessive production of androgens in genetic (XX) females, which leads to Congenital Adrenal Hyperplasia. Or maybe it was because a dude cheated on his wife and left her when she was eight weeks pregnant, causing all kinds of stress on the mother which may have caused the defect in the enzyme.[24]

Or maybe using the fall to explain intersex conditions is wrongheaded to begin with, as many disability theologians have reminded us. Many rich biblical themes relating to vocation or the cross might provide a more fitting lens so that intersex "people can be seen as conduits for God's grace and service rather than … only images of a broken creation in need of 'fixing.'"[25]

I've talked to several intersex friends about this, and I've received mixed opinions. One of my intersex friends strongly believes that her intersex condition *is* caused by the fall, a view she takes great solace in: "Saying intersex is caused by the fall has brought me much comfort! God didn't create me with many hormonal issues, infertile, and needing daily medication just because he wanted to." Others, however, feel dehumanized when non-intersex Christians flippantly declare that intersex conditions are a product of the fall.

Another friend of mine says, "When I hear people say that intersex is caused by the fall, all I hear is that my entire existence is nothing but fallen since my entire existence is affected by my intersex condition on some level. It often feels like people are saying that I am fallen in more severe ways than non-intersex persons." It breaks my heart to think that flippant statements like "intersex is caused by the fall" could rub salt into such deep wounds of societal dehumanization. We need to think long and hard about what we are saying and especially *how* we are saying it.

Now, most Christians believe that every human is touched by the fall in some way. And if they believe that intersex conditions are caused by the fall, they don't necessarily mean that intersex persons are *more* "fallen" than non-intersex persons. But that distinction is sometimes lost in translation. We need to exercise much caution in how we speak about "conditions" and "issues" and "concepts" that are embodied in the lives of real people *who already* have many social cards stacked against them in ways non-intersex persons will never truly understand.

But what about males born with female brains, or females born with male brains? Can this be considered a kind of intersex condition? Do brains come in male and female brands, and if so, could a person's brain be mismatched with their body?

These are tough but relevant questions. Let's take a tour through Brain-Sex Theory.

Chapter 8

MALE BRAIN IN A FEMALE BODY

I recently took a test to see whether I had a male or female brain.[1] The test consisted of thirty different questions with multiple choice answers, such as

What was the last thing that made you cry?
- Death
- Weight gain
- Cute animal videos
- I don't cry.

My masculine mind kicked into gear, and I clicked on "I don't cry." Next question:

Which of the following snacks appeals the most?
- Ice cream
- Cake
- Baked beans and hotdogs
- Anything fried

These all sounded good to me, actually. Did that mean my brain was intersex? Hmmm, if someone had a gun to my head, I'd have to go with "Anything fried." *Boom!* That had to be a manly answer. Next question:

What's your criteria when shopping for jeans?
- That they look normal
- How my butt looks
- That I get it over with quickly
- How they look with my shoes

I was tempted to go with "How my butt looks," since I'd been doing a lot of squats at the gym recently. But a surge of testosterone rushed through my body, and I quickly moused over "That I get it over with quickly." I'm a guy, after all. And all guys hate shopping. Right?

I answered other questions like "How many times a year do you get moody?" and "Are you excited about the Super Bowl or just the half-time show?" and "Do you like to watch *Downton Abbey*?" When all was said and done, my brain-test score was a bit surprising. Apparently, my brain really is intersex: 61 percent male and 39 percent female. I guess I shouldn't have admitted that my favorite part of the Super Bowl is the half-time show.

I had to wonder, though: Do brains come in male and female brands? And if so, do they really cause certain people to love shopping, deep-fried anything, and watching Beyoncé instead of Tom Brady?

THE BRAIN-SEX THEORY

Sonny and Cher's trans* son Chaz Bono has said that though he was born female, he's always had a male brain: "It's just that the sex of your body and the gender of the brain don't match up."[2] And many trans* people describe their experience in similar ways.[3] The average trans* person, when they say they have an opposite-sex brain, is describing how it feels to be trans*. It's a picturesque way of describing their experience rather than a thoroughly researched scientific declaration. We should distinguish, then, between someone describing how it feels to be trans* and someone making a scientific assertion about brains, bodies, and human nature.

As far as the science goes, there's actually an ongoing debate among neuroscientists about whether brains are sexed like our bodies. Those who say that brains are "sexed"—that there are distinct male and female brains—argue for what's called "brain-sex theory." This theory says that some brains are male and others are female.[4] While most peoples' brains are aligned with their bodies, some trans* people have a sort of "intersex condition" of the brain.[5] Their body might be male while their brain is female (or vice versa).[6] This mismatch between brain and body forms the biological basis for why their gender identity—internal sense of self—is incongruent with their biological sex. It's because their brain is sexed differently from their body.

We should distinguish between someone describing how it feels to be trans and someone making a scientific assertion about brains, bodies, and human nature.*

Before we dig into the science of it all, let's hit Pause for a second. Those of us who are at home in our bodies have no clue what it feels like to look at your body in the mirror and think you're looking at another person. To look at people of the opposite sex and think, *That's me.* To think, act, play, relate, and feel emotions that seem typical of a different sex than your own. Whatever the science says about our brains, Christ-followers of all stripes should try to realize how life-giving the brain-sex theory could feel to someone. Some trans* people certainly feel like they have a brain that doesn't match their body. And the brain-sex theory appears to give scientific validation for this incongruence. Let's make sure our posture is soaked with humility as we analyze the science of some people's lived experience.

With that in mind, let's first look at sex differences in the brain, then see how these apply to the brain-sex theory in the trans* conversation.

ARE MEN FROM MARS AND WOMEN FROM PLANET STUPID?

Research into male/female brain differences has a bit of a checkered history—a history that reeks of sexism. Nineteenth-century evolutionary biologist George J. Romanes once wrote, "Seeing that the average brain-weight of women is about five ounces less than that of men ... we should be prepared to expect a marked inferiority of intellectual power in the former."[7] Romanes suggested that this is why women get more exhausted during mentally challenging tasks and why they display "a comparative absence of originality ... especially in the higher levels of intellectual work."[8]

A few decades later, Charles Dana pointed out that "the brain stem of woman is relatively larger" while "the brain mantle and basal ganglia are smaller." Dana didn't think these differences should "prevent a woman from voting" (good call, Doctor). But he argued that these brain differences do "point the way to the fact that woman's efficiency lies in a special field and not that of political initiative or of judicial authority in a community's organization."[9]

So women with their small brains should still be allowed to vote—liberation!—but they certainly shouldn't be able to serve in politics. Such was the state of sex difference and brain research a hundred years ago.

Things have thankfully progressed quite a bit in the last century. We now know that brain size is irrelevant to intellect, and many older theories about sex difference were products of ideological—and sexist—assumptions, rather than science. Yet scientists continue to debate whether brains come in male and female brands.

Some scholars have meticulously combed through brain-research studies (which are plentiful)[10] and pointed out that the supposed sex differences in the brain are overplayed at best and fabricated at worst.[11] Others, however, continue to argue that male and female brains are quite different. One dynamic that throws a wrench into the debate is the issue of neuroplasticity.

NEUROPLASTICITY

Neuroplasticity refers to the brain's ability to physically change throughout a person's life.[12] If a person's brain looks and acts a certain way, this may be because nature made it that way, or it may be because nurture shaped it as such. Various life experiences—from sports to music to dancing to taxi driving—quite literally rewire and reshape our brains.[13]

Imagine a male dancer has a brain that looks similar to a female dancer's brain. Do their brains look similar because both have "female brains"? Or is it because they are both dancers? It's tough to say. "[W]hen researchers look for sex differences in the brain or the mind, they are hunting a moving target. Both are in continuous interaction with the social context."[14]

So even if we were able to see clear differences between "male brains" and "female brains," we'd have to ask this question: Did a "male" brain *cause* someone to act masculine, or did their masculine behavior *cause* their brain to look "male"?

Neuroplasticity plays a significant role in the trans* brain discussion as well. One of the first studies that applied the brain-sex theory to trans* people, directed by neurobiologist Jiang-Ning Zhou in 1995, is titled "A Sex Difference in the Human Brain and Its Relation to Transsexuality." This study is often cited as showing that trans* people have the brains of the opposite sex. Zhou's study was conducted on six post-mortem male-to-female (MtF) transsexuals (this is the term used in the study, though many trans* people don't prefer it) and found that a portion of each subject's hypothalamus (the BSTc) was, on average, smaller than that same portion of the brain in non-trans* genetic males, closer to the brain of an average female. The researchers concluded that the subjects, although they were biological males, had "a female brain structure."[15]

But the scientific community has widely criticized Zhou's study because of its inattention to neuroplasticity (among other methodological problems).[16] The study's six subjects had all taken cross-sex hormones, contracted HIV/AIDS, and lived for years as the sex they identified with—all of which, in light of neuroplasticity, may affect the structure of the brain. Most researchers believe that the credibility of Zhou's study was severely compromised.[17]

More recent studies on male/female brain differences stand on better methodological grounds, though the problem of neuroplasticity poses an enduring challenge.[18] What do these more recent studies say? Do trans* people have opposite-sex brains?

MALE BRAIN IN A FEMALE BODY?

Unfortunately, the studies are mixed. Some showed similarities between the brains of trans* people and the average brains of the sex they identify with (for example, transwomen's brains looked more like average female brains than like average male brains).[19] Other studies, however, showed the opposite: the brains of trans* people were more similar to those of people who shared their biological sex rather than people who shared their gender identity.[20] Other studies found that certain features of trans* people's brains measured in between what is typical for males and females.[21] On top of all this, the problem of *plasticity* continues to plague the research. Does someone's brain cause their gender identity and behavior, or do their gender identity and behavioral patterns rewire their brain?[22] So far, it's impossible to say.

Some researchers have also suggested that certain biological females receive a wash of testosterone in utero, masculinizing their brains. If the brains of biological females are bathed in T, does this cause them to identify as (trans)men when they grow up?

Not usually. Studies show that some of these biological females do end up with masculine-typical *behaviors* and *interests*. For instance, they might be more physically aggressive than your typical female, and many grow up to be attracted to other females. However, according to the research, most of these biological females—quite surprisingly—*don't* end up identifying as male or experiencing gender dysphoria.[23] Sheri Berenbaum, a professor of psychology at Penn State, ran a study that analyzed the relationship between gender identity and prenatal hormone exposure and concluded, "Prenatal androgens apparently have large effects on interests and engagement in gendered activities; moderate effects on spatial abilities; and *relatively small or no effects on gender identity, gender cognitions, and gendered peer involvement.*"[24]

Where does all this leave us? Well, I'm not a neuroscientist or a brain surgeon; I've never even seen a human brain. But based on as many significant studies as I can find, it doesn't appear that the "male brain in a female body" (or vice versa) theory has clear scientific evidence to support it.

Does someone's brain cause their gender identity and behavior, or do their gender identity and behavioral patterns rewire their brain? So far, it's impossible to say.

Now, I'm not going to tattoo this conclusion on my thigh (or anywhere else). The science is still fairly young, and new studies are being performed even as I write. When it comes to brain research, we need to hold our conclusions tentatively, open to the possibility that further research will confirm or correct our current beliefs.

But we can say one thing with a high degree of confidence—something that's not widely disputed: whatever differences might exist between "male brains" and "female brains," these differences are based on generalities, not absolutes.

BRAIN DIFFERENCES: GENERALITIES OR ABSOLUTES?

What does it mean that male and female brain differences are based on generalities, not absolutes? It means that understanding these brain differences is similar to understanding differences among men and women in, say, height. Are women shorter than men? In terms of statistical averages, yes. But is every woman shorter than every man? No. Women are not *absolutely* shorter than men.

We see something similar when it comes to male and female brains. Check out how these specialists who emphasize brain differences between the sexes describe these differences.

Ruben Gur is a professor of psychiatry at the University of Pennsylvania, and he's been eager to emphasize sex differences in the brain. Here's how he describes these differences:

> In a stressful, confusing multi-tasking situation, women *are more likely* to be able to go back and forth between seeing the more logical, analytic, holistic aspects of a situation and seeing the details [while] men *will be more likely* to deal with [the situation] as, "I see/I do, I see/I do, I see/I do."[25]

Gur doesn't say that all female brains will be one way and all male brains another. He says women "are more likely" to holistically analyze a particular situation. For what it's worth, several other studies contradict Gur's claims.[26] But even if Gur is correct, his conclusions only prove generalities, not absolutes. There are some women who are bad at multitasking, and—like women who are six feet tall—they fall outside the dominant pattern of how *most* women are. But they are still female—and so are their brains.

Susan Pinker is a developmental psychologist who argues for the existence of sex differences in the brain. She believes that females have a thicker corpus callosum, which enables quicker left-brain and right-brain interaction. Pinker says that "men *tend to* modulate their reaction to stimuli, and engage in analysis and association, whereas women *tend to* draw more on primary emotional reference."[27] Several scholars have offered blistering critiques on the theory of sex difference in the corpus callosum.[28] In any case, even if Pinker is right and her critics are wrong, notice her language: men "tend to," women "tend to." Pinker is arguing for generalities.

Almost all the studies I've read that argue for sex differences in the brain speak in terms of generalities rather than absolutes:

- During sexual arousal, "men show *comparatively more activity* in the older, more primitive areas of the brain such as the amygdala, thalamus, and hypothalamus, while women show *proportionately more activity* up in the cerebral cortex."[29]
- "[W]omen's sexuality *tends to be* strongly linked to close relationships…. This is *less true* for men."[30]

- "54% of girls will perform above average in facial emotion processing, compared with 46% of boys."[31]

One of the most significant studies on sex differences in the brain was published in 2017.[32] Eighteen experts in the field teamed up to perform "the largest single-sample study of structural and functional sex differences in the human brain" by examining 2,750 females and 2,466 males.[33] Overall, the study found several areas of the brain where males *on average* differed from females. For instance, "the higher male volume ... appeared largest in some regions involved in emotion and decision-making, such as the bilateral orbitofrontal cortex, the bilateral insula, and the left isthmus of the cingulate gyrus," though a few areas showed more similarities than differences between males and females.[34] (For example, there were no sex differences in the volume of the amygdala, hippocampus, thalamus, and caudate.)[35]

If you couldn't explain what any of this means to a six-year-old, don't worry. I couldn't either. Again, I'm not claiming to be an expert in brain science. I'm only telling you what the experts say, and they almost always express their conclusions in terms of generalities—much like the gender stereotypes we talked about in chapter 5. Male and female brains might be somewhat different on average, but even if they are, they also have significant overlap. The brain is not, in fact, sexually dimorphic. In the words of the 2017 study:

Overall, for every brain region that showed even large sex differences, there was always overlap between males

and females, confirming that the human brain cannot—
at least for the measures observed here—be described as
"sexually dimorphic."[36]

Brain differences between males and females, like height differences, are based on generalities, not absolutes. Most women are shorter
than most men, most men are more physically aggressive than most
women, and most women have more gray matter in their brains than
most men. But all these categories have significant overlap.

The same is not true when it comes to the biological sex of
non-intersex humans. It's not as if most non-intersex men have male
reproductive structures while others don't. Biological sex, unlike the
brain, is sexually dimorphic in non-intersex humans.

BRAIN-SEX THEORY AND STEREOTYPES

It's tough to apply the brain-sex theory to trans* experiences without
getting entangled in gender stereotypes. And yet some researchers
don't seem to notice the dilemma. Milton Diamond, for instance, is
a world-renowned (though now retired) professor of anatomy and
reproductive biology who has become one of the foremost researchers
advocating for the brain-sex theory in the gender identity conversation. He believes that "there seems evidence enough to consider trans
persons as individuals intersexed in their brains."[37] Diamond goes on
to argue that transgender persons have "the anatomy of one sex" but
"the emotional awareness of the opposite sex."[38]

But—what does it mean to have "the emotional awareness of
the opposite sex"? Does each sex come prepackaged with its own

particular "emotional awareness"? Ask your feminist lesbian friend, "Hey, do you have a female 'emotional awareness'?" And then duck, because you might get a combat boot thrown at you. (See, there I go with the stereotypes.)

There may be a stereotype about the emotional awareness of females, and it might be based on the *general patterns of female emotions*. But hopefully we're far enough into the twenty-first century to know that not *all* females share the same emotional awareness as the majority in the group. "The notion of a male brain and female brain fits well the popular view of men from Mars, women from Venus," quips neuroscientist Daphna Joel, but "it does not fit scientific data."[39]

It seems that gender stereotypes have crawled into the neuroscience lab. When we use sex-typical behavior to explain the essence of each sex's brain, we empower gender stereotypes to define who we are. You can see why feminists often aren't huge fans of the brain-sex theory. It inevitably relies on gender stereotypes, which is why many feminists consider the brain-sex theory to be little more than "neurosexism."[40]

MAKING SENSE OF IT ALL

The purpose of this chapter has been to explore the possibility that gender identity has an ontological essence that would put it on par with the body. If brains were sexually dimorphic—male and female—and if it were possible, because of the fall or some other reason, for a person's brain to be mismatched with their body, and if this mismatch could be verified somehow, I think this might make a good case for that person having a kind of intersex condition of the brain. Perhaps their brain determines who they are, while their body is a product of the fall and therefore in need of correction.

Given everything we've seen above, however, I don't see much scientific validity to this claim.

No doubt, some people's gender dysphoria has biological roots. It might also have some environmental causes; nature and nurture are often so enmeshed that it's tough to pull them apart. Moreover, trans* experiences come in many shapes and sizes, and everyone's journey is different: remember the different kinds of trans* experiences in chapter 3. For those with early-onset, lifelong gender dysphoria—those who have experienced intense dysphoria from the time they were three or four years old—there's probably a strong biological influence involved with their dysphoria.

But saying biology plays a role is different from saying that a person's brain *is* actually sexed independently from their body. It's one thing to say that biology plays a role in causing a psychological condition in a male or female. It's quite another to draw an ontological conclusion from this that the brain's biology might contradict the body's biology—especially since the science doesn't appear to support this conclusion.

Correct science and correct theology are pointless if we're not willing to love and honor, listen to and learn from, care for **and be cared for by** *the trans* people God has gifted us with.*

I want to hold everything I've said here with an open hand and acknowledge that I'm not a neuroscientist or a psychologist and that the science on brain-sex theory is still fairly young and disputed.

Maybe some massive breakthrough study will change everything, as often happens in science. Or maybe we'll discover something else about the human body and brain that helps us understand gender identity a bit more. Until we do, I want to cautiously say that it doesn't seem like people can be born with the brains of a different sex. Even if there are some sex differences in the brain, all this would show is that some females (for instance) might have stereotypically masculine behaviors, interests, and patterns of thought. But this doesn't mean they have "a male brain."

I also want to have an open heart. All this scientific dissecting of bodies and brains and studies and theories could make a person feel like they're an experiment at a science fair. Those of us who are not trans* need to be sensitive to this dynamic as we interact with scientific data. I think scientific discussions and debates are important, especially when people are making claims about human nature that rely on questionable science (let alone questionable theology). But correct science and correct theology are pointless if we're not willing to love and honor, listen to and learn from, care for and be cared for by the trans* people God has gifted us with. Jesus cherishes them and values them. Would they say the same about you?

Chapter 9

FEMALE SOUL IN A MALE BODY

In the last chapter, we saw that science does not yet support the theory that a person's brain could be sexed differently from their body. But what if we move outside science labs and into the halls of philosophy and theology? What if someone has a male body and a female soul? Are they a man or a woman?[1]

The hard sciences can't offer us much help here; souls don't show up on autopsies. And of course, many secular scholars yawn at the idea of searching for someone's soul. Soul-searching is usually left to the realm of religion. Even so, I am seeing an increasing number of scholars who aren't particularly religious refer to trans* people's inner sense of gender identity as their "true gender self," which sounds almost indistinguishable from the idea of a person's inner soul.[2] Some even go so far as to use the word "soul."[3]

At any rate, I'm a religious person, as are most of you reading this book. So it's worth laying out the theory of the sexed soul (or spirit) and seeing if it has merit. Here's our leading question:

Could someone's soul or spirit be sexed differently than their body?

Most people who answer yes to this question might say that the fall caused incongruence between some bodies and souls. Once we start down the road of soul talk, it takes us into the wide world of theological anthropology.

BODY, SOUL, AND THEOLOGICAL ANTHROPOLOGY 101

Theological anthropology simply means "theological reflection on the human person."[4] It's a complex field of theological and philosophical studies that wrestles with what it means to be human. For our purposes, we're primarily interested in the nature of the soul/spirit and its relationship to the material body.

In general, the spectrum of views about this relationship could be mapped as follows. Those on the left emphasize physicalism (unity of human nature), while those on the right emphasize dualism (distinction between body and soul).

Physicalism	Non-Reductive Physicalism	Soft Dualism	Strong Dualism

- **Physicalism:** There is no spirit/soul, no immaterial part of you. All the stuff that seems immaterial can be explained by neurology. Your emotions, your imagination, and your will are all byproducts of that three-pound chunk of meat called the brain.
- **Non-Reductive Physicalism:** There is an immaterial part of you, but it's inextricably bound to your embodiment. While our existence can't be *reduced*

to our physicality, neither can it be separated from our physicality. There is no body/soul distinction, only ensouled bodies or embodied souls.[5]

- **Soft Dualism:** The body and embodiment are significant to personhood; however, soul and body are "two ontologically distinct substances that are conceivably separable."[6]

- **Strong Dualism:** Not only are the soul and the body "two, fundamentally distinct, 'parts' of the human person,"[7] but the immaterial soul is much more central to who we are than our physical bodies. Extreme versions of this view might even denigrate the body as worthless and evil.

None of these are airtight categories—they are general points along a spectrum. One could conceivably have a view somewhere between Soft Dualism and Strong Dualism, for instance, or between Soft Dualism and Non-Reductive Physicalism.

We can probably nix the first view, Physicalism, since scholars don't consider it a legitimately Christian option. Most Christian philosophers and theologians believe that pure, grade A Physicalism does not resonate with a biblical view of humankind.[8]

The last view, Strong Dualism, is also not a Christian view—despite widespread support from some old hymns and the popular imagination of many Western Christians ("like a bird from prison bars has flown, I'll fly away"). This view borders on the heresy of Gnosticism, or has Gnostic tendencies. Marc Cortez, a renowned expert in theological anthropology, rightly says, "Nearly everyone [in the realm of Christian theology] affirms that human persons are physical, embodied beings and that this is an important feature of God's intended design for human life."[9]

Now, you may think that this settles our question: the "soul sexed differently from the body" view is straight-up Gnosticism and not a serious Christian option. I used to think the same thing. And honestly, when I read statements from some gender-affirming writers, it sounds like they're quoting from an ancient Gnostic hymn. Anyone who takes for granted that your internal, immaterial sense of self is obviously the "real you" while your body is just a pile of neutral (or obnoxious) flesh is not basing their assumption in a Christian view of human nature.

But not every trans* person actually believes they've been "born in the wrong body." Although many trans* people do use the phrase "born in the wrong body" to describe their experience of dysphoria, they aren't necessarily using it as a definitive statement of their theological anthropology.[10] Some trans* people don't like the phrase at all.[11]

Anyone who takes for granted that your internal, immaterial sense of self is obviously the "real you" while your body is just a pile of neutral (or obnoxious) flesh is not basing their assumption in a Christian view of human nature.

In any case, Strong Dualism isn't the only anthropological model that can undergird the "sexed soul" theory. Someone could also argue by way of the Soft Dualist framework that a person's soul might be sexed (or gendered) differently than their body. It's lazy and unthoughtful to simply write off every trans* claim as Gnostic and anti-body. If you pay attention to what actual trans* people are saying, you'll see that at least some of them have thought through and responded to the accusation of Gnosticism.[12] In addition, if trans* people were so anti-body, why would some of them pay $100,000 to alter their bodies? That's a heavy price to pay for something you don't care about. Besides, I've never met a trans* person who immediately changed their view of human nature after being called a Gnostic. Lazy accusations don't embody God's kindness.

SOFT DUALISM AND A SEXED SOUL

How is the Soft Dualist framework used to defend the idea of "sexed souls"? Soft Dualism posits that the "mental and physical realms are both fundamental"[13] to human nature and that "these two parts are fully integrated and interdependent such that the organism as a whole functions properly only when both are working in intimate union."[14] And yet the "mental and physical realms are ontologically distinct" and "can (at least) conceivably exist separate from the other."[15] One of the main arguments for this view comes from the doctrine of an intermediate state; namely, that the soul can be temporarily separated from the body at death and prior to resurrection, in which case "you" still exist apart from the body, albeit temporarily.[16]

A person could argue, therefore, that (because of the fall, or for another reason) someone's soul might be misaligned with their body.[17] The question then becomes, *Is the soul or the body more ontologically significant for a person's status as male or female when there is incongruence?* Because even if the soul and body have been misaligned, this doesn't in itself mean that the soul overrules the body in determining who we are.

CHALLENGES TO THE SEXED-SOUL THEORY

While the "male soul, female body" theory is possible and could draw upon a Soft Dualist perspective (a legitimately Christian view), it runs up against several challenges.

First, non-intersex bodies are clearly sexed. But are our souls *sexed*? Remember what we said about biological sex in chapter 2: "[A]n organism is male or female if it is structured to perform one of the respective roles in reproduction," and "[t]here is no other widely accepted biological classification for the sexes."[18] In other words, the categories of "male" and "female" are by definition descriptions of our bodies, not our souls or any other immaterial aspect of our being. Sex is a material, biological category. Accordingly, immaterial souls can't be sexed.

Second, even if a person's soul were sexed differently than their body, this wouldn't automatically mean the soul overrules the body, *especially* if their body is 100 percent, verifiably, without a doubt biologically male or female. It's one thing to say that the soul is ontologically distinct from the body; that would be Soft Dualism. It's quite another to say that, if there's incongruence, then the immaterial soul obviously overrules the body. That perspective would be much closer to Strong Dualism.

Plus, if a biological male says they have a female soul, how would they know this? By clocking all their hours watching *Downton Abbey*? I mean, I'm sort of joking, but only sort of. We've already seen how cultural stereotypes are intertwined with our conversation. It's hard to discuss male or female souls without running into the same problem of stereotypes. Don't take my word for it. Try it yourself. Describe what it would look like for a person to have a female soul trapped in a male body. How do they dress, or act, or think? What are they interested in? What are their emotions like? Can you answer these questions without drawing on stereotypes about what it means to be feminine?

All the immaterial aspects of personhood are important:
mind, soul, spirit, emotions, personality, likes, and
dislikes. But these don't determine a person's sex.

Third, there's widespread misunderstanding about what the soul really is. It's unfortunate that when we see the word *soul* next to the word *body*, virtually every Westerner associates *soul* with "non-material." Plato would certainly agree with this definition of the soul. So would the Gnostics. But I'm not sure the biblical writers would. The Hebrew and Greek words translated "soul" are much more material than we often think.

Take the Hebrew word *nephesh*, for instance. *Nephesh* is the main word lying behind the English word "soul" in the Old Testament, but it's also translated as "life," "person," "breath," "inner person," "self," "desire," and "throat."[19] *Nephesh* is even used in reference to the "souls" of animals (for example, Gen. 1:24; 9:10), which—unless you're *that* kind of animal lover—throws a wrench into most people's view of the "soul" as something uniquely human.

In the Old Testament, "*nephesh* is used with reference to the whole person as the seat of desires and emotions, not to the 'inner soul.'"[20] In a lengthy study of *nephesh*, Edmond Jacob concludes, "*Nephesh* is the usual term for a man's total nature, for what he is and not just what he has.... Hence the best translation in many instances is 'person.'"[21] *Nephesh* most often includes the body.

The same goes for *ruach*, the Hebrew word for "spirit." We don't need to get into the details, since it's not really disputed among biblical scholars. In short, "*ruach* ... must not be thought of as a separable aspect of man, but as the whole person viewed from a certain perspective."[22]

Greek words for "soul" or "spirit" reveal similar *polysemy* ("many possible meanings"). *Psyche*, for instance, is often translated as "soul" and on a few occasions can refer to immaterial aspects of a person. But it rarely, if ever, refers to the immaterial part of a person *in contrast to the material part. Psyche* in the New Testament, like *nephesh* in the Old, "often stands for the whole person,"[23] not just the immaterial part. Describing Noah's ark, for example, the apostle Peter says, "only a few people *[psychai]*, eight in all, were saved through water" (1 Pet. 3:20).[24] It seems clear here that *psyche* refers to the whole person—material and immaterial.

New Testament scholar Joel Green summarizes the case well:

> Given this polysemy [of words translated as "soul"], we would be mistaken to assume that the word *psyche* ... actually means "soul" (or requires an identification with the concept of "soul"), defined as the spiritual part of a human distinct from the physical or as an ontologically separate entity constitutive of the human "self."[25]

Many scholars have reached conclusions similar to Green's. "Recent scholarship has recognized that such terms as body, soul, and spirit are not different, separable faculties of man but different ways of viewing the whole man," writes biblical scholar George Eldon Ladd.[26] And Mark Cortez says this understanding of the "soul" is one of the things that Christian scholars across the Physicalist-Dualist spectrum agree on, that "'soul' does not refer primarily to the immaterial essence of a human person but to the whole human person as a living being."[27]

It's tough to say, then, that humans have an ontologically distinct immaterial part that ought to overrule the body if the two are at odds.

Now, some might say that I'm wrongly elevating the physical over the psychological. Fraser Watts, a British theologian and psychologist, believes that it's wrong "to suggest that the physical has a theological priority over the psychological or the spiritual." It is, he argues, "theologically unsound to assume that the physical is good, but that the psychological is defective."[28]

Watts raises a good point, but I don't think I'm categorically elevating the physical over the spiritual. I'm simply pointing out that sex categories—male and female—are by definition physical categories. Unless someone has an intersex condition, they are unambiguously male or female in their biology; these are bodily categories. Saying that this assertion *prioritizes* the physical over the spiritual skews the discussion. It assumes that sex is both physical and spiritual. But sex isn't a spiritual category. It's a biological one. All the immaterial aspects of personhood are important: mind, soul, spirit, emotions, personality, likes, and dislikes. But these don't determine a person's sex.

One could talk about a "gendered soul." But what does that mean? As we've seen throughout this book, there's a lot of ambiguity within people's definitions of "gender," and many ideas about gender are entangled with cultural stereotypes. I'm not saying that a case can't be made. I'm only saying that it's going to take a bit of work to argue for a "female soul, male body" without relying on modern, stereotypical assumptions about what constitutes femaleness and maleness.

CONCLUSION

Let's come back to our question of incongruence:

> *If someone experiences incongruence between their biologi-*
> *cal sex and their internal sense of self, which one determines*
> *who they are—and why?*

After refracting our question through the lens of the Bible (chapter 4), stereotypes (chapter 5), several pushbacks (chapter 6), intersex conditions (chapter 7), the brain-sex theory (chapter 8), and now the sexed-soul theory (chapter 9), I would say that the Bible and science offer much more evidence to support the view that our biological sex determines who we are. Our sexed bodies determine whether we are male, female, or both; and our embodiment is an essential part of how we image God in the world. I don't think the Bible or science offers enough evidence to suggest that our gender (identity or role) overrules our sexed identity, even if we experience incongruence.

However, we should never downplay the significance of a person's experiences or their internal sense of who they are. These can feel more real than the air we breathe. Any credible application of the conceptual points I've made must understand this: experiences might not define who we are ontologically, but they are nonetheless very real and significant. We can get the Bible right—but if we get love wrong, we're wrong.

INTERLUDE

In February 2020, I was on the campus of Biola University in California giving a bunch of talks on transgender identities. Speaking is part of my job; few weeks go by when I'm not in front of a crowd. But for various reasons, I was incredibly nervous about giving these talks.

Speaking to faculty members was stressful enough, but I was most anxious about speaking to the students. College students ask hard questions and sniff out lazy answers. They're especially sensitive to tone. Your logic can be sound, but if your words aren't loving, they won't believe what you're saying. And when it comes to LGBT+ questions, they're typically more knowledgeable than most adults. Unlike my Gen X generation, Gen Z college students have many LGBT+ friends, or they are LGBT+ themselves. They're typically skeptical when white, straight, older men wax eloquent about the lives and experiences of their friends—or themselves.

And yet, here I was. A forty-four-year-old white dude with a PhD, gearing up to talk about minority experiences. My opening talk was titled "A Christian Perspective on Transgender Identities." Several hundred college faces stared at me as I began talking about the importance of humanizing this conversation. I told the story of my friend Lesli, the same Lesli from the beginning of this book. I emphasized that those of us who aren't trans* need to very cautiously and humbly engage this topic, knowing that it's never just a topic—it's people. I then talked about sex and gender, Genesis 1:27, the relationship between body and mind, and a few other concepts we've discussed in this book. But I tried extra hard to stay focused on the lives of actual people, which isn't always easy when you're discussing complex concepts.

Several minutes into the talk, I noticed a person to my left in the sea of faces. I wondered if they might be trans*. *What are they thinking?* I asked myself. *Do they agree with anything I'm saying? Do they despise the fact that a non-trans* straight man is talking about their experience? I really hope I don't say anything that will frustrate their faith.*

It's easy to discuss abstract concepts from a stage. But the pastoral rubber meets the personal road when you're able to think deeply, love widely, and speak in a way that embodies God's pleasure and delight. I tried hard to do that during my talk, though I'm sure I said things I could have worded differently or stated more graciously. Sometimes *how* we believe is just as important as *what* we believe. The content of what we say is significant. We should reject lazy thinking, unbiblical theories, and convoluted illogical reasons for what we believe. But if our posture and tone don't communicate love, the content of our ideas will be powerless.

Sometimes how *we believe is just as
important as* what *we believe.*

The evening after my talk, I was scheduled to meet with a couple dozen LGBT+ and same-sex-attracted Christians on campus. This group of students, called "The Dwelling," sought to be "a caring and supportive community where students who identify as LGBTQ or experience same-sex attraction (SSA) can journey together, reconciling their faith and life circumstances as they grow in discipleship to Christ."[1] Some of the students were theologically conservative. Others were not. Still others were just trying to figure things out. Once again, my nerves flared up. *What will they think of a straight married dude invading their sacred space?*

As I entered the room, some were eager to meet me and chat, while others were a bit quieter. I sat down at the only chair available—right beside the trans* person I had noticed in the crowd earlier that day.

We went around the room introducing ourselves and getting to know each other. And then I fielded a bunch of questions from the group. Some reaffirmed everything I had said that morning. Others raised thoughtful challenges. All of them were incredibly gracious, even though I could tell that not everyone agreed with me.

Then the trans* person to my left raised their hand, staring into my eyes. They said,

> I don't know how to say this, but … I was really nervous about hearing you speak. People like me, we're so used to hearing cisgender men like you tell us about our experience. But I want you to know, I was truly shocked by how concerned you were to humanize the conversation. To humanize me. I'm not sure if I agree with everything you said. I'm still just trying to figure myself out. But when you were talking, I felt … seen.

And I felt loved. I felt like you cared. And I can't tell
you how much that means to me. I just needed you to
know that.

My anxious heart was cradled by their kindness. There I was, trying to embody God's kindness to people who were marginalized and
misunderstood. I didn't expect to receive God's kindness in return.
And yet, I was flooded with it.

As I returned home from Biola, I was also preparing to turn in
the manuscript of this book to the publisher. It was in its seventh
draft. But I decided I needed to comb back through the manuscript
one more time with my new friend's face in mind, hovering above
every line of this book.

I know that some of you reading this book are trans*. As I
said in the preface, my primary audience is the general Christian
population, most of whom aren't trans*. But I hope you have felt
dignified and humanized as you have read my words. You may not
have agreed with everything I've said or even *how* I've said it. We're
all on a journey, and mine is an imperfect one. But one day, we might
find ourselves sitting next to each other. And I hope we'll be able to
call each other friends.

LOOKING BACK AND PRESSING ON

We've waded through a lot of biblical, scientific, and philosophical
material so far. We haven't exhausted everything—even if you feel
exhausted by it all!—but we have considered from various angles the
question of incongruence:

If someone experiences incongruence between their gender and their biological sex, which one determines who they are—and why?

We've examined this question through the lens of the Bible, science, a bit of philosophy, and various sociological issues related to femininity and masculinity. I have suggested that if our biological sex is unambiguous, then our bodies should determine who we are, male or female. It's also crucial to understand our gender identity—how we fit (or don't fit) into stereotypical gender roles. But if we are asking an ontological question—who *are* we?—I don't think gender should override sex when there is incongruence. Part of discipleship is learning to embrace our bodies as important aspects of our identity, learning to see them as gifts from God and part of how we bear his image in the world.

In the remaining chapters, we'll focus on more practical aspects of our topic. We'll begin by looking at a social phenomenon that has become a highly publicized part of this conversation: Rapid-Onset Gender Dysphoria, which has to do with the massive increase in teenagers identifying as trans* (chapter 10). We'll then wrestle with whether a disciple of Jesus should transition (chapter 11). Finally, we'll explore various questions related to pronouns, bathrooms, and sleeping spaces (chapter 12).

Please beware: all these topics are incredibly sensitive and shrouded in widespread, dehumanizing, volatile debates. All the more reason to keep our wits about us, always remembering that we're discussing the intimate details of real people.

Chapter 10

RAPID-ONSET GENDER DYSPHORIA

Helena was fourteen when she realized she was attracted to both boys and girls and began to explore what this meant for her through online communities on Tumblr. It was there that she learned about various gender identities. She read story after story of people identifying as trans*. "I eventually started relating to [these stories]," she later explains, "and identifying as trans*."[1]

Helena learned on Tumblr that taking testosterone was the next step she must take as a trans* person. So she began cross-hormone therapy (CHT): "On Tumblr specifically, there's this attitude that if you have the slightest inclination that you might have gender identity confusion, the healthiest thing you can do is explore that and experiment with that."

Getting testosterone was easy.[2] All it took was a one-hour consultation with a counselor who asked about her dysphoria. "I had all these rehearsed answers that I didn't genuinely believe, but it's really popular for the trans* community to ... help each other rehearse answers and tell each other what to say to doctors."

Helena was on CHT for two years. At first, she really enjoyed the experience. But after a while, several problems flared up.

It is a common thing for women on testosterone to experience a lot of anger. Then there's this weird phenomenon where you get upset and want to cry, but you can't cry. Even though I was really elated at first, eventually these kinds of problems started getting more apparent and I started feeling really miserable.... I was angry, like, all the time. Everything made me angry. I felt like I had been put through the wringer with all these emotional changes.... It really messed with my mental health.

Helena also learned that high doses of testosterone in females often cause their ovaries and uterus to atrophy after about five years. "I was aware of this ... but [I assumed that] probably by the time that becomes my problem, the doctors will figure something out."

Helena became passionate about her new identity. "I was a very, very, very radical trans* activist. I was super into this gender ideology." One of her trans* friends detransitioned, which felt like a betrayal. "I viewed it as 'triggering,' so I just blocked her on Tumblr. Everything about detransitioning I saw as 'triggering,' because it made me doubt myself. So I just blocked them out of my view."

Helena was miserable—emotionally, physically, mentally. "At some point," she remembers, "I just had to say: this is not working." She also "started seeing some of the flaws in the trans* ideology as a whole. I saw a lot of parts of the community that were really toxic, and really messed up." Ultimately, she decided to detransition back to female.

Helena is now living as a bisexual female who still wrestles with dysphoria, and she has some strong words to describe her experience identifying as trans*:

> I lost 5 years of my life to gender ideology … 5 years. [O]f believing a lie. [O]f centering all of my identity, friendships, actions, and thoughts on a lie. [A] false-hood. 5 years of repressing my trauma and sexuality in favor of a lie.[3]

Helena's story is one story. And one story is just one story. We should never view an entire idea or concept through the lens of just one story. But in the last few years, stories like Helena's have exploded on the scene. Some call the sudden rise of dysphoria in teens a trend. Others call it an outbreak.[4] Some psychologists have termed it Rapid-Onset Gender Dysphoria (ROGD). Whatever you name it, the percentage of teenagers identifying as trans*—a growing number of whom later detransition—has risen exponentially, especially among female teenagers.

I want to discuss this social phenomenon, since it raises many practical questions about trans* identities, mental health, online influence, and the ethics of medical interventions for adolescents. Let's first get our minds around the recent escalation of teens identifying as trans*.

We should never view an entire idea or concept through the lens of just one story.

WHAT IS RAPID-ONSET GENDER DYSPHORIA?

In many Western countries, we've seen a massive spike in teenagers questioning their gender. For instance, the Tavistock Centre in London, the main gender clinic in the United Kingdom, treated 51 (34 males, 17 females) children and teenagers in 2009 who had gender dysphoria or were identifying as trans*. In 2016, the same clinic saw 1,766 (557 males, 1,209 females) children and teenagers, and in 2019 it saw 2,364 (624 males, 1,740 females).[5] That's more than a 5,000 percent increase among females in ten years. Researchers have documented similar upsurges, among biological females in particular, in many Western countries: Sweden,[6] the United Kingdom,[7] the Netherlands,[8] New Zealand,[9] Canada,[10] and the United States.[11] A growing number of medical practitioners, feminists, parents, detransitioners, and even some older trans* people are deeply concerned about the sudden rise in young people questioning their gender. Through my own organization, the Center for Faith, Sexuality & Gender, I've seen a dramatic increase in emails and phone calls from parents whose child comes out as trans*, seemingly out of the blue, with no prior evidence of gender dysphoria. Many of these stories that I've listened to fit the description of ROGD.

Lisa Littman of Brown University coined the term Rapid-Onset Gender Dysphoria "rapid-onset," because most of these kids announce they are trans* in a way that seems quite sudden to their parents and counselors. A few years ago, Littman published the first peer-reviewed study on ROGD, where she surveyed 256 parents who have kids (83 percent of whom are female) that seem to fit her description of ROGD.[12] As the parents explored the situation a bit more, they found many common factors surrounding their children's apparently sudden trans* identity:

- Few of the children showed any signs of gender dysphoria to their parents growing up.
- Their new identity seemed to appear out of the blue.
- Many, if not all, of their friends at school were trans*, and their coming out often followed their friends' coming out as trans*.[13]
- Many of them became more popular after they came out as trans*.[14]
- They engaged in heavy online and social media activity (more than normal) surrounding their coming out.[15]
- Many of them had other mental health concerns that weren't being dealt with.

That last point about co-occurring mental health concerns is significant. In fact, 63 percent of the kids referred to in Littman's survey "had one or more diagnoses of a psychiatric disorder or neuro-developmental disability preceding the onset of gender dysphoria."[16] These diagnoses included the following:

- 48% had experienced a traumatic or stressful event prior to the onset of their gender dysphoria.
- 45% were engaging in nonsuicidal self-injury prior to the dysphoria.

- 15% had been diagnosed with ADHD.
- 12% had been diagnosed with OCD.
- 12% were on the autism spectrum.
- 7% had an eating disorder.
- 7% were bipolar.

These mental health issues were present *before* the kids came out as trans*. Of those who consulted a gender therapist or physician for the purpose of pursuing transition, only 28 percent of clinicians chose to "explore issues of mental health, previous trauma, or any alternative causes of gender dysphoria before proceeding"—*even after parents informed the clinicians of previously diagnosed mental health issues.*[17] One parent "tried to give our son's trans doctor a medical history of our son," but "she refused to accept it. She said the half hour diagnosis in her office with him was sufficient."[18] Parents were often called "transphobic" or "bigoted" by their kids if they encouraged their child to wait longer before transitioning, if they recommended a comprehensive health evaluation before transitioning, or if they simply expressed concerns about transitioning.[19] Littman said that the majority of the kids in her study thought "transition would solve their problems," and many of them "became unwilling to work on their basic mental health issues before seeking treatment."[20]

Several psychologists and researchers have observed phenomena similar to what we see in Littman's research. What Littman calls ROGD, they've witnessed in their own clinics and communities.[21] Others, however, have criticized Littman's theory, calling it transphobic, hateful, and harmful to trans* kids.[22] One critique is that Littman surveyed parents and not the kids themselves. But parent reports on the well-being of teenagers is a well-established method of research. It's not perfect; Littman and others never said it was. But to dismiss it outright would be naive at best and harmful at worst. Plus—this might not come to a shock to those of you who are parents—kids aren't always the best at self-evaluation. Sometimes, they rewrite their past in their own minds, intentionally or unintentionally. Other times, they simply lie, as Helena and many others now admit.

You could say parents can't be trusted either. And maybe some of them shouldn't be trusted. Perhaps some were aloof parents who were oblivious to their child's lifelong struggle with gender dysphoria. Parental reports are certainly fallible. But Littman did survey over 250 parents, and many of them had strikingly similar stories. Other psychologists and counselors have reported the same kind of ROGD stories among their patients.[23] For what it's worth, almost all the parents Littman surveyed held generally liberal social values. Eighty-six percent favored same-sex marriage, and 88 percent believed transgender people deserve the same rights and protections as others.[24] It's not as if Littman surveyed a bunch of fundamentalist Christians. Plus, a growing number of young women in their late teens or early twenties now say they experienced exactly what Littman showed in her study. Like Helena, these young women say they were influenced by their social environment, both online and in their circle of friends.[25] It's not just parents, then, but the kids themselves who say that ROGD is a real (and concerning) phenomenon.

Some people see the sudden rise in trans*-identifying teenagers as a good thing. A high number of trans* kids have always existed, they argue. Only now do these kids feel safe actually talking about who they are and seeking help.[26]

This dynamic may account for some of the rise in teenagers coming out as trans*. Certainly there's less stigma about being trans* today than in previous years. But it doesn't explain the massive, historically unprecedented spike in *biological females* seeking treatment. Historically, biological males have tended to outnumber biological females in rates of gender dysphoria, including late-onset gender dysphoria. But, as we saw earlier, there's been a stunning reversal in the sex ratio among kids and teenagers identifying as trans*. The United Kingdom, for instance, has witnessed a 1,460 percent increase among males and a 5,337 percent increase among females identifying as trans* compared to the number of referrals ten years prior.[27] "Although a decrease in stigma for transgender individuals might explain some of the rise in the numbers of adolescents presenting for care," says Littman, "it would not directly explain the inversion of the sex ratio."[28]

If we consider that societal influence might play some role here, then the explosion of teenage females with ROGD isn't too surprising. Teenage girls (especially in the West) have often struggled with eating disorders, body dysmorphia, and other conditions related to poor body image—conditions that often spread through social influence.[29] Littman writes,

> There are many insights from our understanding of peer contagion in eating disorders and anorexia that may apply to the potential peer contagion of rapid-onset gender dysphoria. Just as friendship cliques can set the level of preoccupation with one's body, body image, weight, and techniques for weight loss, so too

may friendship cliques set a level of preoccupation with one's body, body image, gender, and the techniques to transition.[30]

Rigid gender stereotypes also seem to play a role in the rising numbers. It's not uncommon for health care professionals and other caretakers to affirm a child's gender identity based on their gender-stereotypical behavior. One doctor in Wales prescribed hormones to a twelve-year-old biological female who had already been on puberty blockers since age nine. The reason? "This child has always been a boy, *never worn a dress, always played with boys*."[31] Another teenager named Sam didn't fit either stereotype. He liked Legos and Pokémon—stereotypical boy interests—but he also liked opera and hated sports. He liked to grow his hair long and wear pink Crocs. When other kids started to harass him at school, the principal advised him either to get rid of his pink Crocs and cut his hair short, or to socially transition and become a girl. He needed to pick one gender or the other.[32]

Once again, the concepts of "boy" and "girl" seem to be entangled with gender stereotypes, which is problematic when you're told that your female child needs medical attention since they love sports and hate dresses.

MEDICALIZING THE YOUTH

I'll be honest, this part of the trans* conversation has me concerned. I've tried hard to keep my wits about me as I've researched all sides of this debate: the debate about whether it's healthy or even ethical to encourage trans* teenagers to medically transition, *especially* when some or many of them might fit the category of ROGD. I've tried to avoid believing sensational reports from extreme right- or left-wing media, which tend to bend the truth in the direction they want it to go. I've sat down with medical professionals, with people who have transitioned and are happy they did, with people who have transitioned and regret it, and with parents of trans* kids. I've tracked how this debate is unraveling in countries like the United States, Canada, the United Kingdom, and Sweden. Through it all—not in spite of, but *because of*, my heart for the well-being of trans* people—I've become deeply disturbed by some of the things gender-affirming health care professionals are promoting.

One of my biggest concerns has to do with the risks of cross-sex hormone therapy (CHT). Some say that CHT is perfectly fine and its psychological benefits far outweigh any minor side effects.[33] In fact, the World Professional Association for Transgender Health (WPATH), a leading authority in the trans* conversation, says that "[f]eminizing/masculinizing hormone therapy—the administration of exogenous endocrine agents to induce feminizing or masculinizing changes—is a *medically necessary* intervention for many transsexual, transgender, and *gender nonconforming* individuals with gender dysphoria."[34]

I'm particularly concerned with the phrase "medically necessary," especially since WPATH includes "gender nonconforming individuals" among the cohort of kids who medically need to transition. "Gender nonconforming" is a broad, elastic category that often includes anyone who doesn't conform to gender stereotypes. A boy who prefers violin over football might be considered gender nonconforming. Twenty-seven percent of California youth (ages twelve to seventeen) are considered gender nonconforming.[35] Is it really "medically necessary" to inject one in every four teenagers full of cross-sex hormones?

Not all health professionals share WPATH's enthusiasm for CHT. Many studies show significant health risks involved with CHT.[36] Side effects include likely adverse changes in cholesterol and blood pressure, increased risk for heart attack and stroke, increased risks for blood clots, and increased risk of cancer.[37] Other possible side effects include risk of diabetes and a lifetime of low energy.[38] Plus, use of CHT for more than two years will most likely produce irreversible changes, such as infertility in both men and women and a deeper voice in biological females.[39] Despite these risks, WPATH considers CHT to be "medically necessary" in many cases, and some doctors are prescribing CHT to kids as young as twelve years old.[40]

Similar questions arise concerning puberty-suppressing hormones. Some say there are no real risks in taking puberty suppressors. "Treatment to delay puberty among adolescents struggling with gender identity seems to boost psychological well-being for those who ultimately pursue sex reassignment," one study suggests.[41] But just as one story is only one story, so also one study is only one study. Several other studies reveal a number of adverse side effects related to puberty suppressors, including the risk of stunted height, diminished bone density, headaches, hot flashes, weight gain, mood and emotion alterations, and negative effects on memory, concentration, flexible thinking, self-control, and IQ levels—along with stunted genitalia (which may make later MtF bottom surgery difficult or impossible).[42]

Not everyone reports adverse effects after taking puberty blockers. But to date, no significant study has been done on the long-term effects of giving puberty blockers to teenagers.[43] "If you suppress puberty for three years," says Russell Viner, a hormone specialist at University College London's Institute of Child Health, "the bones do not get any stronger at a time when they should be, and we really don't know what suppressing puberty does to your brain development. We are dealing with unknowns."[44] Carl Heneghan, director of the Centre for Evidence-Based Medicine at Oxford University, says in a recent review of the scientific research that "puberty blockers are being used in the context of profound scientific ignorance."[45] This lack of "robust evidence" has recently led the United Kingdom's highly respected Royal College of General Practitioners to release a position statement voicing concern about the use of puberty blockers and CHT with young people.[46] This is why some medical professionals say, "In light of the many uncertainties and unknowns, it would be appropriate to describe the use of puberty-blocking treatments for gender dysphoria as experimental ... to expose young people to such treatments is to endanger them."[47]

My point is not that CHT and blockers certainly *will* cause tons of problems. I'm only saying they *might*. But I'm very concerned about the wisdom and ethics of health care professionals prescribing these interventions to teenagers despite the drugs' potential negative short-term and long-term effects, many of which aren't yet fully known by the medical community.

We all make decisions that may have health risks. Maybe it's too much pizza, not enough exercise, way too much ranch dressing for such a small salad. Life is one big health risk. Sometimes we'd rather savor one more slice of Chicago deep dish, even though we might be shortening our life in doing so. But at least we know the risks. We're not surrounded by doctors who tell us, "More pizza, less broccoli!" Should a twelve-year-old girl wrestling with her identity be given puberty blockers without fully understanding how it may permanently damage her body?

It's out of compassion for both these parents and
their kids that I'm deeply disturbed by the eager
medicalization of kids, especially since a growing
number of kids who do transition later regret it.

Even more ethical questions surround the topic of surgically transitioning teenagers. Is a teenager who's wrestling with their gender identity, along with other likely co-occurring mental health concerns, able to make an informed decision about undergoing irreversible surgeries to align their body with their gender identity? Our brains aren't even fully developed until around age twenty-five. It's one thing for an adult to make this decision. I'm not convinced a fifteen-year-old is ready.

But some powerful voices in the medical community disagree with me. Johanna Olson-Kennedy is arguably *the* leading voice in the gender-affirming medical community. She's the director of the Center for Transyouth Health and Development at Children's Hospital Los Angeles, where she has helped more than one thousand patients transition. She received a $5.7 million grant from the National Institutes of Health to test the benefit of giving cross-sex hormones to kids as young as twelve and performing double mastectomies on biological girls as young as thirteen.[48] Olson-Kennedy doesn't see any problem with removing the breasts of a thirteen-year-old wrestling with their gender, since "adolescents actually have the capacity to make a reasoned, logical decision." Plus, says Olson-Kennedy, "If you want breasts at a later point in your life, you can go and get them."[49]

Biological girls are given high doses of testosterone as young as twelve. They're having their uterus and ovaries removed at sixteen, the same age that some biological boys are having their penises removed. And there's an ongoing push to lower the age where kids can get hormones and surgery without their parents' consent. Currently, in Oregon, fifteen-year-olds can medically transition without the consent of their parents.[50]

Even when parental consent is required, it's often not truly "informed." Parents are sometimes told that if their child doesn't transition, the child will probably attempt suicide. (See the appendix for a discussion of suicidality and trans* identities.) *Do you want an alive son or a dead daughter?* In some cases, parents have lost custody of their kids because they didn't think it was wise to give their teenage biological daughter testosterone and consent to having their teen's breasts removed.[51] I talked to one parent the other day whose fourteen-year-old is demanding cross-sex hormones. This parent is being told that if they don't say yes, they are putting their child at risk for suicide and could lose custody. It's out of compassion for both these parents and their kids that I'm deeply disturbed by the eager medicalization of kids, especially since a growing number of kids who do transition later regret it.

DETRANSITIONERS SPEAKING OUT

As the number of trans* teenagers continues to rise, so also does the number of detransitioners. And they're speaking out against what they see as medical malpractice and ideological brainwashing. Charlie Evans, founder of the Detransition Advocacy Network, says,

> There are few studies behind detransition rates, but I can tell you there are thousands of us—our voices are hidden because we are seen by the queer community as an inconvenient consequence of their movement. We are just collateral damage for the 'greater good'.... This generation are guinea pigs, and the fact that scientists and doctors are staying quiet about this is criminal.[52]

Charlie hosted the first ever detransition conference in Manchester, UK, on December 2, 2019. Hundreds of people showed up to spread awareness, share their stories, and protest a gender-affirmative-only approach toward what they see as gender-confused and troubled teens. These detransitioners aren't against transition per se. They are against misdiagnosing every gender nonconforming teen as trans* and rushing them into transition without providing proper information.

Charlie has started a network called the "Detransition Advocacy Network" to support people who decide not to transition or who have transitioned but now regret it. Another organization, the Pique Resilience Project, is a group of detransitioned females in their twenties who testify to the accuracy of Littman's study about Rapid-Onset Gender Dysphoria. And still other websites, YouTube channels, blogs, and online communities are forming quickly.[53]

Other countries are reevaluating their standards of care for trans*-identifying teenagers in light of worldwide concerns about ROGD. A lot of dust has been kicked up recently in Sweden, for instance—a very progressive country where most people are supportive of the trans* community. Sweden's Board of Health and Welfare released a study showing a 1,500 percent increase in Gender Dysphoria diagnoses among thirteen- to seventeen-year-old females between 2008 and 2018. This data sparked widespread concern and is currently causing health care professionals to rethink their approach.[54] A similar conversation is happening in the United Kingdom.

In the United States, by contrast, the gender-affirmative-only model still reigns, and many doctors are reluctant to question this model for fear of losing their jobs. But a growing number of health care professionals are beginning to speak out against what they see as an ideologically driven, unscientific approach to caring for trans*-identified teenagers. If this trend continues, I suspect we'll soon see changes in the medical community. But many teens may be harmed before change comes.

A CHRISTIAN RESPONSE

It's important that Christians become aware of ROGD and all the controversy that surrounds it, but also that we respond to it in a Christlike manner. What does this look like?

First, and I can't say this loudly enough: we shouldn't assume that every trans*-identifying teenager fits the ROGD mold. ROGD describes *one* kind of trans* experience. Some parents could come across the idea of ROGD and think, *Oh good, it's just a phase! My daughter will grow out of this soon enough.* I don't want to give parents the impression that every trans* teenager will grow out of their trans* identity.

ROGD describes *one* kind of trans* experience. Most of my friends who are trans* or gender dysphoric do not have experiences that resonate at all with the ROGD stories they hear. For them, being trans* wasn't trendy. Internet use didn't contribute to their dysphoria. They weren't brainwashed by Tumblr. They simply experienced brutal gender dysphoria from the time they were four years old, and they were ridiculed for it, not applauded.

If someone you know seems to fit the ROGD narrative, then understanding this phenomenon could help you sort out a healthy path forward. But you could do a lot of harm to your friend if you assume they're succumbing to a social trend when they're really wrestling with something quite different. If you've met one transgender person, you've met … one transgender person. And if you've met a teen who seems to fit the ROGD narrative, you've still only met one trans* person.

Second, the church needs to foster better, more authentic, and more life-giving communities for our teenagers. Many kids who appear to fit the ROGD narrative are struggling with other significant challenges in life: anxiety, depression, self-harm. Some have experienced trauma, some have been abused, and most feel isolated and weighed down by social pressures. One reason young people turn to online help is because they haven't found community, love, and authentic relationships elsewhere. If the church simply gets upset about the rise of ROGD and doesn't work to create safe communities of love and listening for teens, then we're not embodying the way of Christ as we ought. People search for community when they don't already have one.

Youth groups can't be satisfied with simply attracting a high number of kids. We need to create spaces where young people can open up, be heard, receive godly wisdom, and learn about God's expansive vision for what it means to be male and female. But if youth groups and churches reinforce cultural stereotypes—to be a woman is to be feminine, to be a man is to be masculine—they will continue to exacerbate the problem.

This goes for our homes as well. Parents need to be aware of the daily lives of our kids. As a parent of three teenage girls, I can say that parenting is both the most wonderful and the most challenging thing in my life right now. Parenting isn't for the fainthearted. But we need to be heavily involved in our kids' lives from a young age and have sex- and gender-related conversations with our kids as soon as they become aware of their bodies (age three? maybe four?). We need to allow for different ways of being boys and girls; we shouldn't demand that our kids fit the stereotypes. Our kids need to see their parents as the safest, most loving people to turn to in time of need.

Third, be aware of excessive internet use. This is a whole topic in itself. But excessive internet, and especially social media, use has been shown to do a lot of harm to teenagers. Anxiety, depression, and suicidality are all on the rise among teenagers; scholars are connecting this rise, in part, to excessive screen time and social media use.[55]

We need to create spaces where young people can open up, be heard, receive godly wisdom, and learn about God's expansive vision for what it means to be male and female.

When it comes to gender and sexuality, the internet is a hot mess. And yet the internet will likely be the first place kids turn for answers if they feel they can't ask their questions at home or at church. Teaching your kids, helping your friends, and pastoring your people to be wise in how much internet media they take in (and *what* they take in) is a necessary component of Christian discipleship in the twenty-first century. But limiting social media use without creating real, vibrant, understanding, nonjudgmental alternatives for community won't work. People *will* gravitate to where they feel seen. Churches and homes that don't become such environments will only push people to seek out community online.

Remember, the manner in which we speak about these things is just as important as what we say. This rings true especially with something as intricate and sensitive as teens questioning their gender.

It's time to return to the question we've danced around in this chapter: Is it ever morally right for a Christian to transition? With truth and grace by our side, let's wrestle with this delicate and complex question.

Chapter 11

TRANSITIONING AND CHRISTIAN DISCIPLESHIP

Should a Christian ever transition?

I almost didn't write this chapter. I wanted to leave it out. I'm not a psychologist or a doctor, and I don't experience gender dysphoria. I've never lain in bed all day with "an electric current through my body that caused my joints to ache, my stomach [to] turn, my hands [to] shake, and nausea in the most severe moments of dysphoria." I've never felt like I had a "creepy serum ... injected all over my body to create an odd, numb yet painful feeling coursing through my blood vessels and seeping into my flesh."[1]

I've never felt the burst of hope, beaming like a ray of sun on a crisp spring day, upon hearing that this misery, these suicidal thoughts, might disappear if I transitioned. I've never scoured the internet chasing this hope to find out if it was real, only to find expert after expert and story after story affirming it. Relief exists. There can be an end to the shaking and nausea and creepy serum coursing through my veins.

I don't know what's it's like to turn to the church for help only to hear nothing. No wisdom, no counsel, no awareness of the conversation. Sermon after sermon, Bible study after Bible study. No one is addressing my situation. Does the Bible say anything about my experience? Does the Bible say anything about *me*? Does anyone care? Does Jesus know that I exist?

"We were all going around talking about our struggles and confessing our sin," Jack told me about a Bible study he was in. He hadn't told anyone his struggles with gender dysphoria. He was scared to death to say anything. But if everyone else could talk about their struggles, why shouldn't he? When it was his turn to talk, with hands shaking and fear welling up inside him, Jack said, "I've never told anyone this, but I ... I sometimes feel like I should have been a woman."

Only it wasn't sometimes. It was most of the time. Day after day, year after year, two things had been true of Jack's life: he was a sold-out believer in Jesus, and he experienced lifelong, and at times debilitating, gender dysphoria. He didn't believe Jesus wanted him to transition. He still believed that he was a man. But he wanted a second opinion. He wanted some guidance, some wisdom, some prayer. He wanted *someone* to walk with him in his journey.

"I experience gender dysphoria," Jack continued. But the more he talked, the quieter the room got. Blank stares and troubled faces. He stammered on. "It's ... I mean ... that's what psychologists call my condition. My experience. Whatever." More silence. "Anyway ... I guess I just wanted to share. Thanks."

Jack received some cordial nods and a few superficial conversations after the Bible study. But no one seemed to care. Jack didn't need them to throw him a party, lifting him up on a chair and parading him around the room. He didn't need them to have all the answers. He didn't need a psychological Gandalf, puffing out wisdom about gender dysphoria through rings of smoke. He just needed someone to care enough to help him navigate the challenges of his life as a Christ-follower.

I didn't want to write this chapter. And yet people like Jack and many other Christians with gender dysphoria—and their families and their pastors—are looking for nuanced, theologically rooted, psychologically informed guidance as they process whether transitioning is something Jesus would want them to do.

With much fear and trepidation, then, here are some thoughts.

TWO POLARIZING APPROACHES

The debate about transitioning is often dominated by two extreme perspectives on opposite ends of the spectrum.

On one end, the narrative is "Transition or suicide!" That is, trans* people are told that if they don't transition, they'll likely end up taking their own lives. Even if they don't, all kinds of self-destructive coping behaviors probably await them—self-harm, drug and alcohol abuse, or destructive relationships—which could also end in death.

Counselors, activists, and medical practitioners often give "transition or suicide" ultimatums to the parents of kids with gender dysphoria. "Our only choice was to have a dead son or a living daughter," one set of parents said.[2] Another parent explains, "Did I want a living son or a dead daughter? I wasn't going to take the risk by waiting around and doing nothing." Transitioning, this parent believed, "is my only option to save my child's life."[3]

We'll come back to the sobering reality of trans* people and suicidality in the appendix. For various reasons, which we'll discuss there, I don't think this binary advice—transition or suicide—is psychologically or ethically responsible.[4]

It's far too easy for us to dismiss the struggles of others, especially if we don't face the same struggles ourselves.

On the opposite end of the spectrum are those who take what I call a "stop it!" approach. If you haven't seen that old Bob Newhart skit, it's worth taking a five-minute break to type "Bob Newhart stop it" into YouTube. Bob Newhart (playing the role of a psychologist) gives a poor woman with all kind of phobias two words of advice: "Stop it!"

Hilarious as the skit is, some people take a similar approach toward people with dysphoria. A five-year-old boy puts on a dress? "Stop it!" A seven-year-old girl wants to cut her hair short? "Stop it!" A ten-year-old boy wants to play the violin instead of football? "What are you, some kind of girl? Stop it!"

For some people, all behavior is either sinful or righteous, and if you read the right verses and pray the right prayers, you'll have enough power to choose the right things. Any psychological experience that might underlie a behavior is ignored or dismissed. Looking for the psychological roots of a person's feelings or actions amounts to blame-shifting.

People who respond like this seem to have never sat down and listened to someone with gender dysphoria. Not just heard a person's words, but really listened. It's far too easy for us to dismiss the struggles of others, especially if we don't face the same struggles ourselves.

For many Christians, the "transition or suicide" approach is too simplistic and lacks scientific backing or theological reflection. The "stop it" approach is also too simplistic and lacks empathy or nuance.

But if all other methods of managing dysphoria don't work, should transition be an option?

THINKING CHRISTIANLY ABOUT TRANSITION

I suggest we view this question through three different lenses. I'll call these (1) the ontological lens, (2) the ethical lens, and (3) the practical lens. We'll discuss each one in order.

1. The Ontological Lens

The *ontological lens* focuses on the question, "Who am I?" More specifically, "Does God consider me to be a man or a woman?" We've spent several chapters looking at this already, so we don't need to rehash it all. As we've seen, quite a bit of biblical, theological, and scientific evidence suggests that a person's biological sex determines whether a person (without an intersex condition) is a man or a woman—even if their gender identity doesn't resonate with this.

Christian discipleship is oriented toward living out the divine image that God created us to be. Sexed bodies are part of that image. Ontologically, then, transitioning would be moving us further away from who we *are*, not bringing us closer to it.

In no way do I want to minimize the real pain and suffering a person with gender dysphoria may experience. I absolutely want to explore ways of relieving their suffering. But I want to do so in a way that resonates with a biblical rhythm of sanctification: embracing the divine image God created us to be, an image that includes our sexed bodies as part of our human identity.[5]

Our sex is not arbitrary. It's part of how we reflect God's image in the world.

Mark Yarhouse and Julia Sadusky are two Christian psychologists who agree with this perspective. They recognize that "pastoral care" should focus on "returning the person to God's creational intent"; namely, helping the person find "the congruence of gender identity with biological sex." And they say, "We prefer this too, if at all possible."[6]

However, they appeal to the brain-sex theory (which we discussed in chapter 8) to suggest that in some rare cases, transitioning may return a person back to God's creational intent: "[I]n rare instances, one's anatomy may have mapped differently than one's brain. Would we then consider that one's gender identity is, in some cases, instructive?"[7]

If the brain-sex theory is true, then perhaps some people might experience an "intersex condition of the brain" whereby their body might be male while their brain is female (or vice versa). One could argue that changing a person's biological sex to align with their brain *is* a return to God's creational intent, which was distorted by the fall.

This might be the strongest Christian argument in favor of sex reassignment surgery. Mark and Julia, whom I consider friends, are solid, biblically minded Christians who not only understand the psychological complexity of what we're talking about but have walked with many people who experience gender dysphoria.

But this perspective largely depends on the validity of brain-sex theory. As we've seen, not only is the science behind this theory widely disputed, but it's also intertwined with cognitive and behavioral stereotypes of how men and women should think and act. Women can have stereotypically masculine interests and behaviors, and these might be rooted in the brain. But these interests and behaviors don't make them into men.

From my vantage point, the ontological lens suggests that we should help people accept their sexed bodies as part of their God-given identity.

2. The Ethical Lens

This lens is closely linked to the previous one. If a person *is* male or female, then they should embrace and honor that identity. But is this a moral decision?

"Moral decision" can mean different things to different people. Some people make a distinction between choices that are *unwise* but not necessarily *morally wrong*, and choices (like whether to sleep with a prostitute) that are clearly morally wrong, not just unwise.

If we embrace our earlier ontological point, then is transitioning morally wrong or just unwise?

This is a tough question. And if you think it's easy, you might not have thought it through carefully enough. Despite the complexity, though, I think a strong ethical case can be made that transitioning is not just unwise but also morally wrong.

I recognize that even reading this might trigger some of you. Some of my friends feel a spiraling sense of shame and rejection when anyone says transitioning might be unethical for a Christian. But this shouldn't prevent us from wrestling with the ethics of it all. As Christians, we must be willing and able to ask, "What does the Bible say about it?" Consider the following points:

First, our biological sex is connected to our status as image bearers of God. "*In the image of God* he created them; *male and female* he created them" (Gen 1:27). Transitioning isn't just tweaking or enhancing our biological sex; it's seeking to change it. Our sex is not arbitrary. It's part of how we reflect God's image in the world.

Second, the cross-dressing prohibition (Deut. 22:5) and Paul's words about maintaining male and female distinctions (1 Cor. 11:2–16) add weight to viewing transitioning as a moral question. So do Paul's words in 1 Corinthians 6:12–20 and other places where he roots ethical behavior in a high view of the body. Paul doesn't believe the body to be a morally neutral canvas.

Third, an overarching biblical theology of sexed embodiment—one that looks back to creation (Gen. 1–2) and forward to our resurrected state—suggests that our sexed bodies are a significant part of human identity and personhood. When we consider the story of Scripture as a whole (not just a few proof texts) and how it informs our theological anthropology, transitioning for non-intersex people seems to go against God's creative intention.[8]

There are two main ethical arguments in favor of Christians transitioning under some circumstances. The first argument, which we discussed earlier in this chapter, has to do with the brain-sex theory: in some rare cases, transitioning is actually aligning a person's body with their brain and therefore *is* the ethically right thing to do.

The second argument has to do with relieving a person's suffering. Transitioning, some say, might be the only thing that will relieve a person's dysphoria. And indeed, bringing comfort to those who are in distress, especially those who have been marginalized by others, is a hallmark of Christian love. Emotionally, I very much resonate with this point. When I sit with people who experience dysphoria, all I want to do is make it go away. And yet, relieving someone's suffering isn't really a strong, stand-alone ethical point. From a Christian perspective, relieving the suffering of a fellow Christian should go hand in hand with helping them embrace the divine image they've been created in. Good, godly, faithful people sometimes walk through life with a thorn in their side. Sometimes God takes it away; other times he doesn't. Removing the thorn isn't always the ethically necessary thing to do. Plus, as we'll see in the next section, there's no guarantee that transitioning *will* relieve someone's suffering. Sometimes trying to remove the thorn just pushes it deeper into your skin.

I think there are good biblical and ethical reasons why a disciple of Jesus should not transition. But I also think we can make an even clearer biblical case for why Christians should care for the poor, the outcast, the immigrant, the downtrodden and oppressed, those who are marginalized and criticized by the religious elite; for why Christians should rebuke those who claim Jesus but are racist, misogynist, unkind, unloving, ungracious, or downright nasty on social media. We can make a strong case for why Christians should confront fellow Christians who embody and promote cultural views of masculinity and femininity, baptizing them in the name of "being biblical" while hanging these stereotypes like millstones around the necks of struggling siblings in Christ. We need to consider questions related to transitioning with a deep commitment to Scripture and a deep distain for hypocrisy.

Good, godly, faithful people sometimes walk through life with a thorn in their side. Sometimes God takes it away; other times he doesn't.

And—I can't emphasize this point enough—if you are a Christian in leadership, or any Christian mentoring or parenting someone who's trans*, we *must* give trans* people space to wrestle with the ethical aspects of transitioning. A top-down, heavy-handed, compassionless approach that gives no room for personal wrestling—"Thus sayeth me and the Lord!"—will most likely push people toward transitioning and away from us. We need to hold our views with humility, graciously prioritizing relationship. We can't force-feed our views to others—no matter how biblical they may be.

3. The Practical Lens

Even if transitioning were ontologically and ethically valid, we'd still have to consider the practical pros and cons of such a decision. Now, I want to be clear: we shouldn't make ethical decisions based on pragmatics, arguing that "the end justifies the means." This approach is more formally called "utilitarian ethics," and it's not really a Christian way of making moral decisions. And yet, Christians sometimes take a utilitarian approach to decision making, even if they don't say, "Hey, I'm going with the utilitarian ethical view on this one." Utilitarian ethics is at work when a church grows from one hundred to one thousand and deems whatever means they used to cause the growth as moral. The end justifies the means.

But we don't see this ethical reasoning in Scripture. Sometimes doing the right thing leads to perceived success. Other times it leads to perceived failure. *Faithfulness*, not *effectiveness*, is what Jesus calls us to. Despite how prevalent utilitarian ethics is in pop Christianity, it's telling that a recent book called *Christian Ethics: Four Views* doesn't even list utilitarianism as one of the four Christian options.[9] In the introduction, the authors explain that they've intentionally excluded it because it's not a Christian view.

I say all this to make sure the practical point I raise in the next few pages isn't taken as the foundational reason why I don't think Christians should transition. Even so, I want to observe that transitioning may not bring the relief some people are promised.

We've already looked at the controversy surrounding puberty blockers and cross-sex hormone therapy (CHT) in the previous chapter. Due to increased risk of heart disease, stroke, blood clots, and cancer (among other things), taking CHT could be replacing one problem with a whole set of other ones.

Sex reassignment surgery (SRS) has also received mixed reviews.[10] Some studies show remarkable success (though "success" is a tricky word). A range of follow-up studies have found that people with gender dysphoria who have medically transitioned are generally happier and healthier than they were before SRS and that their dysphoria has all but gone away.[11]

Other studies have less clear results.[12] Some have found that, while the experience of dysphoria may have decreased, the rates of other mental health issues (including depression, anxiety, and suicidality) often remain relatively high.[13] Most researchers acknowledge that transition outcome studies generally continue to suffer from methodological problems.[14] One common problem is that these studies sometimes rely on "small sample sizes collected by *convenience sampling*."[15] Convenience sampling is like standing outside of a mall and asking all the people whether they like shopping. Your percentages might be a bit higher than if you took the same poll outside the gates of the Indy 500. SRS studies often lack a comparable control group—comparing people who went through SRS with those who didn't. They also usually rely on self-reporting. Any psychologist who still has a job knows that self-reporting, while necessary, is not always a reliable way to determine how someone's really doing.

A severe problem with most studies is that they are not longitudinal in nature. That is, they typically measure the "success" of SRS only up to one year after the procedure. In that first year, most people who go through SRS say they feel much better than they did before. The weight of evidence seems to suggest this (albeit through self-report). But how do they feel two years later? Five years? Ten years?

Only a few studies have been significantly longitudinal. One of the most well-known is a Swedish study published in 2011, which surveyed all 324 sex-reassigned persons in Sweden between 1973 and 2003. This study had a large sample size, it had a control group, it was based on the entire population rather than just a convenience sample, and it was longitudinal, including some participants who had their surgeries up to thirty years prior. This is what the study found:

> Persons with transsexualism, after sex reassignment, have considerably higher risks for mortality, suicidal behavior, and psychiatric morbidity than the general population, [although] surgery and hormonal therapy alleviates dysphoria.[16]

To be clear, this study compared the mental health of trans* people post-SRS with that of *the general population*, not with that of trans* people who chose *not* to pursue SRS. In other words, we don't know whether the mental health of those in the survey got worse, improved, or stayed the same after surgery. All we can say is that the mental health risks of trans* people after surgery are considerably higher than those of non-trans* people.

Another longitudinal study was more precise in how it measured the mental health of its participants. It focused on mental health measures of Danish individuals both before and after they underwent SRS, with data drawn from 1978 to 2010. They found that 27.9 percent of the sample were diagnosed with psychiatric issues before SRS, and 22.1 percent after SRS. Significantly, only 6.7 percent of the sample were diagnosed both before and after SRS, which means that 15.4 percent developed psychiatric issues *after* SRS. These findings led the researchers to conclude that "SRS may reduce psychological morbidity for some individuals while increasing it for others."[17]

Again, we shouldn't make moral decisions based on "success" rates, or lack thereof. But neither should we make life-altering decisions without being well-informed about potential outcomes. This means listening to voices on different sides of the issue, including the voices of those who are dissatisfied with their choice to transition: the detransitioners.

As we saw in chapter 10, detransitioners seem to be coming out of the woodwork in swelling numbers. A few years ago, you could hardly find any such stories. Now, YouTube, Reddit, Tumblr, and other sites are bursting with stories of transition regret. Detransitioners usually don't say transitioning is wrong for everyone. But they do say that way too many people rush to transition (as they did) without realizing all the potential problems their transition could create.

Now, I want to reiterate what I said earlier: We shouldn't use stories of detransitioners to argue that transitioning isn't successful. Rather, we should first think ontologically and ethically about what we mean by "success." In spite of all the stories of detransitioners, I'm going to guess that the majority of people who transition don't regret it. Christians need to make ethical decisions based primarily on what is most *faithful*, not what is—from the world's viewpoint—most *effective*.

The growing number of detransition stories, however, does challenge the narrative that transitioning is the only way (or a surefire way) to be happy. Even if I were a God-hating, Bible-smashing, do-whatever-makes-you-happy kind of guy, I would still encourage trans*-identified people to think long and hard—and do quite a bit of listening from a diverse array of informed voices—before they make an irreversible, lifelong decision.

WHAT IF SOMEONE HAS ALREADY TRANSITIONED?

How should we respond to those who have already transitioned? This question is really tough. I have in my mind faces of friends who have transitioned, friends who searched the Scriptures and spent loads of time in prayer before transitioning, friends who are truly godly, Jesus-following, Bible-believing Christians. The first thing we need to realize is that many different situations could have surrounded a person's decision to transition. Each one might merit a different relational or pastoral response. Here are just a few possibilities:

- A Christian who transitioned and has received nothing but positive affirmation from godly people in their life.
- A Christian who was on the brink of committing suicide (maybe had several attempts) and has been told by religious authorities that transitioning is their only hope.
- A Christian who has decided not to follow gracious, wise counsel backed by theological and scientific evidence that transitioning was not a morally right thing to do. This counsel was coupled with sacrificial, loving fellowship and a commitment to walk with the person through alternative ways of dealing with their dysphoria.
- A Christian who has decided not to follow religious counsel that was very impersonal, trite, and

uninformed. This counsel was *not* offered alongside any relational commitment, love, or guidance.

- A Christian who transitioned before they came to Christ.
- A non-Christian who's been coming to your church and is spiritually seeking.
- A brand-new convert to Christianity.
- A person (Christian or non-Christian) who has transitioned but now might want to detransition.

And on and on the list goes. If you've met one trans* situation, you've met ... one trans* situation. Here are a few general principles to consider.

First, Christians should want trans* people—whether non-transitioned or transitioned—to flood our churches. The more the merrier, I say. It'll create loads of beautifully complex pastoral opportunities, and some Christians will get uncomfortable and leave. So be it. I don't think church should be limited to squeaky-clean Christians who (think they) have all their stuff together or who keep their porn, their greed, their pride, and their lack of concern for the poor hidden behind dusty hymnals. I want churches filled with those who know their brokenness, who don't hide their pain, who ask very hard questions. If a trans* person who has transitioned is coming to your church, praise God. I hope they are treated with the utmost kindness and respect. All the difficult questions about what to do now are secondary to creating communities that embody God's kindness, which draws people to himself (Rom. 2:4)—*especially* those who've been marginalized by the church.

If Jesus were a pastor today, I suspect he'd have plenty of trans* people attending his church. Do they want to attend yours?

Second, meaningful relationship requires taking a good deal of time to get to know and learn from a trans* person. Hear their story. Ask good questions. *Real* questions, not interrogative ones. Remember, people transition for all kinds of different reasons. You have no clue what this person has been going through until you really get to know them. Policies and doctrinal statements might have their place, but they can't replace sharing a meal with a fellow image bearer of God.

I do believe that one long-term goal of discipleship is for all believers to identify with their biological sex. But what this looks like for trans* Christians who have already undergone SRS might be very different than it would for other trans* Christians.

Third, people may come to your church in various shades of transition: social, hormonal, or surgical. Each category presents its own questions. If a biological female has socially transitioned to male, this might mean they have cut their hair short, stopped wearing makeup, and started wearing "men's" jeans. If this person wants to realign with her biological sex, that realignment might be primarily a heart (and mind) change, since makeup and dresses and long hair aren't required to live as female.

Discipleship is a long process.... God doesn't demand overnight sanctification, and we're all thankful that he doesn't.

When it comes to someone who's been on hormones and wants to realign with their biological sex, a new set of challenges arises. As much as taking CHT can be hard on the body and mind, getting off it can be equally difficult. What if medical complications arise? What about the psychological repercussions? Will you be there for your trans* friend as they wrestle through this decision, committing to love and support them no matter what they decide? And if they do choose to stop CHT, will you be there for them all the more? Will you sacrifice your time and money to embody Jesus and bear another person's burdens?

If someone has had invasive surgeries, the choice to detransition is incredibly difficult. Most of these surgeries are irreversible. If a biological male has had their penis removed (penectomy), it's not like you can just stitch it back on. "It" no longer exists. Plus, just as surgical transition is expensive, so are detransitioning surgeries. *If* a person does desire to detransition and can't afford it, then I'd recommend that the Christian community come alongside the person and help (or flat out) pay for it. On the other hand, a person might come to identify with their biological sex mentally, spiritually, and socially, yet physically still have a transitioned body that resembles the opposite sex. It may be impossible, painful, or too expensive (or all of the above) to detransition surgically. And this brings with it another set of complexities—or, as I like to call them, relational opportunities.

Fourth, discipleship is a long process, a journey along a road that runs right through the pearly gates. God doesn't demand overnight sanctification, and we're all thankful that he doesn't. Just think about your own sin. Your anger, your pride, your porn, your greed, your insatiable quest for comfort. How long has it been a struggle? When's the last time you messed up? No matter what you think disciple-ship should look like for a person who's transitioned, let's give them some space and grace to work through their obedience to Jesus in the context of a loving, nonjudgmental community.

My friend Kyla transitioned (FtM) eight years ago. Three years ago, she met Jesus and decided to detransition back to female. It was a grueling process—encountering Christ, having her world turned upside down, concluding that she wasn't really a man. Kyla decided to detransition back to female out of obedience to Christ. But she couldn't do it alone.

A couple at her church knew what she was going through and how impossible it would be for her to walk this road in isolation. They invited Kyla to live with them in their home, so they could be the spiritual family she needed through it all. "I couldn't have done this without them," Kyla said. "I couldn't have gone through this without the family of Christ."

Christians are not solitary individuals called to follow Jesus on our own and demand that others do the same. We're a community of radical misfits, called into a motley family filled with grace and truth where no one should walk alone.

Chapter 12

PRONOUNS, BATHROOMS, AND SLEEPING SPACES

Of all the practical questions Christians ask about trans* identities, these three might be the most common: What pronouns should non-trans* Christians use for trans* people? What bathrooms should a trans* person use? And where do trans* people sleep at, say, high school summer camp? The latter two are very similar, so we'll address those together. But first, let's dive into what might be the most asked—and most contentious—question in this conversation.

PRONOUNS

Should non-trans* Christians use a trans* person's pronouns and chosen name?[1]

In other words, if a biological male identifies as a female, should you use the name they've chosen for themselves or their birth name (what trans* people call their "deadname")? And which pronouns should you use? The set that matches their biological sex, in this case *he/him*? Or the one that matches their gender identity, in this case *she/her?* Or what if a trans* person identifies with *they/them* pronouns rather than *he/him* or *she/her?* Is that okay? Is it grammatically correct? And what about other recently minted pronouns like *ze* or *hir?*

One important way Christians can honor
others is by seeking to understand.

These are tough questions, and committed Christians disagree on what to do. Some might think, *What's the big deal? Isn't it just a pronoun?* I can see how people might roll their eyes at this whole topic. I used to do the same. Then I talked to several trans* people about why pronouns can be such a big deal. I still don't think I fully understand, but I'm trying to. If you've never sat down and genuinely listened to *why* a trans* person considers pronouns to be significant, I would recommend doing so. Even if you still don't agree with their reasoning or resonate with their experience, one important way Christians can honor others is by seeking to understand.

The same goes for those of us who might be frustrated at people who refuse to use a trans* person's chosen name or pronouns. What is *their* reasoning? Some people won't budge in the pronouns they use for others because of their concerns about the ideological roots that underlie language. As they see it, pronoun use is not just about pronouns; it's about fundamental beliefs concerning human nature. If you're frustrated that some people have deep reservations about using a trans* person's pronouns, you might need to listen to them with the same grace and humility that you're asking of them.

This topic is obviously very volatile. But reading this chapter with a white-knuckled grip and an anger-reddened face won't get us very far in actually understanding what both sides are saying. So take a deep breath! Relax. Dump out your coffee and grab a glass of wine (or herbal tea, I guess). Let's try to understand what both sides are saying, beginning with the view that we should only use pronouns that match a person's biological sex.

ARGUMENTS AGAINST USING THE PRONOUNS TRANS* PEOPLE IDENTIFY WITH

First, some argue, using pronouns that don't match a person's biological sex is lying. "I would be lying to call a he a 'she,'" writes John Piper.[2] Sure, Christians are to be loving, but not at the expense of being untruthful. To be untruthful is actually unloving, and using pronouns that *don't* match a person's biological sex is simply untrue.

The Nashville Statement—a series of affirmations regarding sexuality and gender signed by many Christian leaders in 2017—affirms this perspective. Article 11 of the Statement resonates with Piper's concern: "We affirm our duty to speak the truth in love at all times, including when we speak to or about one another as male or female. We deny any obligation to speak in such ways that dishonor God's design of his image-bearers as male and female."[3]

Second, this group argues, using a trans* person's pronouns would be a capitulation to an unbiblical and destructive ideology. If we use the untruthful language of a destructive ideology, we give in to that ideology. "'[T]rans communities use language as a tool to transform culture," writes Laurie Higgins. "They redefine words, emptying them of their former meanings, and invent new words that embody subversive and false assumptions."[4] My good friend Rob Smith, who personally favors pronoun avoidance, agrees that using what he calls "untrue pronouns" risks additional harm. He says, "It communicates (and so potentially endorses and perpetuates) the false claim that gender (in Judith Butler's words) is 'a free-floating artifice.' The reason this ideology is dangerous is because it creates and deepens delusions in confused and vulnerable people, and (in many cases) leads them to destroy their relationships (e.g., marriages) and do irreparable damage to their bodies (e.g., through SRS)."[5]

Third, if we refer to a male as "she" (or vice versa), we're feeding delusion and actually harming a person rather than loving them. Denny Burk sums up this argument well:

> I must never encourage or accommodate transgender fictions with my words. In fact, I have an obligation to expose them. For me, that means that I may never refer to a biological male with pronouns that encourage him to think of himself as a female. Likewise, I may never refer to a biological female with pronouns that encourage her to think of herself as a male.[6]

These three arguments could apply to using a trans* person's chosen name as well as their pronouns. But most Christian leaders who make these arguments about pronouns will still use a trans* person's chosen name. Piper, for instance, believes that names are culturally arbitrary, and therefore it's fine to use a person's chosen name.[7] He recommends using a person's name as a concession, while not using pronouns that don't match their biological sex, since this would be lying.

Personally, I think these three arguments raise some good points. But let's suspend judgment until we hear the other side.

ARGUMENTS FOR PRONOUN HOSPITALITY

Some say that using a person's preferred pronouns is an act of hospitality. You don't have to share all the beliefs a trans* person has about themselves in order to use the pronouns they identify with. It's simply an act of respect. Several arguments bolster this view, arguments that require a bit of explanation.

First, advocates of pronoun hospitality argue, language is flexible and changes over time. Pronouns don't *always* refer to someone's biological sex but can refer to someone's gender identity. You may agree or disagree that gender identity should be separated from biological sex, or you might think it's wrong to prioritize gender over sex. But the fact is, the meaning of words is determined in part by cultural usage, and pronoun usage now includes gender identity, not just biological sex. That's just how language works. You are not *lying* if you use "she" to describe a biological male whose gender identity is female, even if you disagree with this person's choice to identify as female. You're simply using language according to the social flexibility that language has always had.

For instance, the word *nice* didn't always mean what it means today. It comes from the Latin word *nescius*, which means "ignorant," and it was used this way for a few hundred years. But its meaning changed over time through usage. Same with the word *pretty*, which used to mean "crafty" or "cunning." Even the Old English word *girle*, now spelled *girl*, used to mean young people of either sex. When Chaucer said "yonge girles of the diocise" in *The Canterbury Tales*, he meant "young people of the diocese."[8] Imagine ye olde English lads getting their knickers in a bunch when liberals had the audacity to limit the word *girl* to young females.

The meaning of words also changes from culture to culture. If a Brit invited his American friend to the park for a game of "football," we would give the poor American chap a break if he showed up with his helmet and shoulder pads, ready to tackle someone. But we'd quickly appreciate how the term *football* legitimately means different things to different people. Language is shared social space where people of different worldviews come together. We won't get very far in this shared space if we demand that words only be used according to how *we* mean them, without any care for how other people understand the same terms.

Second, as the advocates of pronoun hospitality have observed, we see moments in Scripture where Christ's followers exploit language's flexibility, especially when they are contextualizing a message for a particular culture.

Take Paul's speech in Acts 17, for instance. The apostle quotes from two different pagan texts:

> God did this so that they would seek him and perhaps reach out for him and find him, though he is not far from any one of us. "*For in **him** we live and move and have our being.*" As some of your own poets have said, "*We are **his** offspring.*" (v. 27–28)

The two **bolded** pronouns ***him*** and ***his*** are part of quotes from two pagan poets, Epimenides and Aratus, respectively. In both cases, the original Greek writer used the pronouns to refer to Zeus, the head deity of the Greek pantheon of gods. Yet Paul still quotes these texts, pronouns and all, reframing them to refer to Yahweh.

Paul meets his audience where they are in order to communicate God's message to them. His audience believes *him/his* refers to Zeus. Paul applies the pronouns to Yahweh. Paul speaks in language his listeners can understand, inviting them to a game of soccer by asking them to play football. (Or, if you fancy a British Paul, just flip it around.)

Of course, Paul's use of Zeus' pronouns on Mars Hill doesn't map perfectly onto our current discussion. We can't just quote Acts 17 and think we've solved the pronoun debate. But we do have biblical evidence that Paul *exploited the flexibility of language to meet people where they were at.* He prioritized people over dictionaries.

Third, some people argue, using the pronouns trans* people identify with communicates respect (not necessarily agreement) and is usually necessary for establishing a relationship. Christian psychologist Mark Yarhouse says, "It is an act of respect, even if we disagree, to let the person determine what they want to be called. If we can't grant them that, it's going to be next to impossible to establish any sort of relationship with them."[9] You can respect someone, and use language that communicates your respect, without agreeing with them.

This argument also partially responds to the concern that using a trans* person's chosen name or pronouns will encourage them to have an untrue view of themselves. Greg Coles, who defends the principle of pronoun hospitality, interviewed a bunch of trans* people and asked them how they felt when non-trans* people used the pronouns they identified with. According to Greg,

None of my interviewees were inclined to interpret a cis-gender Christian's pronoun hospitality as an automatic indication that this Christian agreed with everything about the way in which the trans person expressed their gender.... These interviewees saw the cisgender Christian's willingness to define gendered pronouns in terms of *gender identity* rather than *[biological] sex* as an indication that that person was willing show respect for the existence of non-cisgender identities.[10]

Trans* people typically view using their pronouns and chosen name as a basic act of courtesy and respect that's necessary for continuing relationship. Christians should build relational bridges instead of walls, and refusing to use someone's pronouns might as well be a brick wall the height of Babel's tower.

NAVIGATING THE PRONOUN DEBATE

Both sides of this debate raise some good points, and any honest Christian should consider each view. Personally, I side with the case for pronoun hospitality. I'll explain why in a second. But I want to first acknowledge some points in the first view that I consider valid.

The point about ideology lying behind language is a good one. To repeat Rob's point: "The reason this ideology is dangerous is because it creates and deepens delusions in confused and vulnerable people." Anyone who sides with the pronoun hospitality view should linger on this point and make sure we don't dismiss it too quickly. There's a thin line between language and ideology. And, to be frank, some things going on with language in contemporary culture are not only worrisome but could be destructive.

Take Canada's Bill C-16, for instance. This bill seeks to protect trans* people from discrimination and hate speech, which is a good thing. But some people argue that the bill could lead to jailtime for someone who refuses to use the pronouns a trans* person identifies with.[11]

It's one thing for language to change meaning over time (like *nice* or *girl*) or between cultures (like *football*). But this happens naturally and by societal consensus. If a small group of activists demands that people be penalized or imprisoned for calling a biological male "he," this would be closer to fascism than democracy. George Orwell would certainly have a thing or two to say. Calling a transwoman "he" or a transman "she" might be disrespectful, and it might have relational consequences. But it's not necessarily hate speech. Using the pronouns a person identifies with should be a matter of common courtesy, not a legal demand. And I respect those who are wary of caving in to neo-Marxist ideological pressure. Real ideological battles are happening in the world right now, and Christians must navigate these battles in a way that embodies the countercultural, counterpopular, counterpolitical way of our crucified Savior.

But as we're finding our way through the battlefield, we need to make sure we're not stepping on the necks of innocent people in the process.

Yes, there are some activists who want to pressure and shame Christians into agreeing with their way of thinking. But there are also hurting people who live in our neighborhoods and sit in our pews, trapped in patterns of self-harm and suicidal ideation because they've been shunned and shamed so badly by the church that they genuinely believe God hates them. As trivial as pronouns may seem to you, something as simple as using a person's chosen name and pronouns might be the small whisper of grace that nudges them to put the gun down and give this Christian thing one more chance.

Real ideological battles are happening in the world right now, and Christians must navigate these battles in a way that embodies the countercultural, counterpopular, counterpolitical way of our crucified Savior.

This is why I think the pronoun hospitality view is the better of the two approaches. To reiterate the point: language is shared social space that evolves over time and changes between cultures. Even the pronoun *he* has more flexibility than some people realize. According to several dictionaries, *he* can refer to a person whose sex is unknown—a synonym for "that one" or "that person."[12] This use of *he* was very common for centuries, and though it started to lose popularity with the rise of the feminist movement, it continues to be used today. Similarly, if we walk into a room of friends and say, "Hey guys!" and one of our friends who has a vagina says, "Um, I'm not a guy," we typically roll our eyes and say, "Oh come on, you know what I mean!" The term *guy* sometimes indicates maleness, but it's flexible enough to include people without a Y chromosome. And when the King James says, "*He* that hath ears to hear, let him hear" (Matt. 11:15 KJV), this doesn't mean Jesus was letting everyone with ovaries off the hook.

Again, none of this exactly parallels what we're talking about. But it shows that language—even a pronoun like *he* or *she*—is shared social space that's flexible.[13] You could demand that your hearer immediately adopt your worldview, your theological anthropology, and your interpretation of Genesis 1:27 before you enter into relationship with them. Or you could meet them where they are, as a gesture of respect, in order to walk with them along the path of discipleship.

All throughout Scripture, we see God meeting people where they are in order to walk with them toward where he wants them to be. When the Son came to earth, he met us where we were. He entered into our pain, our mess, even our wombs. He didn't speak to us in his native tongue of Heavenese and demand that we learn its grammar. Rather, he spoke our human language in all its imperfection, because that was the language we could understand.

Some trans* people (especially those who identify as nonbinary) use the pronouns *they/them/theirs* instead of *he* or *she*. If you know someone who uses *they/them/theirs*, the best thing you can do is to ask them *why* they identify with these pronouns. One of my friends who identifies as nonbinary uses *they/them* pronouns, and I'm embarrassed to say that I've know this person for quite some time and yet only recently asked them why they use these pronouns. My friend, a biological female, is a sold-out believer in Jesus who struggles with serious gender dysphoria. For whatever reasons, when they hear people refer to them as "she/her," it triggers their dysphoria. If the usage is persistent, it can lead to self-harming behaviors like cutting. "If I had things my way," my friend recently told me, "I'd get top surgery, take cross-sex hormones, and go by *he/him*. But I don't believe this is God's will for me. Using *they/them* pronouns is a neutral way for me to not identify as a man, and yet not spiral into depression and self-harm when I hear *she/her* over and over."

To me, this is an easy one. I think we should do our best to use *they/them* pronouns for the following reasons: One, *they/them* pronouns can be used generically of any human and can be used in the singular. In fact, *Merriam-Webster Dictionary* not only says that *they* can refer to a singular object (including a person) but also recently added that *they/them* can refer to a "single person whose gender identity is nonbinary."[14] Two, *they/them* is gender neutral; it's different than calling a biological male "she" or a biological female "he." Three, on a practical level, it might nudge people to put down the razor blade and not cut themselves. Four, it could make non-binary or trans*-identified people actually want to be around you rather than run the other way.

The most important thing is not perfection
but that people see us trying.

I could keep going, but hopefully these four points are good enough. I admit that using *they/them* pronouns can be difficult at times. I still fail to get it right, especially when I'm on stage giving a talk that includes telling stories about my nonbinary-identified friends. The most important thing is not perfection but that people see us trying.

Back to *he/him* and *she/her*. I think a good case can be made for using these pronouns, even if they don't match a person's biological sex, based on the flexibility of language. In other words, I don't think using the pronouns a trans* person identifies with is necessarily lying, since they might view the pronoun as a reference to their gender identity—whether you agree with that identity or not—rather than their biological sex. Again, language is shared social space. In order for people to communicate with each other, somebody has to give in.

Now, as a long-term goal of discipleship, my preference is that all Christ-followers would come to see their biological sex as a divine gift and part of their identity. And maybe a trans*-identified Christian will come to this conclusion and end up using pronouns that resonate with their biological sex. This might be a long-term goal, but I don't think it should be a short-term prerequisite.

My friend Kat hated to be called "she." Even after Kat had a radical conversion to Jesus, the word *she* was like nails on a chalkboard. All Kat heard in the word *she* was cultural femininity—little pink dresses and hours of *Downton Abbey*. Over time, she began to see things differently, and now she's okay with people referring to her as "she," especially trusted friends. I asked Kat how she would have felt if someone had refused to use the pronouns she identified with (which were *they/them*) early on in her discipleship journey. "I wouldn't have trusted them or wanted to be around them," she said. "I know it seems trivial to some, but this was a big deal for me. I would have taken their persistent use of 'she' *not* as a loving expression of 'the truth' but as a punch in the gut, a sign of disrespect. And I don't want to be around people who keep punching me in the gut."

I'm not saying the pronoun question is an easy one, and I respect people on both sides of the debate. But until I see better reasons to the contrary, I think we should use the pronouns a person identifies with.

BATHROOMS AND SLEEPING SPACES

"I hate going to the bathroom in public," Kat told me. Public bathrooms have always been a thorn in her flesh. "I don't belong in the men's room. And yet, when I go to the women's room, some women think I'm a guy and start yelling at me. It's a lose-lose situation." Kat told me that she will do almost anything to avoid using public bathrooms, which typically means limiting her liquid consumption. "When I'm at church, I don't drink coffee, even though I love coffee. I try to do whatever it takes to avoid that stressful feeling of having to pee."

I don't share Kat's story to argue that we should do away with male and female restrooms. I only share it to help us understand that even the bathroom issue isn't just an issue. Some people talk about the transgender bathroom debate as if trans* people wake up every day conniving like the evil Vector in *Despicable Me* about how they can do away with sex-segregated bathrooms. In my experience, most of them just want to pee.

Kat and other trans* people I've talked to say the first thing they look for when they visit a church is a single-stall bathroom. Some will turn around and leave if they don't see one. Most of us have never thought about this. But that's kind of the point. Trans* people face challenges in life that we have no clue about. I would therefore suggest that, as much as it's in a church community's power, they should install a single-stall bathroom or two in their building, which could also double as family restrooms. (As a father of three daughters, I can say that I loved the option of a family restroom when my girls were young.)

Some churches, of course, won't be able to do this because of budget constraints or space limitations, or because they meet in rented space. But if possible, putting in a single-stall bathroom could be a fine act of hospitality. I mean, put yourself in the shoes of a trans* person who hates using public restrooms. Imagine how it would feel to know that a church went out of its way to accommodate your needs, so that you too can drink coffee at church. Most trans* people already feel out of place and uncomfortable at church. Why wouldn't churches want to go out of our way to show that we care deeply for the one and not just the ninety-nine?

Our desire should be to eliminate any unnecessary barriers that might keep teens from encountering Christ.

Aside from the bathroom question, I think the more pressing question has to do with sleeping arrangements and changing spaces at, say, youth group summer camps. If a teenager is biologically male but identifies as a girl, do they sleep with the boys or the girls? Or do other options exist? And what is the rationale for our policies?

Before we even consider these questions in relation to trans* students, we need to remember that same-sex sleeping arrangements for teens are always complicated, even if none of these teens is trans*. Any time a bunch of teenagers with raging hormones and partially developed brains are pumped full of sugar and adrenaline, then crammed into a cabin together—especially if there's insufficient adult supervision—you have a recipe for trouble. The teens in these spaces might be gay or same-sex-attracted, terrified of undressing in front of their peers or having peers undress in front of them for fear their bodies will betray their attractions. Teens might be dealing with body shame, embarrassed to show off their underdeveloped or unathletic bodies in the presence of older, more attractive peers who boldly flaunt their assets. Their skin might be marked with scars from cutting that they're afraid someone else will notice. They might be survivors of sexual abuse—and whether their abuser was a person of the same sex or the opposite sex, undressing in the same room with *anyone* might be an agonizing experience.

If we want to honor all the diverse needs and concerns of these teens, then, we can't simply assume that placing people in same-sex spaces is enough to ensure everyone's safety. Changing and sleeping spaces that don't give teens the option of bodily privacy can lead to a whole host of problems. Our desire should be to eliminate any unnecessary barriers that might keep teens from encountering Christ. If all the male-bodied teens are getting naked together at camp (and all the female-bodied teens are doing the same), this is probably a bad idea for a whole bunch of reasons that have nothing to do with trans* people.

In short, male-specific and female-specific spaces like bathrooms and sleeping rooms need adequate supervision and the option of bodily privacy for the sake of *all* youth. But what does this mean for trans* students? In cases where a person's sexed body doesn't match their gender identity, should they be in spaces that match their biological sex or spaces that match their gender identity? How do we accommodate the needs of trans* students along with the needs of everyone else?

Regardless of how we approach this question, any categorical rule can create potential challenges. If we separate guys' and girls' spaces by gender identity rather than biological sex (so that a biological female who identifies as a guy stays in a guys' room), this policy could raise concerns for some non-trans* students and their parents. Trans* students themselves might find it difficult being in an opposite-sex space if they know that some of their peers are uncomfortable sharing space with them.

On the other hand, putting trans* students in same-sex spaces (for example, having a biological female who identifies as a guy stay in a girls' room) can put these students at increased risk. Sleeping and changing in a same-sex room might flare up a trans* person's dysphoria, leading to crippling anxiety, self-harm, or suicidal ideation. It's hard for non-trans* people, especially those of us who haven't experienced mental health issues, to wrap our minds around such a chain of events. But this kind of psychological chain reaction is quite common among people with dysphoria, and it should be taken seriously by leaders who are eager to see trans* students encounter Christ.

Trans* people might also feel unsafe around their peers in a same-sex room. Perhaps they've been bullied by same-sex peers, especially if their trans* identity or experience with dysphoria is publicly known. It's not uncommon for biological males who are less stereotypically masculine to be mocked, harassed, or physically or sexually abused by more "masculine" peers. If a trans* person has experienced this kind of bullying or abuse, sleeping in the same room with a group of guys—even if *these guys* would never bully the trans* person—could legitimately unearth a traumatic episode.

Where does this leave us? I do think that sleeping spaces should be based on sex and not, say, gender identity. But I also recommend accommodating the needs of trans* students (or others who might be at risk in a same-sex space) on a case-by-case basis. In conversation with the trans* student and their family, from a posture of mutual respect and trust, look for a creative solution that will help this student—and all your students—encounter Jesus. Here are several possible ways to accommodate a trans* student:

- Depending on facilities, you could see if a cabin has a separate room connected to it where the trans* student could stay. I know of one scenario where this was offered to a trans* student who gladly accepted it.
- Some camps have spaces where leaders stay, usually in smaller and more private rooms. Perhaps the trans* student would feel more comfortable staying with a few leaders rather than with students.
- Some trans* students might feel more comfortable staying in a room with others of the same sex if their parent (of that sex) stays with them. Again, I know of one case where a camp offered this option to a family and they greatly appreciated it.
- Similarly, you could have a leader or counselor who has a heart for LGBTQ people and understands

some of their struggles stay in a same-sex cabin with the trans* student. Having at least one person who truly sees them (and is willing to stand up for them, if needed) might reduce their concerns.

- Commuting to camp may be an option for the trans* student, even if the camp typically requires students to sleep on-site. If they live too far away to commute from home, maybe you can pay for an Airbnb or some other housing facility where the trans* student can stay with a couple of leaders.

Please be aware that some of these suggestions could feel "othering" to certain trans* students or their families. But some might appreciate the options and feel like the camp leaders truly care about their needs, providing a great pathway for an encounter with Christ. The key principle is that these options should be explored *with* the trans* student and their family. I'm not at all advocating for non-trans* leaders to determine which option they will choose *for* the trans* student. It's best to think through several different possibilities ahead of time and let the trans* person and their family choose what's best for them.

Here's one more idea that I think might be the best option, if the camp can swing it:

- Set up a cabin or two where counselors and students (with their parents' knowledge and permission) are eager to stay with the trans* student. Ideally, you would have one such cabin with all male counselors

and students, and another with all female counselors and students. The trans* student could stay in
whichever cabin they felt safest. Many students in
Christian youth groups have a lot of LGBTQ friends
and are very sensitive to the unique challenges their
friends face. Some might be LGBTQ themselves.
Whatever the case, the camp could find out ahead
of time if several students would be willing to stay
in a cabin together where the trans* student would
feel safe, so that this student can have the best possible chance of hearing and experiencing the love
of God.[15]

This wouldn't have to feel "othering," since no one except the
students, parents, and leaders involved needs to know that one cabin
is a "trans*-friendly cabin." It's just a cabin. Parents of students not
sleeping in this cabin, who might otherwise worry about their child
staying in a cabin with a trans* person of the opposite biological sex,
should be fine with this situation. It's possible that a parent whose
kid isn't in this cabin might still refuse to send their kid to camp, if
they learn about a trans* student staying with a group of opposite-sex
peers. In an effort to accommodate *everyone's* needs, I would certainly
want to reach out to this parent, listen to their concerns, and respond
with thoughtfulness and grace. But I don't see a logical (let alone
biblical) reason why they would be concerned about this, since it
doesn't involve their kid in any way.

Some might worry that this scenario puts a trans* person in a
cabin with people of the opposite sex. True, but if you're worried

about sexual relationships developing, let's be clear: most trans* teenagers are attracted to the same biological sex. Besides, when the lines of guys' spaces and girls' spaces are drawn according to sex, this means that gay or same-sex attracted people are in the same cabin as the sex they are attracted to. And, whether you care to admit it or not, this has been going on ever since summer camps were first invented. No policy erases all temptations or possible challenges—and this is one of many reasons why every cabin needs sufficient supervision from responsible leaders.[16]

To repeat an earlier point: it's vital to work with the trans* student and their family ahead of time so that they are involved in the decision about where they should sleep. Listen to their fears. Understand their concerns. Make sure they know that you *see* them and that you eagerly want them at camp.

Christ died for everyone, but he also had a particular
yearning to reach those who had been marginalized
and ignored by the majority—and so should we.

I want to make two closing observations. First, remember the diversity of trans* experiences (from chapter 3). This is why it's important to get to know the trans* individual you're talking to and have several options available. One trans* teenager might have lifelong debilitating dysphoria, while another might experience ROGD or might not have dysphoria at all. One might be attracted to the same sex, while another might experience autogynephilia and be attracted to the opposite sex. And many of them might have mental health concerns related to their dysphoria. The way you accommodate one trans* person might look very different than the way you accommodate another.

Second, our posture through this whole conversation matters enormously. As you work to accommodate the needs and concerns of trans* people (or anyone else) on a case-by-case basis, be sure not to treat these accommodations as a hassle or a distraction from important kingdom work. Meeting the needs of trans* people, removing any barriers that stand between them and the gospel, *is* important kingdom work. Christ died for everyone, but he also had a particular yearning to reach those who had been marginalized and ignored by the majority—and so should we.

The goal of this chapter has not been to solve every practical question that might arise as we enter into relationship with trans* people. Instead, I want us to learn how to ask the right questions and cultivate a biblically faithful and Christlike posture in addressing them. Whether or not you agree with every suggestion I've made, I hope I've at least modeled this kind of approach for you.

Conclusion

OUTRAGEOUS LOVE

Our cultural moment is one of outrage and uncertainty. And sometimes I, too, get caught up in the moment.

I'm deeply concerned about what's being taught to young kids about gender in public schools. It seems at times to advance a single ideological perspective while suppressing other views, which is indoctrination rather than education. I'm grieved when medically invasive and irreversible procedures are performed on adolescents wrestling with their identities—especially those who have additional mental health concerns. And when I listen to some politicians talk about gender and trans*-related questions, I wonder if they even know what they're talking about.

There's plenty of fodder for outrage. But outrage doesn't change the world.

Love changes the world.

Getting furious at our cultural moment doesn't convince people of the truth. Our truth will not be heard until our grace is felt, because the greatest apologetic for truth is love.

Instead of sitting back and fuming over headlines, Christians should exude the outrageous love of Christ toward those struggling with their gender or entangled in the web of deceptive ideologies. Yes, we should resist and deconstruct those ideologies with thoughtfulness and grace. But if that's all we do, we fail to embody the presence of Christ in the world as we ought.

We need less outrage and more outrageous love.

Our truth will not be heard until our grace is felt,
because the greatest apologetic for truth is love.

I'm constantly challenged by the grace/truth tension in Jesus. He had a high ethical standard. So high that nobody can live up to it. And yet Jesus loved those who fell short of it. Just look at the Sermon on the Mount (Matt. 5–7). Jesus' sermon is one of the most ethically rigorous speeches in all religious history. Try reading through the whole thing in the morning and then live that way for the day. You'll fail before breakfast. Jesus had a ridiculously high standard of obedience, yet he excessively loved those who fell short of it.

Jesus wasn't "pro tax collecting," and yet tax collectors flocked to him (Luke 15:1). Jesus opposed adultery, but he stood up for adulterers—not their behavior, but their humanity. Jesus stood against sin, and yet sinners wanted to be in his presence. The marginalized, the hurting, the shamed and shunned—they all wanted to be around Jesus. They wanted to go to his church. Do they want to go to yours?

Christians and churches have a heavenly mandate to stand against destructive ideologies. This includes some of the radical narratives that have emerged from trans* and gender-affirming communities. And it also includes the destructive ideologies of legalism, hypocrisy, and self-righteousness. These latter ideologies could be even more destructive than the former when they're dressed up in religious garb. It's all too easy to vilify the sins of others, to shame them for struggling in ways we do not. But God sees the heart of every person and knows that the ground is level before the cross. The one who stands furthest from the grace of God is the one least willing to extend that grace to others: the religious hypocrite, the legalist, the one tying heavy burdens around the necks of the marginalized.

Christ-followers shouldn't mock the swelling number of people identifying as trans*. If that number keeps rising, then so should the number of trans* people gathering in our homes and around our tables. If Jesus were here today, he'd have more trans* friends, not fewer, as the trans* community grows. He would—and did—challenge the narrow masculine and feminine stereotypes enshrined in so many of our churches today. Some people identify as trans* in part because they don't fit the narrow, artificial boxes of gender stereotypes—unbiblical stereotypes sometimes mandated by so-called "biblical" Christians. Advocating a more expansive, *truly* biblical, view of gender expression might allow trans*-identified believers to express themselves within their male or female sex rather than trying to escape it.

The Bible challenged the stereotypes perpetuated by its own cultures. And it challenges ours. We're not being biblical Christians when we adopt cultural stereotypes and then attempt to stuff our teenagers unceremoniously into them. Saying that a man is actually a woman goes against God's creational design. And so is baptizing cultural stereotypes in pseudobiblical water.

Our cultural moment is an outrageous one. What we need is a different way. A fresh posture. A radically biblical community. One that affirms bodies, rejects stereotypes, pursues truth with humility, and lavishes grace on everyone who fails.

If people—especially marginalized and broken people—come into our communities, they should never want to leave.

Trans*-identified people often have several cards stacked against them: mental health concerns, loneliness, depression, social stigma, and family rejection. And when I say "family rejection," I'm not talking about families who disagree with trans* identities. I'm talking about families who shout mean and nasty things at trans* people, telling them they are despicable, disgusting, and damned to hell. Families who refuse to speak to them, or kick them out of the house, leaving them in the care of the streets.

According to a study of 6,456 trans* adults, 57 percent have family members who refuse to speak to them, 50 percent have experienced harassment at school, 65 percent have suffered physical or sexual violence, and 69 percent have experienced homelessness.[1] These are precisely the people Jesus wants to fill his church with. Jesus created a family for the family-less, a spiritual hospital for those in need. Getting angry about prevailing gender ideologies isn't going to bring trans* people into that family. People don't need more outrage. They need a fresh encounter with love.

Posture is crucial in this conversation. As Christians, we already have many strikes against us. We're known for being anti-gay, judgmental, hypocritical, anti-trans, anti-Target, anti-this, anti-that. Jesus was against many things, but somehow he had a reputation of being *for* people. Somehow Jesus was able to have a clear ethical stance, to speak out clearly against sin, and yet to still draw to himself the very people who were found guilty by his words.

As the number of trans* people in the world increases, our churches should have more trans* people, not fewer. Not because our ethic is weak or unclear, but because it is strong and wholistic—true, courageous, compassionate, and humble. If people—especially marginalized and broken people—come into our communities, they should never want to leave.

We need less outrage and more outrageous love.

My friend Lesli, whom I opened this book with, currently identifies as nonbinary and prefers *they/them* pronouns. Lesli is attracted to the same sex, believes in a traditional view of marriage (one man and one woman), and has a massive heart for LGBTQ people. Lesli has become one of the dearest, wisest, most godly people in my life. Lesli is so godly that they'll *hate* that I just said that.

I've got a lot of straight Christian friends in my life. Pastors, teachers, missionaries, even some who would be considered "Christian celebrities." They are all wonderful in so many ways. But Lesli's the one who checks in when I'm down and celebrates with me when I'm up. Lesli prays for me more than I pray for myself. Few weeks go by where Lesli doesn't ask me how I'm doing. How I'm *really* doing. Lesli asks me authentic questions, knows my kids' names, and preaches Jesus to me when I need it—which is often. If I'm on my death bed, Lesli is going to get a call, and I know Lesli will be there for me. We don't always agree on things. Even in the trans* conversation, Lesli and I don't see eye to eye on a number of questions, including questions I've written about in this book. But one thing's for sure: if I ever need a good dose of Jesus, if I ever need a fresh encounter with the risen Lord, I look to Lesli to embody Jesus to me.

Lesli is not just *needy*; Lesli is *needed*—in my life and in the lives of many others. Lesli is a human, a Christian, a gender-dysphoric person, and a beautiful pinnacle of God's creation. Lesli is a gift to the church, to the world, and to me. And they live their faith in ways I only dream of.

All because one pastor, fueled by the truth of love, reached out to Lesli ten years ago with compassion and grace.

Will you?

Appendix

SUICIDALITY AND TRANS* PEOPLE

The relationship between suicide and trans* people is a delicate topic. I can't think of anything more horrific than a teenage son or daughter taking their own life. I've had friends who have lost children to suicide. And just last year, a friend of mine took his own life, leaving behind his wife and three young children. I can hardly breathe as I write this sentence, recalling the horrors of loved ones taking their own lives.

Suicidality is a complex topic. When it's enmeshed with the trans* conversation, the complexity is quadrupled. It's therefore important to understand some of the complexities of suicidality in the trans* conversation so that we can cultivate a Christlike response.

UNDERSTANDING SUICIDALITY

Suicidality includes four different (but sometimes related) aspects: (1) suicidal ideation, (2) self-harm, (3) suicide attempts, and (4) completed suicide.[1]

Suicidal ideation (1) has to do with any thought a person might have about attempting to take their own life. Data on suicidal ideation is almost always based on self-report. Mental health counselors and research studies might ask someone, "Have you ever thought about taking your own life?" Answers to questions like this are then used to calculate the frequency of suicidal ideation. Percentages of suicidal ideation are much higher than those of suicide attempts or completed suicides.[2]

Self-harm (2) *could* include suicide attempts. But in most cases, the motivation for self-harm is different than the motivation to end one's own life. Although attempted suicide could result in self-harm, few people who engage in self-harming behavior are trying to take their own lives.[3] For instance, "cutting" is rarely a purposeful suicide attempt, but it can be interpreted as a suicide attempt.[4] The line between self-harm and suicide attempts can be blurry.

Actual suicide attempts (3) are much more frequent than completed suicides (4). It has been estimated that one to two hundred suicide attempts take place for every completed suicide.[5]

We should keep these four different aspects of suicidality in mind as we're talking about suicidality among trans* people. All four are worth fighting to diminish. But it would skew our discussion to misinterpret rates of suicidal ideation as rates of self-harm or to confuse suicide attempts with completed suicides.

RATES OF SUICIDALITY AMONG TRANS* PEOPLE

Many studies have been conducted on suicidality rates among trans* people, and they yield fairly diverse percentages. According to one harrowing statistic, 41 percent of trans* adults have attempted suicide. This percentage is based on a 2011 study published by the National

Center for Transgender Equality,[6] and it is on the high end. Most studies yield lower percentages, though again, we have to pay close attention to what aspect or aspects of suicidality they're measuring (ideation, attempts, completion) and the demographic (age) being measured.

For instance, the same team that reported the 41 percent statistic performed another study on suicide attempts among trans* adults in 2017. This second study found that 22 percent of trans* adults had attempted suicide—just over half the percentage reported in their prior study.[7] Other studies yielded similarly divergent results:

- A study of "highly gender nonconformist" students (aged eleven to seventeen) reported a 3 percent rate of attempted suicide. This same study reported that gender nonconforming youth and cisgender youth "did not statistically differ in their rates of lifetime suicidal thoughts and suicide attempts."[8]
- Another study found that 33.73 percent of trans*-identified adolescents reported suicidal ideation, compared to 18.85 percent of non-trans* adolescents.[9]
- Five studies reported the prevalence of self-harm, suicidal ideation, and suicide attempts among clinic-referred adolescents with gender dysphoria.[10] Their percentages yielded the following ranges:

    Self-Harm = 28.8%–41%

    Suicidal Ideation = 17.5%–42.2%

    Suicide Attempts = 11.9%–15.8%

One reason for the diversity in percentages is methodology. Who did the researchers survey? How large was their survey sample size? How did they measure their responses? Did they have a control group? Did they base percentages on self-report, or objective criteria?

No one disputes that suicidality is high among trans* people. Just how high is tougher to say. In any case, one of the most important—yet often neglected—aspects of the high suicidality rates among trans* people is the presence of co-occurring mental health concerns.

SUICIDALITY AND MENTAL HEALTH

Without question, unaddressed mental health issues are the number one cause of suicidality. A recent study based on the National Comorbidity Survey Replication Adolescent Supplement, which sampled 10,148 US adolescents, found that 96.1 percent of those who attempt suicide meet lifetime criteria for at least one *DSM* diagnosis for mental illness.[11] According to Suicide.org, "Over 90 percent of people who die by suicide have a mental illness at the time of their death."[12] As we've seen, trans*-identifying people—especially teenagers—have a rate of co-occurring mental health issues much higher than the average.[13] Does the high rate of suicidality among trans* people result from their experience as trans*, or from other co-occurring mental health concerns, or both?

It's tough to say. Almost every study that reports high suicidality among trans* people does not "control" for mental health issues. That is, they compare trans* people with the general population and not with non-trans* people who have mental health conditions. One recent study, however, did control for mental health conditions and found that the percentages of suicidality (among trans* and non-trans* people with mental health conditions) were roughly the same. The study measured suicidal ideation among trans* adolescents who were being treated at gender clinics in three different cities and found that "the rate of suicidality was, in general, much more similar to that of referred adolescents" with mental health issues.[14] For example, the percentage of FtM trans* adolescents who reported suicidality were as follows: Toronto (32.5 percent), Amsterdam (26.9 percent), and London (33.3 percent).[15] The same study found that 34.9 percent of *non-trans* adolescents with mental health conditions* also reported suicidal ideation. According to this study, mental health concerns were a significant influence on suicidality rates.

The 2011 study from the National Center for Transgender Equality, which reported that 41 percent of trans* adults had attempted suicide, didn't factor co-occurring mental health concerns into their study. In their own words:

> [T]he survey did not directly explore mental health sta-tus and history, which have been identified as important risk factors for both attempted and completed suicide in the general population. Further, research has shown that the impact of adverse life events, such as being attacked or raped, is most severe among people with co-existing mood, anxiety and other mental disorders.... The lack of systematic mental health information in the NTDS data significantly limited our ability to identify the pathways to suicidal behavior among the respondents.[16]

That is, the study didn't conclude that simply being trans* is a direct pathway to suicidality.[17] There are other unexplored reasons that could contribute to suicidality.[18]

SUICIDALITY AND SOCIAL CONTAGION

When the hit Netflix series *13 Reasons Why*—a fictional story about a teenage girl's suicide—was released in 2017, adolescent suicide rates in the United States spiked. While the series very helpfully exposed various social factors that often contribute to suicidality, critics accused the show of increasing suicidality among teens.[19]

Exposure to suicides has been shown to increase suicidality.[20] Keith Hawton and Kathryn Williams of the Centre for Suicide Research in Oxford explain, "Recent systematic reviews ... have found overwhelming evidence for ... the influence of media on suicidal behavior." They say that "[y]ounger people seem to be most vulnerable to the influence of the media."[21] Others agree that youth in particular are susceptible to social contagion surrounding the topic of suicide.[22]

Social contagion is an important piece of the discussion about suicidality and trans* identities. If the suggestion of suicide makes people more prone to attempting suicide, then promoting the idea that trans* people tend to be suicidal may itself increase suicidality among trans* people, especially teenagers. When parents and their trans* kids are given the binary choice between "transition or suicide," this narrative may actually increase suicide rates among trans* people.

We should be very concerned about the high rates of suicidality among trans* people, yet cautious in how we go about addressing it. Quick and flippant references to suicide rates among trans* people, especially in the presence of young people struggling with their gender, might do much more harm than good.

THE IMPACT OF TRANSITION

Some say that transitioning is the best solution to suicidality among trans* people, but this perspective is problematic at best and harmful at worst. Transitioning can introduce a whole new set of physical, emotional, and psychological problems that could contribute to depression and thus suicidality:

- Adverse effects from hormone therapy (such as infertility and cardiovascular problems)[23]
- Disappointment with the results of surgeries[24]
- Negative health effects from surgeries
- Inability to "pass" as the sex you desire even after surgery
- Transition regret[25]

Long-term follow-up studies have shown that completed suicide rates are still much higher for trans* people who transition than among the general population.[26] If other co-occurring or underlying mental health conditions aren't addressed, these are likely to continue even after transition. That is, one should not think that transitioning is an effective way to deal with mental health concerns. Yet the heavy emphasis sometimes placed on the importance of transitioning to reduce suicidality can lead people to overlook other possible mental health concerns. In the conversation about trans* suicidality, ignoring the prevalence of co-occurring mental health concerns and laying emphasis exclusively on transitioning may seem caring and respectful, but it does no favors to the trans* community.

MINORITY STRESS, TRANS* IDENTITIES, AND SUICIDALITY

What if trans* people experience mental health issues (and therefore suicidality) because of minority stress?

Minority stress has to do with the hostile stressors that trans* people (and other LGBTQ people) experience due to their minority identity and the negative effect this has on their mental health.[27] Put simply: social ostracism leads to mental health concerns for trans* people.

Without doubt, minority stress plays at least some role in mental health issues like anxiety and depression among trans*-identified people.[28] And unfortunately, for those raised in the church, minority stress has been magnified. Hearing sermons and conversations about trans* people being disgusting abominations can take a toll on a person's well-being. My friend Lesli was raised in the church and remembers hearing a sermon about "the mentally ill trans community" who were "an abomination in God's eyes." The preacher urged his congregation to "protect our children from their evil ploys" while Lesli's friends "shouted 'Amen' and showed the appropriate levels of disgust." Lesli's response? "I was ashamed that I was such an abomination to the God that I adored." That was thirty years ago. And Lesli still deals with internalized shame on a daily basis.

Minority stress certainly plays a role in many trans* experiences.[29] But minority stress or social rejection can be tough to define.

For example, if a biological male identifies as a female, and their friends and family still believe they're male, does this mean their loved ones don't *accept* them? Certainly, if a person is being mocked or bullied or shamed, this could cause minority stress on anyone. But some people might view disagreement as social rejection. Not everyone who *feels* rejected by society has actually *been* rejected by society. Just what "social acceptance" means is in the eye of the beholder.

Some say that misgendering a trans* person (that is, not using their chosen name or pronouns) causes suicidality. But if someone becomes suicidal after being misgendered, there are likely other mental health concerns that should be explored. Ignoring these concerns is itself harmful. One trans* person named Helen confirms this explicitly:

> People don't just self-harm or commit suicide because they are dead named [that is, called by their birth name rather than their chosen name]. It might be their final straw, but they commit suicide because they are already volatile and unstable. Their self-worth is fragile because it's based on a view of the world that relies on everybody else seeing you the way you see [your]self and doesn't provide any coping mechanisms for when people don't choose to validate your self-perception.[30]

Jonathan Haidt and Greg Lukianoff address a similar idea in their book *The Coddling of the American Mind*.[31] They show that when we isolate ourselves from opposing viewpoints and challenging perspectives, we get weaker rather than stronger. Some scholars call this "antifragility": the idea that mental and physical challenges in life makes us resilient or "antifragile," while trying to create a world where everyone agrees with us makes us fragile.[32] Helen's perspective reflects this principle of antifragility:

> I'm not saying it's OK to dead-name someone or to misgender them on purpose. It's rude and inconsiderate at best and dangerous at worst. Doing this might indeed be the final straw that pushes someone over the edge and that's totally not OK. Of course, it's always important to be aware of the potential repercussions of our actions and be aware that people are fragile. But I truly believe that identity based politics causes as many problems as it solves and the hypersensitivity to dead-naming and misgendering is one of these things. The trans community actively promotes the view that dead-naming is an act of violence and I can't help but think that this only exacerbates the negative impact on somebody when they hear this.

Helen isn't speaking from a distance. She's speaking from experience: "I've personally known trans people who have committed suicide. I nearly did so myself a few years ago." But from her perspective, dead-naming and misgendering weren't the main issues.

In short, minority stress certainly plays a role in higher rates of suicidality among trans* people. But it's probably intertwined with a complex set of emotional and psychological factors that also play a role. Weaponizing suicidality to push a particular ideological point might actually increase suicide attempts among trans* people rather than reducing them.

A CHRISTIAN RESPONSE TO SUICIDALITY AMONG TRANS* PEOPLE

The Christian response to suicidality among trans* people must be multifaceted.

First, we should understand some of the complexities of suicidality and trans* experiences. If you or someone you know is suicidal, you might want to explore more thoroughly some of the themes discussed here.

Second, suicidality can be socially contagious, which means we need to be extra sensitive in how we talk about it. We need to be aware of how our publicized concerns could actually increase suicidality rates still higher.

Third, if we care about suicidality—and if you're a Christian, or a human, you should care—we cannot weaponize high suicide rates to promote an ideology. I appreciate the expressed concern of the "transition or suicide" narrative, which is to help people struggling with dysphoria. Still, I worry that this oversimplified binary intensifies the problem instead of mitigating it.

Fourth, if you or someone you know is wrestling with suicidal thoughts, it's essential to get help immediately. Suicide.org is a great resource to look into (among others). The National Suicide Prevention Lifeline is 1-800-273-8255. The Trans Lifeline is 1-877-565-8860.

I asked a friend of mine who runs an organization aimed at addressing suicidality to close us out with some pieces of advice. Here's what he says:

DON'T BE AFRAID TO ASK ABOUT SUICIDE

Talking to someone about suicide is always a difficult thing to do. However, if you are concerned that someone you love is contemplating suicide, it's okay to ask them directly. While this might feel counterintuitive, it opens up the conversation and is often a source of relief for the person struggling. You can ask them:

- "Have you been thinking about killing yourself?"
- "Are you contemplating suicide?"

SEEK IMMEDIATE HELP

If the person you are speaking with says they are contemplating suicide, it's important to ask if they have made a plan. If they have, there is a much higher risk that they will attempt it, and you should get them help immediately. Here are a few ways to help:

- ***Call a local crisis response team.*** Most major cities have teams that are designed to respond to a mental health crisis. A simple search on the internet for

"Crisis Response Team" in your city should provide a number.

- ***Contact a local mental health hospital.*** These are independent outpatient mental health care facilities where people can stay for a period of time to receive evaluations and counseling.
- ***Take them to the emergency room.*** If the above two options are not available and the crisis is peaking, you can always take a loved one to a hospital ER. Doctors will perform evaluations and ask many questions of the patient, giving them ample time to think through their situation.
- ***Call 911.*** If you believe that the person may attempt suicide and you are concerned for their well-being, 911 is always an option. First responders will be dispatched to their location to perform a well check.

EQUIP YOURSELF

Suicide rates are increasing across all demographics of Western society. As a Christian, how can you prepare to respond to someone who is suicidal?

- ***Take a mental health first aid course.*** MHFA is like CPR for mental health. It will provide you with tools to recognize and respond to a mental health crisis in a helpful way. See mentalhealthfirstaid.org for details.

- **_Learn to recognize the signs._** Signs of possible suicidality include:

Talk. A person may be suicidal if they talk about these things:

> Killing themselves
> Feeling hopeless
> Having no reason to live
> Being a burden to others
> Feeling trapped
> Unbearable pain

Behavior. Certain behaviors may signal risk:

> Increased use of alcohol or drugs
> Looking for a way to end their lives, such
>> as searching online for methods
> Withdrawing from activities
> Isolating from family and friends
> Sleeping too much or too little
> Visiting or calling people to say good-bye
> Giving away prized possessions
> Aggression
> Fatigue

Mood. People who are considering suicide often display one or more of the following moods:

Depression

Anxiety

Loss of interest

Irritability

Humiliation/Shame

Agitation/Anger

Relief/Sudden Improvement

We could say much more about these important matters, but I hope these give you some foundational starting points for additional care. Suicidality should be addressed with the utmost precaution and thoughtfulness. May we all hope and pray that the church will embody Jesus more vibrantly, working tirelessly to reduce the suicide rate among the people God has entrusted to us.

NOTES

PREFACE

1. The Editorial Board, "The Next Civil Rights Frontier," *New York Times*, July 31, 2013, www.nytimes.com/2013/08/01/opinion/the-next-civil-rights-frontier.html.

CHAPTER 1: PEOPLE

1. Lesli prefers "they/them" pronouns, hence the reason I use these pronouns in retelling Lesli's story. See chapter 12 for a longer discussion of pronoun use for transgender people. Also, I'm retelling this story from Lesli's perspective, how they described their feelings and internal sense of who they were growing up. I'll discuss later what it means to think and play "like a boy."

2. Quotations attributed to Lesli are taken from my personal communication with Lesli.

3. You can read about this story, and others like it, here: "In Their Own Words: Parents of Kids Who Think They Are Trans Speak Out," *Public Discourse*, February 26, 2019, www .thepublicdiscourse.com/2019/02/49686/. The names Stephanie and Carol are pseudonyms I have chosen.

4. We'll discuss this in more detail in chapter 11.

5. Alan (pseudonym) tells his story in a blog post titled "If I Hadn't Been Shown Grace, I'd Be a Trans Woman Right Now," Center for Faith, Sexuality & Gender, October 30, 2018, www.centerforfaith.com/blog/if-i-hadn-t-been-shown-grace-i-d-be-a-trans-woman -right-now.

6. This is well documented in the provocative book by Yale scholar Paul Bloom, *Against Empathy: The Case for Rational Compassion* (New York: HarperCollins, 2016).

7. Steve Corbett and Brian Fikkert, *When Helping Hurts: How to Alleviate Poverty without Hurting the Poor ... and Yourself* (Chicago: Moody, 2009).

CHAPTER 2: TEN THOUSAND GENDERS

1. Mark Yarhouse, *Understanding Gender Dysphoria: Navigating Transgender Issues in a Changing Culture* (Downers Grove, IL: IVP Academic, 2015), 20.

2. Taken from my personal correspondence with a friend.

3. One of my friends posted this in the comments section on my blog post "Sex, Gender, and Transgender Experiences: Part 2—Biological Sex and Gender Role," Center for Faith, Sexuality & Gender, July 29, 2019, www.centerforfaith.com/blog/sex-gender-and-transgender-experiences-part-2-biological-sex-and-gender-role. The comment, titled "Generalities vs. Absolutes," was posted by Addie on July 31, 2019.

4. Alex Bullard, answer posted on *Quora*, November 5, 2018, www.quora.com/Whats-the-best-way-you-can-think-of-to-describe-how-gender-dysphoria-feels?redirected_qid=31089569.

5. Ian T. Nolan, Christopher J. Kuhner, and Geolani W. Dy, "Demographic and Temporal Trends in Transgender Identities and Gender Confirming Surgery," *Translational Andrology and Urology* 8(3), June 2019, www.ncbi.nlm.nih.gov/pmc/articles/PMC6626314/.

6. See, for instance, Lisa A. Urry et al., *Campbell Biology*, 11th ed. (New York: Pearson, 2016), 298–99. This is one of the leading textbooks in biology.

7. Hilary Lips, *Sex and Gender: An Introduction*, 6th ed. (Long Grove, IL: Waveland, 2008), 5–6.

8. Rebecca Reilly-Cooper, "Sex and Gender: A Beginner's Guide," 2015, https://sexandgenderintro.com.

9. American Psychological Association and National Association of School Psychologists, "Resolution on Gender and Sexual Orientation Diversity in Children and Adolescents in Schools" (2015). Retrieved from www.apa.org/pi/lgbt/resources/sexuality-definitions.pdf.

10. Paul R. McHugh and Lawrence S. Mayer, "Sexuality and Gender: Findings from the Biological, Psychological, and Social Sciences," *New Atlantis* No. 50 (Fall 2016): 90.

11. Anne Fausto-Sterling, *Sexing the Body: Gender Politics and the Construction of Sexuality* (New York: Basic Books, 2000), 20.

12. This is from Yarhouse, *Understanding Gender Dysphoria*, 17, but also reflected in most other scholars I've read.

13. The idea of *gender role* was developed by sexologist and gender guru John Money, who said that "gender role ... is defined as *everything* that one says and does to indicate that one is either male or female, or androgyne" (*Sin, Science and the Sex Police* [Amherst, NY: Prometheus Books, 1998], 347). Others describe gender role in similar terms. It is the "adoptions of cultural expectations for maleness or femaleness" (Yarhouse, *Understanding Gender Dysphoria*, 17). "*Gender roles* govern the way we're expected to act, depending on our gender" (Austen Hartke, *Transforming: The Bible and the Lives of Transgender Christians* [Louisville, KY: Westminster

John Knox, 2018], 23). "Gender roles in society means how we're expected to act, speak, dress, groom, and conduct ourselves based upon our assigned sex" ("What Are Gender Roles and Stereotypes?" Planned Parenthood, www.plannedparenthood.org/learn/gender-identity /sex-gender-identity/what-are-gender-roles-and-stereotypes). Robert Stoller first proposed the term *core gender identity*—later shortened to *gender identity*—to refer to a person's "fundamental sense of belonging to one sex" (Robert Stoller, "The Hermaphroditic Identity of Hermaphrodites," *Journal of Nervous and Mental Disease* 139 [1964]: 453).

14. Quoted in Margaret Hartmann, "The History of Pink for Girls, Blue for Boys," *Jezebel*, April 10, 2011, https://jezebel.com/the-history-of-pink-for-girls-blue-for-boys-5790638.

15. To add more proof to the nurture view, some cross-cultural studies show that boys and girls raised in different cultures differ on the level of masculine and feminine traits, suggesting that culture has something to do with shaping these traits in children. See, for instance, J. H. Block, "Conceptions of Sex Roles: Some Cross-Cultural and Longitudinal Perspectives," *American Psychologist* 28 (1973): 512–26; Margaret Mead, *Sex and Temperament in Three Primitive Societies* (New York: Morrow, 1935); cf. Lips, *Sex and Gender*, 157.

16. See, for instance, Melissa Hines and Francine R. Kaufman, "Androgen and the Development of Human Sex-Typical Behavior: Rough-and-Tumble Play and Sex of Preferred Playmates in Children with Congenital Adrenal-Hyperplasia (CAH)," *Child Development* 65 (1994): 1042–53. See also Tracy Collins-Stanley et al., "Choice of Romantic, Violent, and Scary Fairy-Tale Books by Preschool Girls and Boys," *Child Study Journal* 26 (1996): 279–302; Kai von Klitzing et al., "Gender-Specific Characteristics of 5-Year-Olds' Play Narratives and Associations with Behavior Ratings," *Journal of the American Academy of Child and Adolescent Psychiatry* 39 (2000): 1017–23; Melissa Hines, "Sex-Related Variation in Human Behavior and the Brain," *Trends in Cognitive Science* 10 (2010): 448–56. For an informed yet accessible summary and discussion, see Leonard Sax, *Why Gender Matters*, 2nd ed. (New York: Harmony, 2017), 47–68. One study even showed different toy preferences among male and female monkeys that are associated with typical human male and female behavior. Obviously, these preferences can't be due to some cultural construct in Monkeyville (see Janice M. Hassett, Erin R. Siebert, and Kim Wallen, "Sex Differences in Rhesus Monkey Toy Preferences Parallel Those of Children," *Hormones and Behavior* 54, no. 3 (2008): 359–64.

17. See Cordelia Fine, *Delusions of Gender: How Our Minds, Society, and Neurosexism Create Difference* (New York: Norton, 2010), 97–106, for a good discussion of different views. For a critique of putting too much stock in the effect that testosterone has on behaviors, see Fausto-Sterling, *Sexing the Body*, 146–232, or more recently, Cordelia Fine, *Testosterone Rex: Myths of Sex, Science, and Society* (New York: Norton, 2018).

18. I say "typically" because some females with an intersex condition known as Congenital Adrenal Hyperplasia (CAH) overproduce the androgen hormone called androstenedione, which seems to have some kind of masculinizing effect on the brain. Females with this condition typically "grow into tomboys, with more rough-and-tumble play, a greater interest

in trucks than dolls, better spatial abilities, and, when they get older, more sexual fantasies and attraction involving other girls" (Steven Pinker, *The Blank Slate: The Modern Denial of Human Nature* [New York: Penguin Books, 2002], 238). The number of studies on girls affected with CAH is enormous, and the results are somewhat mixed. Some have found very few behavioral differences between girls with CAH and unaffected girls (see Fausto-Sterling, *Sexing the Body*, 74–75), while other studies document many behavior differences. In spite of the mixed results, virtually all studies agree that as children, girls with CAH prefer rough-and-tumble play and male-typical toys much more than unaffected girls (for a review and discussion, see Rebecca Jordan-Young, *Brain Storm: The Flaws in the Science of Sex Differences* [Cambridge, MA: Harvard University Press, 2010], 69–74, cf. 255–68).

19. The case was documented in John Colapinto's bestselling book *As Nature Made Him: The Boy Who Was Raised as a Girl* (Nashville: HarperCollins, 2000) and is talked about in virtually every book on sex and gender. David's original birth name was Bruce.

20. Pinker, *Blank Slate*, 349.

21. Susan. J. Bradley et al., "Experiment of Nurture: Ablatio Penis at 2 Months, Sex Reassignment at 7 Months and a Psychosexual Follow-Up in Young Adulthood," *Pediatrics* 102, no. 1 (1998). Research has not focused only on isolated cases. W. G. Reiner studied a cohort of twenty-nine (XY) males with similar conditions: damaged male anatomy, surgically transitioned to female, raised as girls. The result? "Nearly half of them have declared themselves male." See William. G. Reiner, "Psychosexual Development in Genetic Males Assigned Female: The Cloacal Exstrophy Experience," *Child and Adolescent Psychiatric Clinics of North America* 13 (2004): 657–74 [657]); see also H. Meyer-Bahlburg, "Gender Identity Outcome in Female-Raised 46,XY Persons with Penile Agenesis, Cloacal Exstrophy of the Bladder, or Penile Ablation," *Archives of Sexual Behavior* 34 (2005): 423–38.

22. According to the Human Rights Campaign, gender identity is "[o]ne's innermost concept of self as male, female, a blend of both or neither—how individuals perceive themselves and what they call themselves. One's gender identity can be the same as or different from their sex assigned at birth" (Robert Stoller, *Presentations of Gender* [New Haven, CT: Yale University Press, 1985]) 10; cited in Christina Beardsley and Michelle O'Brien, eds., *This is My Body: Hearing the Theology of Transgender Christians* [London: Darton, Longman & Todd, 2016], 12.). Trans* writer Austen Hartke defines gender identity in the same way: "Your internal sense of being male, female, both, or neither" (Hartke, *Transforming*, 21).

23. Sheila Jeffreys, *Gender Hurts: A Feminist Analysis of the Politics of Transgenderism* (New York: Routledge, 2014), 6. The classic presentation of this perspective is Janice Raymond, *The Transsexual Empire: The Making of the She-Male* (New York: Teachers College Press, 1979).

24. Jeffreys, *Gender Hurts*, 6.

25. Rhiannon Williams, "Facebook's 71 Gender Options Come to UK Users," *Telegraph*, June 27, 2014, www.telegraph.co.uk/technology/facebook/10930654/Facebooks-71-gender -options-come-to-UK-users.html.

26. Maggi Price and Avy Skolnik, "Gender Identity," in *The SAGE Encyclopedia of Psychology and Gender*, ed. Kevin L. Nadal (Thousand Oaks, CA: SAGE, 2017), 663–67.

27. Patrick Sweeney, "Gender Versus Sex," in *The SAGE Encyclopedia of Psychology and Gender*, ed. Kevin L. Nadal (Thousand Oaks, CA: SAGE, 2017), 769–71.

CHAPTER 3: WHAT DOES IT MEAN TO BE TRANS*?

1. Melina Sevlever and Heino F. L. Meyer-Bahlburg, "Late-Onset Transgender Identity Development of Adolescents in Psychotherapy for Mood and Anxiety Problems: Approach to Assessment and Treatment," *Archives of Sexual Behavior* 48, no. 7 (2019): 1993–2001.

2. This "desistance" rate has been the subject of much controversy. For a detailed and lengthy review of the literature and controversy, see Paul Eddy, "Reflections on the Debate Concerning the Desistance Rate among Young People with Gender Dysphoria," Center for Faith, Sexuality & Gender, 2020, www.centerforfaith.com/resources?field_product_category _tid=10. See also James Cantor's survey of research, "Do Trans- Kids Stay Trans- When They Grow Up?" *Sexology Today!*, January 11, 2016, www.sexologytoday.org/2016/01/do-trans -kids-stay-trans-when-they-grow_99.html.

3. Jessie Earl, "Do You Need Gender Dysphoria to Be Trans?" *Advocate*, January 18, 2019, www.advocate.com/commentary/2019/1/18/do-you-need-gender-dysphoria-be-trans. Some states in the United States (for example, California) and several countries (Malta, Norway, Denmark, Portugal, Ireland, and Belgium) have adopted self-identification as the legal basis for gender recognition. No medical diagnosis is necessary to legally change a person's gender; see Nick Duffy, "California Adopts Self-ID Gender Recognition Law," *Pink News*, January 3, 2019, www.pinknews.co.uk/2019/01/03/california-gender-self-id/.

4. "I Am Transgender (Female to Male)," YouTube, posted by blndsundoll4mj, October 7, 2019, https://youtu.be/HLtAF5KDChE. Paytas got a ton of criticism for this video and offered an apology but still identifies as trans* (and a gay man, and several other identities).

5. According to the *DSM-5*, the authoritative resource for psychiatric practice, the prevalence rate of gender dysphoria is 0.014 percent. See "Gender Dysphoria," in *Diagnostic and Statistical Manual of Mental Disorders*, 5th ed. (Washington, DC: American Psychiatric Association, 2013), 454. At least 0.6 percent of adults in the United States identify as transgender ("How Many Adults Identify as Transgender in the United States?," Williams Institute, June 2016, https://williamsinstitute.law.ucla.edu/publications/trans-adults-united -states/) and 1.8 percent of high schoolers in the United States identify as transgender (Michelle M. Johns et al., "Transgender Identity and Experiences of Violence Victimization, Substance Use, Suicide Risk, and Sexual Risk Behaviors Among High School Students—19 States and Large Urban School Districts, 2017," *Morbidity and Mortality Weekly Report* 68, no. 3 (2019): 67–71, www.cdc.gov/mmwr/volumes/68/wr/mm6803a3.htm). By now, these numbers are likely higher. The point is, not everyone identifying as transgender experiences gender dysphoria. Nondysphoric people are included under the trans* umbrella.

6. There's a big difference between the ontological questions raised in the trans* conversation and those raised in certain evangelical conversations about same-sex sexuality. Concerning the latter, some argue that the phrase "I am gay" is an unhelpful (or even heretical) ontological statement, while others say that the phrase "I am gay" simply refers to a person's experience of attraction to the same sex. These are interesting points of view and worth discussing, but they are very different from the ontological question in the trans* conversation. Ontologically, some people really are gay—or, if you prefer, attracted to the same sex. People might dispute whether attraction to the same sex is a core or peripheral aspect of a person's humanity. But in either case, it is still an ontological reality; there is no question about whether some people are attracted to the same sex.

7. Reddit, post by u/axel_yo, "I don't wanna be a woman, I just want a woman's body," December 3, 2019, www.reddit.com/r/asktransgender/comments/e5oyjo/i_dont_wanna_be _a_woman_i_just_want_a_womans_body/. The poster goes on to say, "when i imagine myself naked after transition (smooth skin, breasts, feminine face, penis maybe or maybe not) my thoughts are 'heck yes gimme all the HRTs now'. when i imagine myself as a woman after transition just in the store or with friends having a conversation my thoughts are '/shrug.'"

8. Lawrence's book *Men Trapped in Men's Bodies: Narratives of Autogynephilic Transsexualism* (New York: Springer, 2013) analyzes dozens of narratives from transwomen who are autogynephilic. She breaks down autogynephilia into several subtypes, including (a) transvestic (wearing women's clothes), (b) anatomic (a desire to possess female anatomy— sometimes top, sometimes bottom, sometimes both), (c) physiologic (a desire to engage in female functions, like being pregnant, breastfeeding, and menstruating), and (d) behavioral (behaving in ways that are stereotypical of females). On the desire to engage in female functions like breastfeeding and menstruating, see Blaire White's discussion about a group of transwomen (biological males) who say they have a menstrual cycle and PMS ("'Trans Women Are 100% REAL WOMEN' - Okay..," YouTube, September 24, 2019, https://youtu.be/cTSd5PS4-JY).

9. Blanchard is like the master Yoda of autogynephilia research, publishing over a dozen articles on the topic, and is recognized as the foremost voice for understanding this kind of trans* experience (see, for example, R. Blanchard, "Varieties of Autogynephilia and Their Relationship to Gender Dysphoria," *Archives of Sexual Behavior* 22 [1993]: 241–51).

10. See his controversial book *The Man Who Would Be Queen: The Science of Gender-Bending and Transsexualism* (Washington, DC: Joseph Henry, 2003).

11. Subtitle: *Heretics, Activists, and the Search for Justice in Science* (New York: Penguin, 2015).

12. For an argument against the classification of autogynephilia, see Julia M. Serano, "The Case Against Autogynephilia," *International Journal of Transgenderism* 12 (2010):176–87, www.juliaserano.com/av/Serano-CaseAgainstAutogynephilia.pdf. For an argument that virtually all MtF's are autogynephilic, even though many don't care to admit it, see Miranda

Yardley, "A History of Autogynephilia," June 17, 2017, https://mirandayardley.com/en/a-history-of-autogynephilia/. Both Serano and Yardley are MtF trans* people.

13. M. D. Connolly et al., "The Mental Health of Transgender Youth: Advances in Understanding," *Journal of Adolescent Health* 59, no. 5 (2016): 489–95.

14. R. P. Rajkumar, "Gender Identity Disorder and Schizophrenia: Neurodevelopmental Disorders with Common Causal Mechanisms?," *Schizophrenia Research and Treatment* (2014), www.hindawi.com/journals/schizort/2014/463757/.

15. Annelou L. C. de Vries et al., "Autism Spectrum Disorders in Gender Dysphoric Children and Adolescents" *Journal of Autism and Developmental Disorders* 40, no. 8 (2010): 930–36. Another study found that young people diagnosed with ASD were 7.76 times more likely to report gender variance than a control group; see A. Janssen, H. Huang, and C. Duncan, "Gender Variance among Youth with Autism Spectrum Disorders: A Retrospective Chart Review," *Transgender Health* 1, no. 1 (2016).

16. Riittakerttu Kaltiala-Heino et al., "Two Years of Gender Identity Service for Minors: Overrepresentation of Natal Girls with Severe Problems in Adolescent Development," *Child and Adolescent Psychiatry and Mental Health* 9, no. 9 (2015). Another study found that 44.9 percent of children with gender dysphoria were also on the autism spectrum; VanderLaan et al., "Autism Spectrum Disorder Risk Factors and Autistic Traits in Gender Dysphoric Children," *Journal of Autism and Developmental Disorders* 45, no. 6 (2015). For a thorough review and analysis of other studies, see Anna I. R. van der Miesen et al., "Autistic Symptoms in Children and Adolescents with Gender Dysphoria," *Journal of Autism and Developmental Disorders* 48, no. 5 (2018).

17. Sydney Wright, "I Spent Years as a Trans Man. Doctors Failed Me at Every Turn," *Daily Signal*, October 7, 2019, www.dailysignal.com/2019/10/07/i-spent-a-year-as-a-trans-man-doctors-failed-me-at-every-turn/.

18. See Lucy Bannerman, "It Feels like Conversion Therapy for Gay Children, Say Clinicians: Ex-NHS Staff Fear that Homophobia Is Driving a Surge in 'Transgender' Young People," *Times*, April 8, 2019, www.thetimes.co.uk/article/it-feels-like-conversion-therapy-for-gay-children-say-clinicians-pvsckdvq2. Some therapists wonder if certain parents who are highly supportive of their child identifying as transgender could be motivated by a homophobic fear about their child being gay. See Terry Patterson, "Unconscious Homophobia and the Rise of the Transgender Movement," *Psychodynamic Practice* 24, no. 1 (2018): 56–59.

19. Dan Littauer, "Iran Performed over 1,000 Gender Reassignment Operations in Four Years," *Gay Star News*, December 4, 2012, www.gaystarnews.com/article/iran-performed-over-1000-gender-reassignment-operations-four-years041212/. The BBC documentary "Iran's 'Sex-Change' Solution" shows many testimonies that connect the high rate of sex reassignment surgeries with statewide homophobia (YouTube, posted by Ali Hamedani, November 13, 2014, https://youtu.be/Wg51RnpGn9k).

20. In 2007, the president of Iran at the time, Mahmoud Ahmadinejad, told the students at Columbia University, "In Iran, we don't have homosexuals, like in your country" (Hristian Byrnes, "13 Countries where Being Gay Is Legally Punishable by Death," *USA Today*, June 19, 2019).

21. For example, in an informal 2017 online survey of 359 non-transitioned females experiencing gender dysphoria, over 82 percent reported that processing internalized misogyny eased their dysphoria—this was the single most effective strategy mentioned among the respondents. See Hailey Mangelsdorf, "Female/AFAB Dysphoria Management Survey—Analysis and Results," https://docs.google.com/document/d /1nc5X96PwzyfIfpvKi8RQR5t9AQe9SVl76aWZL30rVLY/.

22. Kenneth J. Zucker et al., "A Developmental, Biopsychosocial Model for the Treatment of Children with Gender Identity Disorder," *Journal of Homosexuality* 59, no. 3 (2012): 369–97 (381).

23. Bethel Music, "No Longer Slaves," by Jonathan David Helser and Melissa Helser, track 4 on *We Will Not Be Shaken*, 2014.

CHAPTER 4: MALE AND FEMALE IN THE IMAGE OF GOD

1. See the review of interpretations in J. Richard Middleton, *The Liberating Image: The Imago Dei in Genesis 1* (Grand Rapids, MI: Brazos, 2005), 17–34.

2. *Demut* (the Hebrew word for "likeness") overlaps with the meaning of *selem* but typically highlights the appearance or form of something that resembles something else. The terms are probably meant to be used interchangeably, since they are used in tandem in Genesis 1:26: "Let us make mankind in our image (*selem*), in our likeness (*demut*)." They appear again in tandem but in reverse order in Genesis 5:3: "he had a son in his own likeness (*demut*), in his own image (*selem*)."

3. Middleton, *Liberating Image*, 25.

4. Marc Cortez, *ReSourcing Theological Anthropology: A Constructive Account of Humanity in the Light of Christ* (Grand Rapids, MI: Zondervan, 2017), 109.

5. Karl Löning and Erich Zenger, *To Begin with, God Created: Biblical Theologies of Creation*, trans. Omar Kaste (Collegeville, MN: Liturgical, 2000), 108. Similarly, Joseph Blenkinsopp points out that the strong polemic against idols in Isaiah 40–48 "suggests that creation in the image of God implies polemic against the cult of other images, idolatrous images, in the sense that the human being is to be the only replica and representative of God on earth; see Blenkinsopp's *Creation, Un-creation, Re-creation: A Discursive Commentary on Genesis 1–11* (New York: Clark, 2011), 28. For two other important works on this topic, see Catherine L. McDowell, *The Image of God in the Garden of Eden: The Creation of Humankind in Genesis 2:5—3:24 in Light of the mīs pî, pīt pî, and wpt-r Rituals of Mesopotamia and Ancient Egypt* (Winona Lake, IN: Eisenbrauns, 2015); and Stephen Herring, *Divine Substitution: Humanity*

as the Manifestation of Deity in the Hebrew Bible and the Ancient Near East (Bristol, CT: Vandenhoeck and Ruprecht, 2013).

6. "Clearly, 'male and female' correspond structurally to 'the image of God,' and this formal parallelism indicates a semantic correspondence" (Phyllis Trible, *God and the Rhetoric of Sexuality* [Philadelphia: Fortress, 1978], 17). On the importance of the connection between the image of God—specifically God's "likeness" (*demut*)—and humans as male and female, see W. Randall Garr, *In His Own Image and Likeness: Humanity, Divinity and Monotheism* (Boston: Brill, 2003), 167–69.

7. Phyllis Bird, "'Bone of My Bone and Flesh of My Flesh,'" *Theology Today* 50, no. 4 (1994): 531.

8. See John H. Walton, *The Lost World of Adam and Eve: Genesis 2–3 and the Human Origins Debate* (Downers Grove, IL: IVP Academic, 2015), 77–81.

9. For example, in Ezekiel 41 alone, the word *tsela* is used nine time to refer to the "side rooms" of the temple (vv. 5–11, 26).

10. W. D. Davies and Dale C. Allison, *A Critical and Exegetical Commentary on the Gospel according to Saint Matthew*, 3 vols. (Edinburgh: Clark, 1988–97), III, 10.

11. For an insightful look at how Paul's logic in this passage is driven by a high view of the body, see Gordon Fee, *The First Epistle to the Corinthians* (Grand Rapids, MI: Eerdmans, 2014), 275–94; Bruce N. Fisk, "Porneuein as Body Violation: The Unique Nature of the Sexual Sin in 1 Corinthians 6.18," *New Testament Studies* 42 (1996): 540–58. Rudolph Bultmann argued that Paul only refers to personhood or the self here and not to the physical body (Theology, 1.192), but most scholars reject this interpretation (see the thorough critique by Robert H. Gundry, *Sōma in Biblical Theology: With Emphasis on Pauline Anthropology* [Cambridge: Cambridge University Press, 1976]). Bruce Fisk sums it up well: "Bultmann found difficulties in this passage precisely because it so clearly affirmed what he felt compelled to deny—that the physical body played a very significant role in Paul's theology.... Paul's use of *soma* always draws attention to man's *physique*, his corporality ..." ("Porneuein," 548).

12. "Do not let sin reign *in your mortal body*" (Rom. 6:12, emphasis added) ... "for sin will have no dominion over *you*" (Rom. 6:14 ESV, emphasis added); cf. Rom. 8:11; 2 Cor. 4:10–2; Eph. 5:28–29.

13. See, for instance, James D. G. Dunn, *The Theology of Paul the Apostle* (Grand Rapids, MI: Eerdmans, 1998), 55–61.

14. For a brief theological overview of this point, see Marc Cortez, *Theological Anthropology: A Guide for the Perplexed* (New York: Continuum, 2010), 70.

15. Some people dispute the NIV's translation of *keli geber* as "men's clothing," since *geber* often means "warrior" and, they say, *keli* never means clothing. Some therefore say that the command prohibits woman from dressing up in a warrior's armor and therefore might not have much to do with cross-dressing *per se* (see Linda Tatro Herzer, *The Bible and the Transgender*

Experience: How Scripture Supports Gender Variance [Cleveland OH: The Pilgrim Press, 2016], 34–37). This interpretation is problematic for several reasons. First, while the adjective *gibbor* most often means "warrior," Deuteronomy 22:5 uses the noun *geber*, which often overlaps with the normal word for "man," *ish* (see, for example, Ex. 10:7, 11; 12:37). Second, the word *keli* doesn't typically refer to clothing, but it does refer more generally to various things associated with men, including certain ornaments, weapons, hunting equipment, gear, and also clothing (1 Sam. 21:5; 1 Kings 10:21; Gen. 24:53; Num. 19:18). The translation "the things of men" is probably a better and more inclusive translation of the phrase by itself. However, the parallel statement, "nor a man wear women's *clothing*" (*shimlat*) specifies an article of clothing, which suggests that the former reference to *keli geber* probably does have clothing in mind. In any case, the point made here goes much deeper than mere clothing, to the fundamental differences between men and women. Clothing is the external expression of those differences. In most cultures of every era, clothing carries powerful signs of class, style, modesty, status, and— especially—of sex difference. According to two experts on the history of cross-dressing, "Dress traditionally has been a ubiquitous symbol of sexual differences, emphasizing social conceptions of masculinity and femininity. Cross dressing, therefore, represents a symbolic incursion into territory that crosses gender boundaries" (Vern L. Bullough and Bonnie Bullough, *Cross Dressing, Sex, and Gender* [Philadelphia: University of Pennsylvania Press, 1993], viii; cited in Nili Sacher Fox, "Gender Transformation and Transgression: Contextualizing the Prohibition of Cross-Dressing in Deuteronomy 22:5," in *Mishneh Todah: Studies in Deuteronomy and Its Cultural Environment in Honor of Jeffrey H. Tigay*, ed. Nili Sacher Fox, David A. Glatt-Gilad, and Michael J. Williams [Winona Lake, IN: Eisenbrauns, 2009], 51). In short, "the prohibition of the wearing of clothes of members of the opposite sex was … to safeguard the division between male and female" and was rooted in God's concern for diversity and order as reflected in the creation account of Genesis 1–2 (P. J. Harland, "Menswear and Womenswear: A Study of Deuteronomy 22:5," *Expository Times* 110, no. 3 [1998]: 76).

Determining whether this command still applies today is particularly difficult, however. There's little in the surrounding context that helps us determine its lasting relevance. The verses before (vv. 1–4) talk about straying oxen, and the verses after (vv. 6–8) talk about taking care of birds in their nests. The next set of verses (vv. 9–11) talks about mixing seeds, animals, and fabrics, which could be correlated with the concerns about mixing gender in verse 5. The near context doesn't give us much help in determining modern applications of this verse.

Some people say that the prohibition is probably limited to cultic activity (Herzer, *Bible and the Transgender Experience*, 37). But nothing in the near context of Deuteronomy seems particularly concerned with cultic practices, and the generic terms *geber* ("man") and *ishah* ("woman") would be an odd choice if cultic practices were meant. It seems rather hasty, therefore, to punt to some cultic context of the command, since this isn't stated and can't just be assumed.

In terms of New Testament usage, while the prohibition isn't explicitly cited, we do see similar concerns about clothing and male/female difference in 1 Corinthians 11:2–16. We also see Paul prohibiting same-sex sexual relations in light of his concerns about gender confusion (in particular, Rom. 1:26–27 and 1 Cor. 6:9, as stated above). This suggests that while we shouldn't just thoughtlessly cite Deuteronomy 22:5 as if it self-evidently applies to the church, we can say that the driving principle of the command very much resonates with how the rest of Scripture celebrates maintaining certain differences between the sexes.

16. William Loader, *The New Testament on Sexuality* (Grand Rapids, MI: Eerdmans, 2012), 327–32.

17. See Judith M. Gundry-Volf's extensive study of this passage, where she interacts with dozens of different ways scholars have understood this passage: "Gender and Creation in 1 Corinthians 11,2-16: A Study of Paul's Theological Method," in *Evangelium—Schriftauslegung—Kirche: Festschrift für Peter Stuhlmacher zum 65. Geburstag*, ed. O. Hofius et al. (Göttingen, Germany: Vandenhoeck und Ruprecht, 1997), 151–71. The only interpreter I've found who doesn't think that Paul is arguing to maintain sex differences is Elizabeth Schüssler Fiorenza, *In Memory of Her: A Feminist Theological Reconstruction of Christian Origins* (New York: Crossroad, 1983), 229.

18. Classicist Kyle Harper makes the same point and shows that Paul was truly unique among other Greco-Roman writers by making same-sex sexual behavior about male-female differences rather than power differentials, age differences, or exploitation: "The very language of 'males' and 'females' stood apart from the prevailing idiom of 'men' and 'boys', 'women' and 'slaves.' By reducing the sex act down to the most basic constituents of male and female, Paul was able to redescribe the sexual culture surrounding him in transformative terms" (Kyle Harper, *From Shame to Sin: The Christian Transformation of Sexual Morality in Late Antiquity* [Cambridge, MA: Harvard University Press, 2013], 95, cf. 96–99).

19. Cortez, *ReSourcing*, 114. See also Stanley Grenz, "Jesus as the *Imago Dei*: Image-of-God Christology and the Non-Linear Linearity of Theology," *Journal of the Evangelical Theological Society* 47 (2004): 617–28; Rikk E. Watts, "The New Exodus/New Creational Restoration of the Image of God," in *What Does it Mean to Be Saved? Broadening Evangelical Horizons of Salvation*, ed. John G. Stackhouse, Jr. (Grand Rapids, MI: Baker Academic, 2002), 15–41.

20. Cortez, *ReSourcing*, 197.

21. Feminist interpreters have been particularly concerned with the importance of Christ's maleness. Does this mean that males bear more of God's image, since they are closer to Christ's body? Paul seems to say this in 1 Corinthians 11:7: "A man ought not to cover his head, since he is the image and glory of God; but woman is the glory of man." Yikes! Did Paul really say that? Despite how it looks, it's unlikely that Paul means women *don't* bear God's image, since in every other instance where Paul talks about the "image of God," he associates it with all people regardless of sex. Plus, Paul's statement in Galatians 3:28 balances out his seemingly misogynistic statement here in 1 Corinthians 11:7. For an overview of the maleness of Christ and some questions this raises for theological anthropology, see Cortez, *ReSourcing*, 190–211; Julia Baudzej, "Re-telling the Story of Jesus: The Concept of Embodiment and Recent Feminist Reflections on the Maleness of Christ," *Feminist Theology* 17, no. 1 (2008): 72–91; Eleanor McLaughlin, "Feminist Christologies: Re-Dressing the Tradition," in *Reconstructing the Christ Symbol: Essays in Feminist Christology*, ed. Maryanne

Stevens (New York: Paulist Press, 1993), 118–49; Rebecca D. Pentz, "Can Jesus Save Women?," in *Encountering Jesus: A Debate on Christology*, ed. Stephen T. Davis (Atlanta: Knox, 1988), 77–90.

22. Oliver O'Donovan, *Resurrection and Moral Order: An Outline for Evangelical Ethics*, 2nd ed. (Downers Grove, IL: InterVarsity Press, 1994), 13.

23. O'Donovan, *Resurrection and Moral Order*, 31.

24. See Beth Felker Jones, "Embodied from Creation through Redemption: Placing Gender and Sexuality in Theological Context," in *Beauty, Order, and Mystery: A Christian Vision of Human Sexuality*, ed. Gerald Hiestand and Todd Wilson (Grand Rapids: InterVarsity Press, 2017), 21–30.

25. Some early theologians like Origen and Gregory of Nyssa believed that sex differences would be done away with in the resurrection, while Augustine argued that our resurrected bodies will be sexed; see Jones, "Embodied," 24–25.

26. For example, the reference to "heavenly bodies" and "earthly bodies" (1 Cor. 15:40) alludes to Genesis 1:14–18; 1 Corinthians 15:45 quotes from Genesis 2:7; the reference to sun, moon, and stars (1 Cor. 15:41) draws on Genesis 1:16; the seed-bearing plants after their kind (1 Cor. 15:36–38) draws on Genesis 1:11–12; the reference to birds, animals, and fish (1 Cor. 15:39) finds resonance in Genesis 1:20–22. See N. T. Wright, *The Resurrection of the Son of God: Christian Origins and the Question of God*, vol. 3 (Minneapolis: Fortress Press, 2003), 341.

27. For a thorough study of 1 Corinthians 15:35–49, see Wright, *Resurrection of the Son*, 340–61.

28. Ross Hastings, "The Trinity and Human Sexuality: Made in the Image of the Triune God," *CRUX* 54, no. 2 (2018): 10–24 (10).

CHAPTER 5: GENDER STEREOTYPES

1. For a critical assessment of the claim that David and Jonathan were in a same-sex sexual relationship, see Markus Zehnder, "Observations on the Relationship between David and Jonathan and the Debate on Homosexuality," *Westminster Theological Journal* 69: 1 (2007): 127–74.

2. Myles McDonnell, *Roman Manliness: "Virtus" and the Roman Republic* (Cambridge: Cambridge University Press, 2009), 10–11.

3. See, for example, Craig A. Williams, *Roman Homosexuality*, 2nd ed. (Oxford: Oxford University Press, 2010), 137–76.

4. Marc Cortez, *ReSourcing Theological Anthropology: A Constructive Account of Humanity in the Light of Christ* (Grand Rapids, MI: Zondervan, 2017), 203.

5. Many people today uncritically assume that the ancient world of the Bible was nothing but patriarchy on steroids. But a number of third-wave feminist biblical scholars have challenged this assumption. See Carol L. Meyers, "Was Ancient Israel a Patriarchal Society?," *Journal of Biblical Literature* 133, no. 1 (2014): 8–27.

6. Naomi Greenaway, "'When I Was a Girl': Transgender Men Share Pictures of Themselves before Transition and Reveal What It's REALLY Like to Change Sex," *Daily Mail*, October 13, 2015, www.dailymail.co.uk/femail/article-3270572/Transgender-men-share-pictures -transition-reveal-s-REALLY-like-change-sex.html.

7. Aron Hirt-Manheimer, "'A Dead Son or a Living Daughter': A Conversation with the Mother of a Transgender Child," *Reform Judaism*, July 15, 2016, https://reformjudaism.org /blog/2016/07/15/dead-son-or-living-daughter-conversation-mother-transgender-child.

8. "Transgender Kids—Who Knows Best," *BBC Documentary* (2017) available here: https://vimeo.com/256415639. The documentary discusses transgender summer camps for trans* kids at around the 18:55 mark. This scene illustrates rigid stereotypes of what it means to be a girl or a boy. The documentary is very balanced in terms of expressing the views of those who are advocates of a gender-affirmative approach along with those who are critical of it. Nevertheless, it was widely criticized as harmful and transphobic. See Jesse Singal, "You Should Watch the BBC's Controversial Documentary on the Gender-Dysphoria Researcher Kenneth Zucker," *The Cut*, January 13, 2017, www.thecut.com/2017/01/you-should-watch -the-bbcs-kenneth-zucker-documentary.html.

9. "Transgender Kids," https://vimeo.com/256415639 at the 19:40 mark.

10. Anne Lawrence, *Men Trapped in Men's Bodies: Narratives of Autogynephilic Transsexualism* (New York: Springer, 2013), 96.

11. Lawrence, *Men Trapped*, 96.

12. Miranda Yardley, "What Does It Mean to Be Caitlyn?" Medium.com, August 11, 2017, https://medium.com/@mirandayardley/what-does-it-mean-to-be-caitlyn-31e11670a6c2.

13. According to Bill Mounce, "'working at home' contrasts with the conduct of the younger Ephesian widows who were lazy and ran from house to house (1 Tim 5:13); it does not require a woman to work only at home (cf. Prov 31), but it does state that she does have duties at home" (William D. Mounce, *The Pastoral Epistles*, Word Biblical Commentary, vol. 46 [Nashville: Thomas Nelson, 2000], 411).

14. See the previous chapter, including the endnotes, for a discussion of these two passages.

15. See Judith M. Gundry-Volf, "Gender and Creation in 1 Corinthians 11,2–16: A Study of Paul's Theological Method," in *Evangelium—Schriftauslegung—Kirche: Festschrift für Peter Stuhlmacher zum 65. Geburtstag*, ed. O. Hofius et al. (Göttingen, Germany: Vandenhoeck und Ruprecht, 1997), 151–71.

CHAPTER 6: BUT WHAT ABOUT THE EUNUCH? AND OTHER QUESTIONS ...

1. See, for instance, Lewis Reay, "Towards a Transgender Theology: Que(e)rying the Eunuchs," in *Trans/Formations*, ed. Marcella Althaus-Reid and Lisa Isherwood (London: SCM Press, 2009), 148–67 (152–53); Megan DeFranza, *Sex Difference in Christian Theology: Male, Female, and Intersex in the Image of God* (Grand Rapids, MI: Eerdmans, 2015), 177; Austen Hartke, *Transforming: The Bible and the Lives of Transgender Christians* (Louisville, KY: Westminster John Knox, 2018), 47–58; Justin Sabia-Tanis, "Holy Creation; Holy Creative: God's Intention for Gender Diversity," in *Understanding Transgender Identities: Four Views*, ed. James K. Beilby and Paul Rhodes Eddy (Grand Rapids, MI: Baker, 2019), 195–98.

2. Tara K. Soughers disagrees: "Perhaps it is not biological sex that is referred to in this passage, but gender—a gender that does not depend upon sexual differentiation" (*Beyond a Binary God: A Theology for Trans* Allies* [New York: Church Publishing, 2018], 65).

3. The phrase "male and female" is used only a few times in the Old Testament: in Genesis 1:27 (cf. Matt. 19:4; Gal. 3:28) and 5:2, in reference to the creation of humans as male and female, and in Genesis 6:19; 7:3, 9, 16, referring to animals going into the ark "two by two."

4. Linda Tatro Herzer, *The Bible and the Transgender Experience: How Scripture Supports Gender Variance* (Cleveland, OH: Pilgrim Press, 2016), 71.

5. Herzer, *Bible and the Transgender Experience*, 84.

6. Herzer, *Bible and the Transgender Experience*, 89.

7. Herzer, *Bible and the Transgender Experience*, 92.

8. The Hebrew meaning of Joseph's coat (*ketonet passim*) is uncertain. It could mean "tunic of many colors" or "long tunic with long sleeves." The only other time we see such a coat is on a woman, Tamar, who "was wearing a long robe with sleeves, for thus were the virgin daughters of the king dressed" (2 Sam. 13:18 ESV). Some people therefore say that Joseph's coat is evidence he was cross-dressing. But this analysis is questionable for several reasons. First, we only have two references in Scripture, making it difficult to know whether Joseph was wearing a women's tunic, or whether Tamar and the virgin daughters were wearing men's tunics, or whether they were both wearing a unique kind of garment that was gender neutral. Second, keep in mind that Tamar lived one thousand years after Joseph. Was the *ketonet passim* even the same kind of coat after all those years? Third, it's not like Joseph went out to some ancient H&M, passed over all the male coats, and picked out a women's coat. His father gave him the coat. As Gordon Wenham says, "[W]hatever the tunic looked like, it marked Jacob's special affection for Joseph and served as a perpetual reminder to his brothers" (*Genesis 16–50*, Word Biblical Commentary, vol. 2 [Nashville: Thomas Nelson, 1987], 351). This would be an odd display of "special affection" if Jacob stuffed Joseph into a girl's coat in a society where he would be been ridiculed for it. Fourth, and moreover, his brothers didn't tease him for wearing the coat. Instead, they were jealous. Were all his brothers aspiring cross-dressers?

9. Justin Sabia-Tanis, *Trans-Gender: Theology, Ministry, and Communities of Faith* (Eugene, OR: Wipf and Stock, 2003), 72.

10. The word is only used in two passages in the New Testament (Matt. 19:12 and Acts 8:27–39). In the Septuagint, *eunouchos* translates the Hebrew term *saris* thirty-one times. See Francois P. Retief and Louise Cilliers, "Eunuchs in the Bible," *Acta Theologica Supplementum* 7 (2005): 247–58.

11. Xenophon, *Cyropaedia* 7.60–65; Cassius Dio, *Roman History* 75.14.

12. Esther 1:10, 12, 15; 2:3, 14, 21; 4:4–5; 6:14; 7:9; Cassius Dio, *Roman History* 76.14.4–5.

13. 2 Kings 25:19; Jeremiah 39:3, 13.

14. Juvenal, *Satire* 6.366–378; Martial, *Epigram* 3.81; 4.67; 6.2, 21, 39, 67; 10.91; 11.81; Hieronymus, *Adversus Iovinianum* 1.47; Tertullian, *Ad Uxorem* 2.8.4; Claudian, *In Eutropium* 1.105–109.

15. See, for instance, Lucian of Samosata, *The Eunuch*: "[A] eunuch was neither man nor woman but something composite, a hybrid, and monstrous, alien to human nature" (cf. Claudian, *In Eutropium* 1.468; see J. David Hester, "Eunuchs and the Postgender Jesus: Matthew 19.12 and Transgressive Sexualities," *Journal for the Study of the New Testament* 28, no. 1 [2005]: 13–40 [20]). The eunuch in question in Lucian's writing is one who had his penis cut off. Lucian's perspective seems to reflect his phallocentric view of maleness: men have penises, and the bigger they are, the more manly a person is. Similarly, Augustine said that a castrated eunuch was "a man" who "is so mutilated that he is neither changed into a woman nor remains a man" (*City of God*, 7.24). Notice that Augustine said it was a "man" who had been mutilated. When one considers a mutilated man no longer a man, this reflects cultural assumptions about manhood. These perspectives seem to assume rigid, cultural stereotypes of what it means to be a man or a woman—a problem today just as much as it was back then.

16. Of course, external genitalia is *part* of the evidence used to determine whether someone is male or female, and eunuchs often were castrated; therefore, at least part of the evidence for their biological sex was, to be frank, no longer apparent. A person's biological sex, though, can't be reduced to whether they have testicles or not, any more than a person's humanness can be determined by whether they have two legs or not—even though humans, categorically, are two-legged mammals. In any case, some ancient writers spoke of eunuchs as neither male nor female because they had their "manhood" cut off (see the previous note).

17. This is especially true if Matthew 19:12 alludes to the eunuch prophecy in Isaiah 56, which clearly highlights infertility: "[L]et not the eunuch say, 'Behold, I am a dry tree' … I will give in my house and within my walls a monument and a name better than sons and daughters; I will give them an everlasting name that shall not be cut off" (vv. 3–5).

18. Isaiah 56:3–5; Wisdom of Solomon 3:13–14; implied in Philo, *Joseph* 153.

19. Herzer, *Bible and the Transgender Experience*, 47.

20. Herzer, *Bible and the Transgender Experience*, 25.

21. Hartke, *Transforming*, 108.

22. Some people argue that since eunuchs didn't fit the narrow Roman and Jewish assumptions about masculinity, therefore Jesus didn't consider eunuchs to be male. Linda Tatro Herzer, for instance, says that transgender people "have no interest in carrying out the roles and expectations typically assigned to someone with their genitals" (*Bible and the Transgender Experience*, 46) and are therefore gender variant. She then says that eunuchs (and therefore trans* people) people fall outside the categories of "male and female" in the context of Genesis 1 and Matthew 19: "Jesus discusses marriage, divorce, male, female, *and* eunuchs," she writes, and "Jesus was well aware that there were more than just two ways to live out one's gender—that male and female were not the only two realities" (*Bible and the Transgender Experience*, 47). I find it really hard to believe that Jesus would have agreed with these cultural stereotypes—that since eunuchs were viewed as unmanly and feminine, they therefore weren't *male*.

23. The best evidence for this interpretation is that the phrase "male *and* female" probably refers back to Genesis 1:27, where God created humanity as "male and female." Notice that Paul says, "*nor is there* male and female," which raises the question: What is it about Genesis 1:27 that Paul seems to overturn? One scholar writes, "[O]nce it is recognized that Galatians 3:28c is a citation of Genesis 1:27c the implication is that Paul ... envisions that the creation ordinance which differentiates and separates humanity on the basis of sex has been negated in Christ" (Wayne Litke, "Beyond Creation: Galatians 3:28, Genesis and the Hermaphrodite Myth," *Studies in Religion* 24, no. 2 [1995]: 173–78 [178]). Also, there was a popular myth in Paul's time that humanity originally existed as an androgynous human and was only later split into two different sexes, male and female. Perhaps, then, Paul had this myth in mind when he penned Galatians 3:28. In resurrection, we will return to our original, pristine, androgynous state. For this creation myth, see Plato's *Symposium* 189D–193D. For early interpretations of Galatians 3:28 along these lines, see *Gospel of Thomas* 22; 2 Clement 12:2–6; *Gospel of Philip* 70; cf. the *Gospel of the Egyptians* as quoted by Clement of Alexandria, *Stromata* 3, 13.92–93. The first scholar I can find who connects Galatians 3:28 with this myth of an androgynous original human is Wayne Meeks, "The Image of the Androgyne: Some Uses of a Symbol in Earliest Christianity," *History of Religions* 13, no. 3 (1974): 165–208. For one of many critiques of this view, see Judith Gundry-Volf, "Christ and Gender: A Study of Difference and Equality in Gal 3,28," in *Jesus Christus als die Mitte der Schrift: Studien zur Hermeneutik des Evangeliums*, ed. Christof Landmesser, Hans-Joachim Eckstein, and Hermann Lichtenberger (Berlin, Germany: Walter de Gruyter, 1997), 439–77.

24. With regard to Jew/Gentile and slave/free, therefore, it's clear that Paul is saying that these ethnic and socioeconomic statuses do not diminish your salvation status. "For you are *all* one in Christ Jesus," Paul says in his next breath (Gal. 3:28), which is the climactic point in Paul's argument.

25. So what do we do with Paul's seemingly negative allusion to Genesis 1:27? The phrase
arsen kai thelu ("male and female") is exactly the same as the Greek translation (LXX) of
Genesis 1:27. (In the Old Testament, it's only used elsewhere of humans in Genesis 5:2
and then of all animals in Genesis 6:19–20; 7:2, 3, 9, 16.) What is it about Genesis 1:27
that Paul is seeking to overturn? One interpretive direction that's gained a lot of support
from a variety of scholars is to look at how Genesis 1:27 was *interpreted* by Jews in Paul's
day. Sometimes verses take on an interpretive life of their own through cultural usage.
(Think about how John 3:16 has taken on a life of its own in American football stadiums as
evangelistic sports fans hold up signs with "John 3:16" written on them.)

When we look at Paul's wider culture, we see that the phrase "male and female"
was used as a catchphrase that denoted marriage. For instance, one Jewish text (*Damascus
Document* 4:20–5:2) condemned polygamy by appealing to what the author called "the
principle of creation," that is, "male and female he created them"—a quote from Genesis
1:27. In this context, "male and female" stands in for (monogamous) marriage. Jesus
himself quotes Genesis 1:27 and even tethers it to Genesis 2:24 (the famous "leave and
cleave" marriage passage) in Matthew 19—a context that's all about marriage. Plus, the
specific construction Paul uses, "male *and* female," treats the two words as a collective unit,
a structure different from the other two contrasting pairs Paul mentions in the same verse:
"*neither* Jew *nor* Gentile, *neither* slave *nor* free."

It's quite possible, then, that Paul's short reference to "male and female" is not intended
to throw shade on Genesis 1:27, nor to do away with sex differences altogether. Rather,
Paul might be saying that *women don't need to get married to be valuable in the kingdom.*
This would make sense if Genesis 1:27 was understood in Paul's day as a statement about
marriage, and it also fits in perfectly with what Paul is arguing for in Galatians 3. He's
leveling the playing field of people considered to be socially unequal—slaves and free, Jews
and Gentiles, male and female. In Paul's day, women were often considered to be valuable
as long as they were married and had lots of children. Infertile women, especially widows or
divorced women, were considered less valuable. But not in God's kingdom! Paul challenged
such social hierarchical structures. "For you are all"—married or unmarried, fertile or
infertile—"one in Christ" (Gal. 3:28).

I wouldn't take a bullet for this interpretation. It assumes that Paul has this wider
cultural understanding of Genesis 1:27 in mind, which is precisely that—an assumption. But
it is an informed assumption, one that makes sense of both Paul's culture and his argument
in Galatians 3. From my vantage point, the other interpretive options (for example, that
sex differences will be done away with in the new creation) are far less compelling than this
one in light of Paul's argument in Galatians. Plus, several scholars both liberal and more
conservative see this reading as the best way to understand what Paul is saying. For instance,
Ben Witherington, "Rite and Rights for Women—Galatians 3:28," *New Testament Studies*
27, no. 5 (1981): 595–96; Elisabeth Schüssler Fiorenza, *In Memory of Her: A Feminist
Theological Reconstruction of Christian Origins* (New York: Crossroad, 1983), 211; Judith M.
Gundry-Volf, "Male and Female in Creation and New Creation: Interpretations of Galatians
3:28c in 1 Corinthians 7," in *To Tell the Mystery: Essays on New Testament Eschatology*,
ed. Thomas E. Schmidt and Moises Silva, *Journal for the Study of the New Testament* 100

(Sheffield: JSOT, 1994). Also, my friend Bruce Hansen spends a portion of his PhD dissertation unpacking Galatians 3:28 and comes to the same conclusion; see his "'All of You Are One': The Social Vision of Gal 3:28, 1 Cor 12:13, and Col 3:11," (PhD diss. University of St. Andrews, 2007).

26. "The Laws of Science and the Laws of Ethics," in *The Theory of Relativity, and Other Essays* (New York: Philosophical Library, 1950), 75–77. Confusing the "is" of science with the "ought" of ethics is known as the Naturalistic Fallacy.

27. Martti Nissinen, *Homoeroticism in the Biblical World: A Historical Perspective* (Minneapolis: Fortress, 1998), 30.

28. Nissinen, *Homoeroticism*, 30.

29. "Because of their emasculation they would never return to the past but had to live the rest of their lives in a permanently changed social and gender role" (Nissinen, *Homoeroticism*, 32).

30. *Metamorphoses* 9.669–797. Ovid's story, of course, is a fictional tale. But ancient fiction often mirrored, and was drawn from, real-life experiences (see Kyle Harper, *From Shame to Sin: The Christian Transformation of Sexual Morality in Late Antiquity* [Cambridge, MA: Harvard University Press, 2013], 10, 16, 193, 236).

31. Ovid, *Metamorphoses* 9.791–92.

32. Cassius Dio, *Roman History* 80.13.1–17.1; cf. Aelius Lampridius, *SHA Elagabalus* 8.6–7, 10.5–7, 11.7—12.2.

33. For other comments about cross-gender behavior, see for example Martial, *Epigram* 7.67, though it's difficult to know whether writers and poets like Martial thought that all lesbians simply wanted to be men.

34. Sabia-Tanis, *Trans-Gender*, 78–79.

CHAPTER 7: WHAT ABOUT INTERSEX?

1. You can watch the dialogue on YouTube: "Homosexuality 'Debate': Justin Lee and Preston Sprinkle Dialogue," posted by GeekyJustin, July 8, 2019, https://youtu.be/SHs2SHdSz_Q.

2. The most pressing question surrounding intersex discussions has to do with whether doctors should surgically align a baby's body with typical male or female anatomy in cases where there's a severe intersex condition. If a child's health is at risk, surgery should certainly be performed. But what if a child's intersex condition doesn't affect their health? Should doctors still surgically align the child's body without their consent? Is a parent's consent enough? Or should everyone wait until the child is old enough to decide whether they want (or don't want) a cosmetic surgery? Intersex activists argue for the latter, and I think they're right. These questions are outside the purview of this book, so we won't have space to consider them at length, but they are highly important to many intersex people.

3. If you want to hear some of these conversations, you can listen to episodes 743 and 760 of my podcast *Theology in the Raw* (www.prestonsprinkle.com/podcast).

4. Megan K. DeFranza, "Good News for Gender Minorities," in *Understanding Transgender Identities: Four Views*, ed. James K. Beilby and Paul Rhodes Eddy (Grand Rapids, MI: Baker, 2019), 150.

5. Linda Tatro Herzer, *The Bible and the Transgender Experience: How Scripture Supports Gender Variance* (Cleveland, OH: The Pilgrim Press, 2016), 56–57.

6. The "since intersex, therefore transgender" argument can be seen throughout Austen Hartke, *Transforming: The Bible and the Lives of Transgender Christians* (Louisville, KY: Westminster John Knox, 2018); Tara Soughers, *Beyond a Binary God: A Theology for Trans* Allies* (New York: Church Publishing, 2018); Cheryl Evans, *What Does God Think: Transgender People and the Bible* (Cheryl Evans, 2017); several essays in Christina Beardsley and Michelle O'Brien, eds., *This Is My Body: Hearing the Theology of Transgender Christians* (London: Darton, Longman and Todd, 2016); Herzer, *Bible and the Transgender Experience*; Justin Sabia-Tanis, "Holy Creation, Wholly Creative," in *Understanding Transgender Identities: Four Views*, ed. James K. Beilby and Paul Rhodes Eddy (Grand Rapids: Baker, 2019), 195–222.

7. "An Open Letter to Prof. Alice Roberts on the Subject of DSDs and Kindness," @ *MRKHVoice – The Blog of Claire Graham*, September 12, 2019, https://mrkhvoice.com /index.php/2019/09/12/an-open-letter-to-prof-alice-roberts-on-the-subject-of-dsds-and -kindness. Graham goes on to point out that "every single intersex org has been clear that intersex is nothing to do with gender nor identity," listing as examples statements from Intersex Human Rights Australia, Accord Alliance, the Intersex Society of North America, and DSD (Differences of Sex Development) Families ("Further Down the Rabbit Hole with Alice, Another Open Letter," *@MRKHVoice – The Blog of Claire Graham*, September 15, 2019, https://mrkhvoice.com/index.php/2019/09/15/further-down-the-rabbit-hole-with-alice -another-open-letter/).

8. See "What Is Intersex?" Intersex Society of North America, www.isna.org/faq/what _is_intersex.

9. For the 1.7 percent statistic, see Anne Fausto-Sterling, *Sexing the Body: Gender Politics and the Construction of Sexuality* (New York: Basic Books, 2000). This 1.7 percent statistic has been repeated in many news outlets, including *USA Today* (Susan Miller and Mary Bowerman, "What Does It Mean to Be Intersex?" *USA Today*, January 23, 2017, www .usatoday.com/story/news/nation-now/2017/01/23/what-does-mean-intersex/96939238/) and the *Washington Post* (Nora Caplan-Bricker, "Their Time," *Washington Post*, October 5, 2017, www.washingtonpost.com/sf/style/2017/10/05/the-intersex-rights-movement-is-ready- for-its-moment/). The 0.022 percent statistic comes from a consensus statement constructed by a team of almost fifty specialists who concluded that about 0.022 percent (1 in every 4,500) of all live births are intersex; see Ieuan A. Hughes et al., "Consensus Statement on Management of Intersex Disorders," *Pediatrics* 118, no. 2 (2006): 488–500.

10. See the critique by Leonard Sax, "How Common Is Intersex?" *Journal of Sex Research* 39, vol. 3 (2002): 174–8.

11. For the breakdown of how common each condition is and for a description of each, see Sax, "How Common Is Intersex?," and Fausto-Sterling, *Sexing*. See also the Intersex Society of North America's website (www.isna.org) for more information. Even though the ISNA closed down in 2008 (and the website hasn't been updated since then), it still remains a good source for understanding intersex conditions.

12. Characteristics: Two or more X chromosomes in males (for instance, XXY or XXXY), small and sometimes poorly functioning testicles, less body hair, and possible breast growth. Infertility is also a common symptom.

13. Characteristics: Females are missing an X chromosome; they are typically infertile and are at higher risk for heart disease and diabetes.

14. Characteristics: The vagina doesn't fully develop, and the uterus may develop only partially or not at all.

15. Sax, "How Common Is Intersex?"

16. Gynecomastia actually occurs in around 70 percent of all adolescent males (not only those with Klinefelter's), though it typically goes away within two years without treatment.

17. It's rare for someone with XXY chromosomes to have a female phenotype, but some cases have been documented; see E. Saavedra-Castillo, "47,XXXY Female with Testicular Feminization and Positive SRY: A Case Report," *Journal of Reproductive Medicine* 50, no. 2 (2005): 138–40.

18. Sax, "How Common is Intersex?"

19. Graham, "Open Letter."

20. Emi Koyama, "From 'Intersex' to 'DSD': Toward a Queer Disability Politics of Gender," *Intersex Initiative*, February 2006, www.intersexinitiative.org/articles/intersextodsd.html.

21. Characteristics: A defect in an enzyme leads to an excessive production of androgens in genetic (XX) females, which produces either male genitalia or genitalia that appear somewhere in between male and female.

22. Characteristics: Similar to CAIS, PAIS typically causes some atypical features in the sexual anatomy of genetic males (XY). Some people with PAIS exhibit underdeveloped male and female sexual anatomy, while in less severe cases they may have male anatomy with a very small penis and be infertile.

23. Characteristics: As the name suggests, people with ovotestes are born with both ovarian and testicular tissue.

24. For what it's worth, even some scholars and medical professionals who don't believe in the fall use language to describe intersex conditions that suggests something went wrong in fetal development. Hilary Lips, a world-renowned expert in theories surrounding sex and

gender, describes CAH as a "genetically transmitted syndrome" that "causes the adrenal glands of the fetus to *malfunction*, resulting in a release of *excess androgens* from the prenatal period onward" (*Sex and Gender: An Introduction*, 6th ed. [Long Grove, IL: Waveland, 2008], 192). Lips describes AIS as "a genetically transmitted *disorder* that makes their cells *partially or completely unable to respond* to their high prenatal levels of androgens" (*Sex and Gender*, 196). Suzanne Kessler believes that the existence of intersex persons challenges the male/female sex binary, and she describes CAH as an "*inherited enzyme deficiency condition*, causing a *malfunction* of the fetus's adrenal gland, which results in the *overproduction* of fetal androgen" (*Lessons from the Intersexed* [New Brunswick, NJ: Rutgers University Press, 1998], 165–66; cited in Megan DeFranza, *Sex Difference in Christian Theology: Male, Female, and Intersex in the Image of God* [Grand Rapids, MI: Eerdmans, 2015], 30). And Christian theologian Megan DeFranza, who also believes that male and female aren't the only two sexes, says that "people with AIS are *unable to process* male hormones" and "their cells *lack the proper receptors*" (*Sex Difference*, 25). (Emphasis added to all quotes in this note.)

25. Kelby Carlson quoted in Anna Sutherland, "The Theology of Disability," *First Things*, January 24, 2013, www.firstthings.com/blogs/firstthoughts/2013/01/the-theology -of-disability.

CHAPTER 8: MALE BRAIN IN A FEMALE BODY

1. "How Male/Female Is Your Brain?" Brainfall.com, https://brainfall.com/quizzes/how -malefemale-is-your-brain/.

2. Quoted in Alyssa Litoff and Lauren Effrom, "Chaz Bono's 'Transition': Bono Talks About Gender Reassignment Surgery and What It's Done for His Sex Life," ABC News, May 9, 2011, https://abcnews.go.com/Entertainment/chaz-bonos-transition-sonny-chers-child-man -sex/story?id=13561466.

3. Based on this idea, legal scholar Blaise Vanderhorst has argued that "'neurological sex,' expressed as gender identity" should serve as "the sole criterion for legal sex" (Blaise Vanderhorst, "Whither Lies the Self: Intersex and Transgender Individuals and a Proposal for Brain-Based Legal Sex," *Harvard Law and Policy Review* 9 [2015]: 274).

4. Some of the commonly cited differences are the volume and density of gray/white matter and certain neurochemical differences; L. S. Allen et al., "Two Sexually Dimorphic Cell Groups in the Human Brain," *Journal of Neuroscience* 9, no. 2 (1989): 497–506; Akira Matsumoto, ed., *Sexual Differentiation of the Brain* (New York: CRC, 1999).

5. Milton Diamond, "Transsexualism as an Intersex Condition," in *Transsexuality in Theology and Neuroscience: Findings, Controversies, and Perspectives*, ed. Gerhard Schreiber (Boston: de Gruyter, 2016), 43–53. Other potential mechanisms being explored include genetic and epigenetic pathways. See Thomas E. Bevan, *The Psychobiology of Transsexualism and Transgenderism: A New View Based on Scientific Evidence* (Santa Barbara, CA: Praeger, 2014), chs. 5–7.

6. For example, some researchers have found that transmen have about the same number of neurons in a part of the hypothalamus (the BSTc) as non-trans* males in the control group, while transwomen have a number similar to the non-trans* females in the control group; J. N. Zhou et al., "A Sex Difference in the Human Brain and Its Relation to Transsexuality," *Nature* 378 (1995): 68–70; F. P. M. Kruijver et al., "Male-to-Female Transsexuals Have Female Neuron Numbers in a Limbic Nucleus," *Journal of Clinical Endocrinology and Metabolism* 85, no. 5 (2000): 2034–41. For a broader review of this type of claim, see E. S. Smith et al., "The Transsexual Brain—A Review of Findings on the Neural Basis of Transsexualism," *Neuroscience and Biobehavioral Reviews* 59 (2015): 251–66.

7. George J. Romanes, "Mental Differences between Men and Women," *Education Papers: Women's Quest for Equality in Britain, 1850–1912*, ed. D. Spender (London and New York: Routledge and Kegan Paul, 1887/1987); cited in Cordelia Fine, *Delusions of Gender: How Our Minds, Society, and Neurosexism Create Difference* (London: W. W. Norton, 2010), 140.

8. See Fine, *Delusions of Gender*, 141.

9. Fine, *Delusions of Gender*, 130.

10. In the last fifty years, more than 50,000 papers have been published on sex differences in psychology (Daphna Joel, "TEDxJaffa—Daphna Joel—Are Brains Male or Female?" YouTube, posted by TEDx Talks, October 8, 2012, www.youtube.com/watch?v=rYpDU040yzc). Needless to say, our discussion in this chapter won't be able to survey all the data.

11. For instance, see Fine, *Delusions of Gender*; Rebecca Jordan-Young, *Brain Storm: The Flaws in the Science of Sex Differences* (Cambridge, MA: Harvard University Press, 2010); Anne Fausto-Sterling, *Sexing the Body: Gender Politics and the Construction of Sexuality* (New York: Basic, 2000), ch. 5; Gina Rippon, *The Gendered Brain: The New Neuroscience that Shatters the Myth of the Female Brain* (London: The Bodley Head, 2019).

12. On neuroplasticity, see also Moheb Costandi, *Neuroplasticity* (Cambridge, MA: MIT Press, 2016).

13. See Cordelia Fine et al., "Plasticity, Plasticity, Plasticity ... and the Rigid Problem of Sex," *Trends in Cognitive Science* 17, no. 11 (2013): 550–51; Tomáš Paus, "How Environment and Genes Shape the Adolescent Brain," *Hormones and Behavior* 64, no. 2 (2013): 195–202.

14. Fine, *Delusions of Gender*, 236.

15. Zhou et al., "Sex Difference," 68–70.

16. The authors recognize that neuroplasticity wasn't accounted for in their study, but not everyone who cites the study realizes this limitation; some cite the study as if it were more definitive than it really is.

17. See Jordan-Young, *Brain Storm*, 104–106; Anne Lawrence, "A Critique of the Brain-Sex Theory of Transsexualism," *Transsexual Women's Resources* (2007). A recent study by

neurologist Stephen Gliske concludes that "anatomic incongruence (i.e., having a size/shape more like the opposite gender) in limited [brain] regions is typical in individuals without gender dysphoria and is not likely to be sufficient to cause gender dysphoria" (Stephen V. Gliske, "A New Theory of Gender Dysphoria Incorporating the Distress, Social Behavioral, and Body-Ownership Networks," *eNeuro* 6, no. 6 [2019]).

18. Studies by a Spanish research team alleviated at least one of these methodological problems by comparing brain structures (for example, white matter volume) of trans* persons *prior to cross-sex hormone therapy* (CHT) with male and female controls. See Giuseppina Rametti et al., "White Matter Microstructure in Female to Male Transsexuals Before Cross-Sex Hormonal Treatment: A Diffusion Tensor Imaging Study," *Journal of Psychiatric Research* 45, no. 2 (2011): 199–204; Giuseppina Rametti et al., "The Microstructure of White Matter in Male to Female Transsexuals before Cross-Sex Hormonal Treatment. A DTI Study," *Journal of Psychiatric Research* 45, no. 7 (2011): 949–54.

19. For example, F. P. Kruijver et al., "Male-to-Female Transsexuals Have Female Neuron Numbers in a Limbic Nucleus," *Journal of Clinical Endocrinology and Metabolism* 85, no. 5 (2000): 2034–41; Dick F. Swaab, "Sexual Differentiation of the Human Brain: Relevance for Gender Identity, Transsexualism, and Sexual Orientation," *Gynecological Endocrinology* 19, no. 6 (2004): 301–12; Simon Lajos et al., "Regional Grey Matter Structure Differences between Transsexuals and Healthy Controls—A Voxel Based Morphometry Study," *PLoS One* 8, no. 12 (2013); Elke Stefanie Smith et al., "The Transsexual Brain—A Review of Findings on the Neural Basis of Transsexualism," *Neuroscience and Biobehavioral Reviews* 59 (2015), 251–66; B. P. C. Kreukels and A. Guillamon, "Neuroimaging Studies in People with Gender Incongruence," *International Review of Psychiatry* 28, no. 1 (2016): 120–28; A. Guillamon, C. Junque, and E. Gómez-Gil, "A Review of the Status of Brain Structure Research in Transsexualism," *Archives of Sexual Behavior* 45, no. 7 (2016): 1615–48.

20. Emiliano Santarnecchi et al., "Intrinsic Cerebral Connectivity Analysis in an Untreated Female-to-Male Transsexual Subject: A First Attempt Using Resting-State fMRI," *Neuroendocrinology* 96, no. 3 (2012): 188–93; Ivanka Savic and Stefan Arver, "Sex Dimorphism of the Brain in Male-to-Female Transsexuals," *Cerebral Cortex* 21, no. 11 (2011): 2525–33.

21. G. S. Kranz et al., "White Matter Microstructure in Transsexuals and Controls Investigated by Diffusion Tensor Imaging," *Journal of Neuroscience* 34, no. 46 (2014): 15466–75; B. Clemens et al., "Male-to-Female Gender Dysphoria: Gender-specific Differences in Resting-state Networks," *Brain and Behavior* 7, no. 5 (2017). Incidentally, although much has been made of comparisons of the hypothalamus (BSTc), critics have pointed out that this part of the brain doesn't become sexually dimorphic until adulthood, which means it isn't able to explain the trans* experience of children; see, for example, W. C. J. Chung, G. J. De Vries, and D. F. Swaab, "Sexual Differentiation of the Bed Nucleus of the Stria Terminalis in Humans May Extend into Adulthood," *Journal of Neuroscience* 22, no. 3 (2002): 1027–33.

22. Most studies supporting the claim that trans* people's brains are like those of the gender they identify with are based on comparisons of the volume and size of various brain structures. But as we've seen, research has increasingly shown that experiences and behaviors can change the size and volume of brain structures. As one research team puts it, "Our findings provide supportive evidence that socio-cultural experiences of learned independent-interdependent orientations may play a role in regional brain volumes" (C. M. Huang et al., "Culture-Related and Individual Differences in Regional Brain Volumes: A Cross-Cultural Voxel-Based Morphometry Study," *Frontiers in Human Neuroscience* [September 10, 2019]). In addition, epigenetic studies have shown that such things as "[e]arly stress events severely impact brain and behavior" (Raúl Ventura-Junca and Luisa M. Herrera, "Epigenetic Alterations Related to Early-Life Stressful Events," *Acta Neuropsychiatrica* 24, no. 5 [2012]: 255–65). Some studies are beginning to apply these insights to the issue of gender dysphoria. See, for example, Mohammad Reza Mohammadi and Ali Khaleghi, "Transsexualism: A Different Viewpoint to Brain Changes," *Clinical Psychopharmacology Neuroscience* 16, no. 2 (2018): 136–43.

23. To put it in scientific terms: "[P]renatal androgenization of 46,XX fetuses leads to marked masculinization of later gender-related behavior but does not lead to gender confusion/dysphoria" (Louis Gooren, "The Biology of Human Psychosexual Differentiation," *Hormones and Behavior* 50, no. 4 [2006]: 589). See also Bevan, *Psychobiology*, 111–15; Paul Rhodes Eddy, "Understanding Transgender Experiences and Identities: An Introduction," in *Understanding Transgender Identities: Four Views*, ed. James K. Beilby and Paul Rhodes Eddy (Grand Rapids, MI: Baker, 2019), 30–31.

24. Sheri A. Berenbaum, "Beyond Pink and Blue: The Complexity of Early Androgen Effects on Gender Development," *Child Development Perspectives* 12, no. 1 (2018): 58. See also Sheri A. Berenbaum et al., "Gendered Peer Involvement in Girls with Congenital Adrenal Hyperplasia: Effects of Prenatal Androgens, Gendered Activities, and Gender Cognitions," *Archives of Sexual Behavior* 47, no. 4 (2018): 915–29.

25. Cited in Fine, *Delusions of Gender*, 139.

26. See the list and review of studies in Fine, *Delusions of Gender*, 137–40.

27. Susan Pinker, *The Sexual Paradox: Men, Women and the Real Gender Gap* (New York: Scribner, 2009), 116, emphasis added.

28. For example, Anne Fausto-Sterling, *Sexing the Body*, 115–45; K. M. Bishop and D. Wahlsten, "Sex Differences in the Human Corpus Callosum: Myth or Reality?" *Neuroscience and Biobehavioral Reviews* 21, no. 5 (1997): 581–601; Fine, *Delusions of Gender*, 138, 156–57.

29. Leonard Sax, *Why Gender Matters: What Parents and Teachers Need to Know about the Emerging Science of Sex Differences*, 2nd ed. (New York: Harmony, 2017), 122.

30. Letitia Anne Peplau, "Human Sexuality: How Do Men and Women Differ?" *Current Directions in Psychological Science* 12, no. 2 (2003): 37–44; cited in Sax, *Why Gender Matters*, 123.

31. Fine, *Delusions of Gender*, 159, summarizing the study by Erin McClure, "A Meta-Analytic Review of Sex Differences in Facial Expression Processing and Their Development in Infants, Children, and Adolescents," *Psychological Bulletin* 126, no. 3 (2000): 424–53.

32. Stuart Ritchie et al., "Sex Differences in the Adult Human Brain: Evidence from 5216 UK Biobank Participants," *BioRxiv,*, April 4, 2017, 1–19, www.biorxiv.org/content/10.1101/123729v1.full.pdf.

33. Ritchie et al., "Sex Differences," 2.

34. Ritchie et al., "Sex Differences," 8.

35. Ritchie et al., "Sex Differences, 9."

36. Ritchie et al., "Sex Differences," 8. Other studies come to similar conclusions; see D. Marwha, M. Halari, and L. Eliot, "Meta-Analysis Reveals a Lack of Sexual Dimorphism in Human Amygdala Volume," *NeuroImage* 147 (2017): 282–94; A. Tan et al., "The Human Hippocampus is Not Sexually-Dimorphic: Meta-Analysis of Structural MRI Volumes," *NeuroImage* 124 (2016): 350–66; Daphna Joel et al., "Sex Beyond the Genitalia: The Human Brain Mosaic," *Proceedings of the National Academy of Sciences* 112, no. 50 (2015): 15468–73. In the words of cognitive neuroscientist Lutz Jäncke, most "sex/gender differences are not large enough to support the assumption of sexual dimorphism in terms of brain anatomy, brain function, cognition, and behavior. Instead, I suggest that many brain and cognitive features are modulated by environment, culture, and practice (and several other influences)" ("Sex/Gender Differences in Cognition, Neurophysiology, and Neuroanatomy," *F1000 Research* 7 [2018]).

37. Milton Diamond, "Transsexualism as an Intersex Condition," in *Transsexualität in Theologie und Neurowissenschaften: Ergebnisse, Kontroversen, Perspektiven,* ed. Gerhard Schreiber (Berlin and Boston: De Gruyter, 2016), www.hawaii.edu/PCSS/biblio/articles/2015to2019/2016-transsexualism.html. The dichotomy between something being hardwired in the brain and being a "social choice" seems like a false one to me. I didn't make a "social choice" to speak English, yet my brain isn't hardwired to speak English instead of French. I think we could theoretically affirm that a person doesn't choose to experience gender incongruence—and that such incongruence is biologically shaped—without believing that they have a cross-sex or intersex brain. What Diamond does, unfortunately, is interpret generalities as absolutes. If a brain or behavior is more typically feminine, he classifies it as a female brain. Milton was also fascinated that biological males who identified as female responded like typical females during the "viewing of erotic film clips." Maybe this was because they were biological males with female brains. Another explanation could be that they were gay.

38. Diamond, "Transsexualism."

39. From her TEDx talk "TEDxJaffa—Daphna Joel—Are Brains Male or Female?" YouTube, posted by TEDx Talks, October 8, 2012, www.youtube.com/watch?v=rYpDU040yzc.

40. Ginger A. Hoffman and Robyn Bluhm, "Neurosexism and Neurofeminism," *Philosophy Compass* 11 (2016): 716–29. See also Sigrid Schmitz and Grit Höppner, "Neurofeminism and Feminist Neurosciences: A Critical Review of Contemporary Brain Research," *Frontiers in Human Neuroscience* 8 (2014).

CHAPTER 9: FEMALE SOUL IN A MALE BODY

1. For various narratives along these lines, see LeeRay Costa and Andrew Matzner, *Male Bodies, Women's Souls: Personal Narratives of Thailand's Transgendered Youth* (Binghamton, NY: Haworth Press, 2007).

2. Diane Ehrensaft, "From Gender Identity Disorder to Gender Identity Creativity: True Gender Self Child Therapy," in *Treating Transgender Children and Adolescents: An Interdisciplinary Discussion*, ed. Jack Drescher and William Byne (New York: Routledge, 2013), 43–62 (see especially 46–49).

3. Laura Edwards-Leeper and Norman P. Spack, "Psychological Evaluation and Medical Treatment of Transgender Youth in an Interdisciplinary 'Gender Management Service' (GeMS) in a Major Pediatric Center," in *Treating Transgender Children and Adolescents*, ed. Drescher and Byne, 28. Sahar Sadjadi, a physician and anthropologist of medicine, critiques this secular use of soul language to describe the inner essence of trans* children: "I was perplexed by this merging of science, magic, and religion in explaining children's gender transition" ("Deep in the Brain: Identity and Authenticity in Pediatric Gender Transition," *Cultural Anthropology* 34, no. 1 [2019]: 104). See also Enrico Facco et al., who point out that "even materialist monists keep a latent dualism, in that they accept the dualistic ontologic separation of between brain and mind, while simply disregarding the latter a priori or equating it to its physical aspects" ("In Search of the True Self," *Journal of Theoretical and Philosophical Psychology* 39, no. 3 [2019]: 160).

4. Marc Cortez, *Theological Anthropology: A Guide for the Perplexed* (New York: Continuum, 2010), 5.

5. This view became prominent in biblical scholarship in the mid-twentieth century through the work of Rudolph Bultmann, who famously said, "Man does not *have* a body; he *is* body." Many other scholars have argued for some kind of non-reductive physicalism since Bultmann, including J. A. T. Robinson, F. F. Bruce, Brevard Childs, K. G. Kümmel, Anthony Hoekema, and Joel Green. Green boldly observes, "[A] constellation of issues and concerns has coalesced in biblical studies over the last century with the result that theories of body-soul dualism are today difficult to ground in the Bible" (*Body, Soul, and Human Life: The Nature of Humanity in the Bible* [Grand Rapids, MI: Baker, 2008], 22). One of the issues Green refers to is the development of neuroscience in recent years.

6. Cortez, *Theological Anthropology*, 73. Some recent proponents of this view (or a version of it) include Scott Rae, J. P. Moreland, John Cooper, and William Hasker.

7. Cortez, *Theological Anthropology*, 70.

8. As always, there are exceptions. See, for example, Gary Long, "'Yankee Go Home!': The Cognitive Sciences and Implications for Western-Influenced Thinking and the Mind-Brain-Soul Problem," *Asian Journal of Pentecostal Studies* 13, no. 2 (2010): 180–202.

9. Cortez, *Theological Anthropology*, 70.

10. Trans* writer Christina Beardsley says that those who pursue sex reassignment surgery are not on a quest toward "a Gnostic rejection of the body, or a denial of its importance, but a quest for fuller embodiment" ("Taking Issue: The Transsexual Hiatus in 'Some Issues in Human Sexuality,'" in *This Is My Body: Hearing the Theology of Transgender Christians*, ed. Christina Beardsley and Michelle O'Brien [London: Darton, Longman and Todd, 2016], 75). I'm not sure if this completely alleviates the Gnostic allegations, since "a quest for fuller embodiment" through surgery is, in a sense, a rejection of the body a person was born with. However, some surgical interventions (as, for example, cochlear implants) are not usually regarded as a rejection of the body. The point is, we need more conversations that truly seek to understand what someone else actually believes and fewer labels tossed around that oversimplify complex issues.

11. See, for example, Janet Mock, "Trans in the Media: Unlearning the 'Trapped' Narrative and Taking Ownership of Our Bodies," JanetMock.com, July 9, 2012, https://janetmock.com/2012/07/09/josie-romero-dateline-transgender-trapped-body/.

12. See, for example, Beardsley and O'Brien, "Taking Issue," 75.

13. Cortez, *Theological Anthropology*, 72.

14. Cortez, *Theological Anthropology*, 73.

15. Cortez, *Theological Anthropology*, 73.

16. See especially John Cooper, *Body, Soul, and Life Everlasting: Biblical Anthropology and the Monism-Dualism Debate*, 2nd ed. (Grand Rapids, MI: Eerdmans, 2000). Non-reductive physicalists respond to this argument in various ways. Some will deny that there is an intermediate state where people exist in disembodiment. Others say that if there is a disembodied intermediate state, it's the exception to the rule, not the norm. Our earthly life is embodied. Our resurrection life will be embodied. These bookends of our existence should be the primary lenses through which we understand human nature in the here and now.

17. Theologian Terrance Tiessen has explored an argument along these lines in a thoughtful blog post: "A Female Soul in a Male Body? A Theological Proposal," *Thoughts Theological*, June 20, 2015, www.thoughtstheological.com/a-female-soul-in-a-male-body-a-theological-proposal/.

18. Paul R. McHugh and Lawrence S. Mayer, "Sexuality and Gender: Findings from the Biological, Psychological, and Social Sciences," *New Atlantis* 50 (2016): 90.

19. Green, *Body, Soul, and Human Life*, 54.

20. Green, *Body, Soul, and Human Life*, 54.

21. "Nephesh," in Gerhard Kittel and Gerhard Friedrich, eds., *Theological Dictionary of the New Testament* (Grand Rapids, MI: Eerdmans, 1971), 9:620; cited in Anthony Hoekema, *Created in God's Image* (Grand Rapids, MI: Eerdmans, 1986), 210.

22. Hoekema, *Created in God's Image*, 211.

23. Hoekema, *Created in God's Image*, 213.

24. "Then fear came over every *soul (psyche)*" (Acts 2:43 NKJV); "Every *soul (psyche)* who does not listen to that prophet shall be destroyed from the people" (Acts 3:23 ESV); see also Romans 2:9; 13:1. Along with referring to the whole person, *psyche* (like *nephesh*) can be used to refer to many different aspects of human nature, such as the "life" of a person (Rom. 11:3; Phil. 2:30; 1 Thess. 2:8) or our "emotions" (Mark 14:34; Luke 2:35; used of God's emotions in Matt. 12:18). On at least one occasion, *psyche* refers to an aspect of embodied life that might survive death, as in Matthew 10:28: "Do not fear those who kill the body but cannot kill the soul. Rather fear him who can destroy both soul and body in hell." This statement borders on a more Platonic understanding of the soul as the part of "you" that survives death but won't survive in hell. (And all the annihilationists said, "Amen!") It would be odd, I think, for Jesus to side with Plato rather than with his own Hebrew Scriptures. So perhaps the phrase isn't as Platonic as it may seem—pitting the soul, as the superior immaterial part of you, up against the body. It's quite possible, perhaps even likely, that *psyche* here simply refers to a person's true life as opposed to their earthly life only, as it does in other passages (Mark 10:45; Acts 20:10). R. T. France understands *psyche* in this passage in the sense of "true life" (*The Gospel of Matthew, The New International Commentary of the New Testament* [Grand Rapids, MI: Eerdmans, 2007], 403). But even if you think Matthew 10:28 is a slam dunk in favor of Soft Dualism, you'd still have to acknowledge (because it's a plain fact) that Greek and Hebrew terms for "soul" are polysemous and often refer to material aspects of human nature.

25. Green, *Body, Soul, and Human Life*, 57.

26. George Eldon Ladd, *A Theology of the New Testament* (Grand Rapids, MI: Eerdmans, 1993), 457; cited in Hoekema, *Created in God's Image*, 210.

27. Cortez, *Theological Anthropology*, 70.

28. Fraser Watts, "Transsexualism and the Church," *Theology and Sexuality* 9, no. 1 (2002): 63–85 (80).

INTERLUDE

1. "The Dwelling," *Biola University*, updated August 29, 2018, https://studenthub.biola.edu/the-dwelling.

CHAPTER 10: RAPID-ONSET GENDER DYSPHORIA

1. Helena retells her story in an interview on YouTube: "Teen Transition and Social Media | with Helena," YouTube, posted by Benjamin A. Boyce, February 28, 2019, https://youtu.be /tJ-dEQunjMA. All quotes from Helena are taken from this interview unless otherwise noted.

2. Helena documents this in two lengthy Twitter threads under her username @lacroicsz (https://twitter.com/lacroicsz) on May 9, 2019, and July 16, 2019.

3. Twitter thread posted by @lacroicsz, February 17, 2019, at 1:09 p.m., https://twitter.com /lacroicsz/status/1097196342768816128.

4. See Lisa Marchiano, "Outbreak: On Transgender Teens and Psychic Epidemics," *Psychological Perspectives* 60, no. 3 (2017): 345–66.

5. See Nastasja M. de Graaf et al., "Sex Ratio in Children and Adolescents Referred to the Gender Identity Development Service in the UK (2009–2016)," *Archives of Sexual Behavior* 47, no. 5 (2018): 1301–4; Ken Zucker, "Adolescents with Gender Dysphoria: Reflections on Some Contemporary Clinical and Research Issues," *Archives of Sexual Behavior* 48, no. 5 (2019): 1983–92; "Referrals to GIDS, 2015–16 to 2019–20," Gender Identity Development Service, www.gids.nhs.uk/number-referrals. For a lengthy discussion, see "Why Are So Many Females Coming Out as Trans/Non-Binary?" Gender Health Query, www.genderhq.org /increase-trans-females-nonbinary-dysphoria.

6. Madison Aitken et al., "Evidence for an Altered Sex Ratio in Clinic-Referred Adolescents with Gender Dysphoria," *Journal of Sexual Medicine* 12, no. 3 (2015): 756–63.

7. de Graaf et al., "Sex Ratio."

8. Aitken et al., "Evidence for an Altered Sex Ratio."

9. John W. Delahunt et al., "Increasing Rates of People Identifying as Transgender Presenting to Endocrine Services in the Wellington Region," *New Zealand Medical Journal* 131, no. 1468 (2018): 33–42.

10. Aitken et al., "Evidence for an Altered Sex Ratio"; L. N. Chiniara, H. J. Bonifacio, and M. R. Palmert, "Characteristics of Adolescents Referred to a Gender Clinic: Are Youth Seen Now Different than Those in Initial Reports?" *Hormone Research in Paediatrics* 89, no. 6 (2018): 434–41.

11. With regard to the wider United States, the estimates of two recent studies taken together suggest that between 0.7 percent and 3.2 percent of young people now identify as "transgender," which is higher—perhaps much higher—than the 0.6 percent of US adults who identify as transgender; see J. L. Herman et al., *Age of Individuals Who Identify as Transgender in the United States* (Los Angeles: Williams Institute, 2017), 2; B. D. M. Wilson and A. Kastanis, "Sexual and Gender Minority Disproportionality and Disparities in Child Welfare: A Population-Based Study," *Children and Youth Services Review* 58 (2015): 12. See also "The Rapidly Growing Medicalization of Children and Young People," Kelsey Coalition, December 17, 2019, www.kelseycoalition.org/facts. The adolescent trans* sex ratio

favoring biological females over biological males now appears to be a broad, cross-cultural phenomenon. In the most thorough analysis of this phenomenon to date, Ken Zucker and Madison Aitken perform a meta-analysis of data drawn from fifty-seven different samples, using three distinct source types: clinical referrals, representative population samples, and nonrepresentative population samples. Strikingly, they discovered that "[a]cross the three sample types (N=14,484), the male:female sex ratio (1:2.13) favored birth-assigned females in 39 of the 44 samples" (Kenneth J. Zucker and Madison Aitken, "Sex Ratio of Transgender Adolescents: A Meta-Analysis," paper presented at the meeting of the European Association for Transgender Health 3rd Biennal EPATH Conference Inside Matters. On Law, Ethics, and Religion, April 11, 2019, Rome, Italy, https://epath.eu/wp-content/uploads/2019/04/Boof-of-abstracts-EPATH2019.pdf).

12. Lisa Littman, "Parent Reports of Adolescents and Young Adults Perceived to Show Signs of a Rapid Onset of Gender Dysphoria," *PLoS One* 13, no. 8 (2018).

13. According to Littman's survey, 44 percent came out as transgender after one of their friends did, 28 percent after two of their friends did, 15 percent after three of their friends did, 4 percent after four of their friends did, and 5 percent after five of their friends did.

14. More than 60 percent of the kids Littman studied "experienced an increased popularity within their friend group when they announced a transgender identification" (Littman, "Rapid Onset," 16).

15. Sixty-four percent of parents report an increase in social media use that focused on transgender-related topics. Littman ("Rapid Onset," 19) summarizes the advice they received online: how to tell if they were transgender (54 percent); the reasons that they should transition right away (35 percent); that if their parents did not agree for them to take hormones, the parents were "abusive" and "transphobic" (34 percent); that if they waited to transition, they would regret it (29 percent); what to say and what not to say to a doctor or therapist in order to convince them to provide hormones (22 percent); that if their parents were reluctant to take them for hormones, they should use the "suicide narrative" to convince them (21 percent); that it is acceptable to lie or withhold information about their medical or psychological history from a doctor or therapist in order to get hormones/get hormones faster (18 percent).

16. Littman, "Rapid Onset," 10.

17. Littman, "Rapid Onset," 24.

18. Littman, "Rapid Onset," 26

19. Littman, "Rapid Onset," 21.

20. Littman, "Rapid Onset," 33.

21. Anna Hutchinson, Melissa Midgen, and Anastassis Spiliadis, "In Support of Research Into Rapid-Onset Gender Dysphoria," *Archives of Sexual Behavior*, July 17, 2019; Marina Bonfatto and Eva Crasnow, "Gender/ed Identities: An Overview of Our Current Work

as Child Psychotherapists in the Gender Identity Development Service," *Journal of Child Psychotherapy* 44, no. 1 (2018): 43; R. Kaltiala-Heino et al., "Gender Dysphoria in Adolescence: Current Perspectives," *Adolescent Health, Medicine and Therapeutics* 9 (2018): 31–41; Heino F. L. Meyer-Bahlburg, "Diagnosing Gender? Categorizing Gender-Identity Variants in the Anthropocene," *Archives of Sexual Behavior* 48, no. 7 (2019): 2029–30; Kenneth J. Zucker, "Adolescents with Gender Dysphoria: Reflections on Some Contemporary Clinical and Research Issues," *Archives of Sexual Behavior* 48, no. 5 (2019): 1986–87; J. Michael Bailey and Ray Blanchard, "Gender Dysphoria Is Not One Thing," 4thWaveNow, December 7, 2017, https://4thwavenow.com/2017/12/07/gender-dysphoria-is-not-one-thing/; Debra Soh, "Don't Treat All Cases of Gender Dysphoria the Same Way," *Globe and Mail*, January 24, 2018, www.theglobeandmail.com/opinion/dont-treat-all-cases-of-gender-dysphoria-the-same-way/article37711831/; Lee Jussim, "Rapid Onset Gender Dysphoria: A Saga of Outrage and Science Reform," *Psychology Today* (March 20, 2019), www.psychologytoday.com/us/blog/rabble-rouser/201903/rapid-onset-gender-dysphoria; Roberto D'Angelo and Lisa Marchiano, "Response to Julia Serano's Critique of Lisa Littman's Paper: Rapid Onset Gender Dysphoria in Adolescents and Young Adults: A Study of Parental Reports," gdworkinggroup.org (August 27, 2018), http://gdworkinggroup.org/2018/08/27/response-to-julia-seranos-critique-of-lisa-littmans-paper-rapid-onset-gender-dysphoria-in-adolescents-and-young-adults-a-study-of-parental-reports/.

22. Brynn Tannehill, "'Rapid Onset Gender Dysphoria' Is Biased Junk Science," *Advocate*, February 20, 2018, www.advocate.com/commentary/2018/2/20/rapid-onset-gender-dysphoria-biased-junk-science; Arjee Javellana Restar, "Methodological Critique of Littman's (2018) Parental-Respondents Accounts of 'Rapid-Onset Gender Dysphoria,'" *Archives of Sexual Behavior* 49, no. 1, April 2019; Julia Serano, "Rapid Onset Gender Dysphoria, Scientific Debate, and Suppressing Speech," Medium.com, August 29, 2018, https://medium.com/@juliaserano/rapid-onset-gender-dysphoria-scientific-debate-and-suppressing-speech-fd88a83bcd60. For a recent response by Littman to her critics, see Lisa Littman, "The Use of Methodologies in Littman (2018) Is Consistent with the Use of Methodologies in Other Studies Contributing to the Field of Gender Dysphoria Research: Response to Restar (2019)," *Archives of Sexual Behavior* 49, no. 3, January 2020, https://doi.org/10.1007/s10508-020-01631-z (Epublication ahead of print).

23. See, for example, Lisa Marchiano, "Outbreak," and Sasha Ayad's counseling practice Inspired Teen Therapy, which specializes in helping female teens with ROGD (https://inspiredteentherapy.com).

24. Littman, "Rapid Onset," 6.

25. See the Pique Resilience Project (www.piqueresproject.com) and the Detransition Advocacy Network (www.detransadv.com).

26. See, for example, Julia Serano, "Everything You Need to Know About Rapid Onset Gender Dysphoria," Medium.com, August 23, 2018, https://medium.com/@juliaserano/everything-you-need-to-know-about-rapid-onset-gender-dysphoria-1940b8afdeba.

27. de Graaf et al., "Sex Ratio in Children and Adolescents"; Zucker, "Adolescents with Gender Dysphoria."

28. Littman, "Rapid Onset," 31.

29. See, for instance, S. J. Paxton et al., "Friendship Clique and Peer Influences on Body Image Concerns, Dietary Restraint, Extreme Weight-Loss Behaviors, and Binge Eating in Adolescent Girls," *Journal of Abnormal Psychology* 108 (1999): 255–66; S. Allison, M. Warin, and T. Bastiampillai, "Anorexia Nervosa and Social Contagion: Clinical Implications," *Australian and New Zealand Journal of Psychology* 48 (2014): 116–20.

30. Littman, "Rapid Onset," 32.

31. Kate Lyons, "UK Doctor Prescribing Cross-Sex Hormones to Children as Young as 12," *Guardian*, July 11, 2016, www.theguardian.com/society/2016/jul/11/transgender-nhs -doctor-prescribing-sex-hormones-children-uk. Emphasis added.

32. M. Talbot, "About a Boy," *New Yorker*, March 18, 2013; Marchiano, "Outbreak," 350.

33. One of the studies most often cited in support of favorable outcomes for the adolescent use of puberty blockers and CHT is A. L. C. de Vries et al., "Young Adult Psychological Outcome after Puberty Suppression and Gender Reassignment," *Pediatrics* 134, no. 4 (2014): 696–704. See also Esther Gómez-Gill et al., "Hormone-treated Transsexuals Report Less Social Distress, Anxiety and Depression," *Psychoneuroendocrinology* 37, no. 5 (2012): 662–70; Gary Butler, Bernadette Wren, and Polly Carmichael, "Puberty Blocking in Gender Dysphoria: Suitable for All?," *Archives of Disease in Childhood* 104, no. 6 (2019): 509–10.

34. World Professional Association for Transgender Health, "Standards of Care for the Health of Transsexual, Transgender, and Gender Nonconforming People," 7th version (WPATH 2001), 33, www.wpath.org/media/cms/Documents/SOC%20v7/SOC%20V7 _English.pdf.

35. B. D. M. Wilson et al., *Characteristics and Mental Health of Gender Nonconforming Adolescents in California: Findings from the 2015–2016 California Health Survey* (Los Angeles: The Williams Institute and UCLA Center for Health Policy Research, December 13, 2017), http://healthpolicy.ucla.edu/publications/search/pages/detail.aspx?PubID=1706.

36. The Endocrine Society's most recent (2017) revision of its clinical guidelines states, "[C]linicians should persistently monitor adverse effects of [CHT].… Clinicians should avoid harming individuals (via hormone treatment) who have conditions other than gender dysphoria/gender incongruence and who may not benefit from the physical changes associated with this treatment." W. C. Hembree et al., "Endocrine Treatment of Gender-Dysphoric/Gender-Incongruent Persons: An Endocrine Society* Clinical Practice Guideline," *Journal of Clinical Endocrinology and Metabolism* 102, no. 11 (2017): 3869–903.

37. U. Boehmer et al., "Transgender Individuals' Cancer Survivorship: Results of a Cross-Sectional Study," *Cancer*, March 5, 2020, https://doi.org/10.1002/cncr.32784 (Epublication ahead of print); C. G. Streed Jr. et al., "Cardiovascular Disease Among Transgender Adults

Receiving Hormone Therapy: A Narrative Review," *Annals of Internal Medicine* 167, no. 4 (2017): 256–67; E. Moore, A. Wisniewski, and A. Dobs, "Endocrine Treatment of Transsexual People: A Review of Treatment Regimens, Outcomes, and Adverse Effects," *Journal of Endocrinology and Metabolism* 88, no. 8 (2003): 3467–73; Talal Alzahrani et al., "Cardiovascular Disease Risk Factors and Myocardial Infarction in the Transgender Population," *Circulation: Cardiovascular Quality and Outcomes* 12, no. 4 (2019); D. Getahun et al., "Cross-Sex Hormones and Acute Cardiovascular Events in Transgender Persons: A Cohort Study," *Annals of Internal Medicine* 169, no. 4 (2018): 205–13.

38. J. L. Feldman, "New Onset of Type 2 Diabetes Mellitus with Feminizing Hormone Therapy: Case Series," *International Journal of Transgenderism* 6, no. 2 (2002); J. Defreyne et al., "Is Type 1 Diabetes Mellitus More Prevalent than Expected in Transgender Persons? A Local Observation," *Sexual Medicine* 5, no. 3 (2017): e215–e218.

39. S. Bewley et al., "Safeguarding Adolescents from Premature, Permanent Medicalization," *BMJ* 364 (2019); L. Nahata et al., "Low Fertility Preservation Utilization among Transgender Youth," *Journal of Adolescent Health* 61, no. 1 (2017): 40–44; G. J. Cler et al., "Longitudinal Case Study of Transgender Voice Changes Under Testosterone Hormone Therapy," *Journal of Voice*, April 13, 2019, https://doi.org/10.1016/j.jvoice.2019.03.006 (Epublication ahead of print); M. S. Irwig, K. Childs, and A. B. Hancock, "Effects of Testosterone on the Transgender Male Voice, *Andrology* 5, no. 1 (2017): 107–12.

40. Johanna Olson-Kennedy et al., "Physiologic Response to Gender-Affirming Hormones among Transgender Youth," *Journal of Adolescent Health* 62, no. 4 (2018): 397–401. Both WPATH and the Endocrine Society recommend waiting until age sixteen for CHT and age eighteen for gender-related surgeries. But a number of gender-affirmative clinicians, including Olson-Kennedy, are pushing for even younger ages.

41. Alan Mozes, "Transgender Teens Become Happy, Healthy Young Adults," CBS News, September 10, 2014, www.cbsnews.com/news/transgender-teens-become-happy-healthy -young-adults/. See also de Vries et al., "Young Adult Psychological Outcome," 696–704; R. Costa et al., "Psychological Support, Puberty Suppression, and Psychosocial Functioning in Adolescents with Gender Dysphoria," *Journal of Sexual Medicine* 12, no. 11 (2015): 2206–14.

42. M. Biggs, "Britain's Experiment with Puberty Blockers," in *Inventing Transgender Children and Young People*, ed. Michele Moore and Heather Brunskell-Evans (Newcastle upon Tyne, UK: Cambridge Scholars, 2019), 40–55; C. Richards, J. Maxwell, and N. McCune, "Use of Puberty Blockers for Gender Dysphoria: A Momentous Step in the Dark," *Archives of Disease in Childhood* 104, no. 6 (2019): 611–12; T. Brik et al., "Trajectories of Adolescents Treated with Gonadotropin-Releasing Hormone Analogues for Gender Dysphoria," *Archives of Sexual Behavior*, March 9, 2020, https://doi.org/10.1007/s10508-020-01660-8 (Epublication ahead of print); Paul Hruz et al., "Growing Pains: Problems with Puberty Suppression in Treating Gender Dysphoria," *New Atlantis*, Spring 2017, www.thenewatlantis.com/publications /growing-pains; Guido Giovanardi, "Buying Time or Arresting Development? The Dilemma

of Administering Hormone Blockers in Trans Children and Adolescents," *Porto Biomedical Journal* 2, no. 5 (2017): 15–56; Sahar Sadjadi, "The Endocrinologist's Office—Puberty Suppression: Saving Children from a Natural Disaster?," *Journal of Medical Humanities* 34, no. 2 (2013): 255–60. On top of these potential problems, most preteens who go on puberty blockers will end up going on CHT, which brings its own set of health risks. In a recently published study, 125 of 143 (= 87 percent) children who were placed on puberty suppression drugs chose to go on to CHT (see Brik et. al., "Trajectories of Adolescents," 3). This is quite remarkable, since 61–88 percent of children with dysphoria will end up desisting after they go through puberty. Puberty itself most often plays a significant role in diminishing or even fully alleviating a child's dysphoria. Blocking puberty might be halting the very biological mechanism that takes dysphoria away, and the statistics above bear this out.

43. Brik et al., "Trajectories of Adolescents," 2.

44. Paul Bracchi, "Mixed-Up Five-Year-Olds and the Alarming Growth of the Gender Identity Industry," *Daily Mail*, February 25, 2012, www.dailymail.co.uk/news/article -2106215/Mixed-year-olds-alarming-growth-gender-identity-industry.html.

45. Carl Heneghan, "Gender-Affirming Hormone in Children and Adolescents," *BMJ EBM Spotlight*, February 25, 2019, blogs.bmj.com/bmjebmspotlight/2019/02/25/ gender-affirming-hormone-in-children-and-adolescents-evidence-review/.

46. "The Role of the GP in Caring for Gender-Questioning and Transgender Patients: RCGP Position Statement," June 2019, Royal College of General Practitioners, www.rcgp.org.uk /-/media/Files/Policy/A-Z-policy/2019/RCGP-transgender-care-position-statement-june -2019.ashx?la=en.

47. Hruz et al., "Growing Pains."

48. Olson-Kennedy et al., "Physiologic Response," 397–401; Johanna Olson-Kennedy et al., "Chest Reconstruction and Chest Dysphoria in Transmasculine Minors and Young Adults: Comparisons of Nonsurgical and Postsurgical Cohorts," *JAMA Pediatrics* 172, no. 5 (2018): 431–36.

49. "Dr. Johanna Olson-Kennedy Explains Why Mastectomies for Healthy Teen Girls Is No Big Deal," YouTube, November 5, 2018, https://youtu.be/5Y6espcXPJk. The CEO of the UK-based Gendered Intelligence trans* advocacy organization recently defended allowing adolescents to make irreversible medical alterations of their bodies by comparing it to getting a tattoo or becoming pregnant (Jay Stewart, "Frequently Asked Questions about Children's Gender Identity and Expression," *Journal of Child Psychotherapy* 44, no. 1 [2018]: 52).

50. See the "Guideline for Gender Dysphoria: Frequently Asked Questions" sheet put out by the Oregon state government: www.oregon.gov/oha/HPA/DSI-HERC/FactSheets/Gender -dysphoria.pdf. See also Christine Milrod and Dan H. Karasic, "Age Is Just a Number: WPATH-Affiliated Surgeons' Experiences and Attitudes Toward Vaginoplasty in Transgender Females Under 18 Years of Age in the United States," *Journal of Sexual Medicine* 14, no. 4 (2017): 624–34.

51. Here are three separate cases: (1) "Mother Describes Why California Social Workers Put Her Daughter in Foster Care," Kelsey Coalition, October 31, 2019, www.kelseycoalition.org /pubs/Mother-Describes-Why-California-Social-Workers-Put-Her-Daughter-in-Foster-Care--. (2) Bradford Richardson, "Religious Parents Lose Custody of Transgender Teen for Refusing Hormone Treatment," *Washington Times*, February 20, 2018, www.washingtontimes.com /news/2018/feb/20/religious-parents-lose-custody-transgender-teen/. (3) Lucas Holtyluwer, "Ohio Father Loses Custody of 14-Year-Old Transgender Child, Could Lose Right to Object to Injections or Surgery," *Post Millennial*, May 2, 2019, www.thepostmillennial.com/ohio -father-loses-custody-of-14-year-old-transgender-child-could-lose-right-to-object-to -injections-or-surgery/.

52. Charlie Evans, "The Medicalization of Gender Nonconforming Children, and the Vulnerability of Lesbian Youth," Medium.com, September 8, 2019, https://medium.com /@charlie.evans/the-medicalization-of-gender-non-conforming-children-and-the -vulnerability-of-lesbian-youth-10d4ac517e8e.

53. Other websites that bolster the findings of Littman's study include transgendertrend .com, 4thwavenow.com, parentsofrogdkids.com, kelseycoalition.org, and youthtranscriticalprofessionals.org.

54. One of the catalysts for this concern was the release of a documentary titled *The Trans Train* (season 20, episode 12, of a Swedish documentary series called *Uppdrag Granskning*), which can now be viewed on YouTube (with English subtitles): https://youtu.be/ sJGAoNbHYzk. For a brief overview, see Richard Orange, "Teenage Transgender Row Splits Sweden as Dysphoria Diagnoses Soar by 1,500%," *Guardian*, February 22, 2020, www.theguardian.com/society/2020/feb/22/ssweden-teenage-transgender-row-dysphoria -diagnoses-soar.

55. See, among others, Jean Twenge, *iGen: Why Today's Super-Connected Kids Are Growing Up Less Rebellious, More Tolerant, Less Happy—and Completely Unprepared for Adulthood—and What That Means for the Rest of Us* (New York: Atria Books, 2017).

CHAPTER 11: TRANSITIONING AND CHRISTIAN DISCIPLESHIP

1. Both of these quotes are taken from the descriptions of gender dysphoria documented in chapter 2.

2. Aron Hirt-Manheimer, "'A Dead Son or a Living Daughter': A Conversation with the Mother of a Transgender Child," Reform Judaism, July 15, 2016, https://reformjudaism.org /blog/2016/07/15/dead-son-or-living-daughter-conversation-mother-transgender-child.

3. "Parents of a Transgender Child Ask, 'Did We Want a Living Son or a Dead Daughter?'," *National Post*, February 25, 2016, https://nationalpost.com/life/parents-of-a-transgender -child-ask-did-we-want-a-living-son-or-a-dead-daughter.

4. Many experts in the field push back against the "transition or suicide" narrative. See Susan Bradley, Ken Zucker, Hayley Wood, Stephen Levine, Heino Meyer-Bahlburg, Susan

Coates, Marina Bonfatto, James Cantor, Robert D'Angelo, Lisa Marchiano, Paul McHugh, J. Michael Bailey, Anastassis Spiliadis, Ray Blanchard, and Paul Hruz, among others.

5. For a review of psychological approaches to relieving gender dysphoria, see Paul Rhodes Eddy, "Reflections on the Debate Concerning the Desistance Rate among Young People with Gender Dysphoria," Center for Faith, Sexuality & Gender, April 2020, www.centerforfaith .com/resources.

6. Mark Yarhouse and Julia Sadusky, "The Complexities of Gender Identity," in *Understanding Transgender Identities: Four Views*, ed. James K. Beilby and Paul Rhodes Eddy (Grand Rapids, MI: Baker, 2019), 113.

7. Yarhouse and Sadusky, "Complexities of Gender Identity," 112.

8. Scholars in the trans* conversation are giving increasing attention to ethical concerns. See, for example, L. J. Vrouenraets et al., "Early Medical Treatment of Children and Adolescents with Gender Dysphoria: An Empirical Ethical Study," *Journal of Adolescent Health* 57, no. 4 (2015): 367–73; M. R. Bizic et al., "Gender Dysphoria: Bioethical Aspects of Medical Treatment," Biomed Research International (2018), 9652305, https://pubmed.ncbi.nlm.nih. gov/30009180/. This is certainly a trend to be welcomed. But the nature of ethical lenses is an important question, because not all ethical systems are created equal. Human ethical systems are generally built around three primary pillars: individual autonomy, community, and divinity (R. A. Shweder et al., "The 'Big Three' of Morality (Autonomy, Community, and Divinity), and the 'Big Three' Explanations of Suffering," in *Morality and Health*, ed. A. Brandt and P. Rozin [New York: Routledge, 1997], 119–72). Most contemporary Western secular ethical systems privilege individual autonomy, give little attention to values of community (such as authority and loyalty), and neglect—or outright reject—consideration of the divine. This makes for a significantly lopsided ethical system. By contrast, a Christian ethic of care for trans* people is anchored in the trinitarian God (the divine), formed within the context of Christian community, and woven into the lives of individual Christ-followers, for whom the modern quest for autonomous liberty should be submitted to the lordship of Jesus and his call to "seek first the kingdom of God and His righteousness" (Matt. 6:33 NKJV).

9. Steve Wilkens, ed., *Christian Ethics: Four Views* (Downers Grove, IL: IVP Academic, 2017).

10. SRS and CHT go hand in hand, since CHT is a lifelong therapy. Much of what I say about SRS in this section equally applies to CHT.

11. Peggy T. Cohen-Kettenis and S. H. M. van Goozen, "Sex Reassignment of Adolescent Transsexuals: A Follow-Up Study," *Journal of the American Academy of Child and Adolescent Psychiatry* 36, no. 2 (1997): 263–71; A. Johansson et al., "A Five-Year Follow-Up Study of Swedish Adults with Gender Identity Disorder," *Archives of Sexual Behavior* 39, no. 6 (2010): 1429–37; Lea Karpel et al., "Psychological and Sexual Well Being of 207 Transsexuals after Sex Reassignment in France" [French], *Annales Medico Psychologiques* 173 (2015): 511–19; Anne A. Lawrence, "Factors Associated with Satisfaction or Regret Following Male-to-Female

Sex Reassignment Surgery," *Archives of Sexual Behavior* 32, no. 4 (2003): 299–315; Tim C. van de Grift et al., "Surgical Satisfaction, Quality of Life, and Their Association After Gender-Affirming Surgery: A Follow-Up Study," *Journal of Sex and Marital Therapy* 44, no. 2 (2018): 138–48.

12. One such study led to the discontinuation of SRS at Johns Hopkins Hospital while the hospital was under the direction of Paul McHugh. See Jon K. Meyer and Donna J. Reter, "Sex Reassignment. Follow-Up," *Archives of General Psychiatry* 36, no. 9 (1979): 1010–15. See also Paul R. McHugh, "Surgical Sex: Why We Stopped Doing Sex Change Operations," First Things (November 2004), www.firstthings.com/article/2004/11/surgical-sex.

13. B. Udeze et al., "Psychological Functions in Male-to-Female Transsexual People Before and After Surgery," *Sexual and Relationship Therapy* 23, no. 2 (2008): 141–45; J. Barrett. "Psychological and Social Function before and after Phalloplasty," *International Journal of Transgenderism* 2, no. 1 (1998): 1–8; M. W. Ross and J. A. Need, "Effects of Adequacy of Gender Reassignment Surgery on Psychological Adjustment: A Follow-Up of Fourteen Male-to-Female Patients," *Archives of Sexual Behavior* 18, no. 2 (1989): 145–53.

14. A number of studies on medical transition outcomes highlight the challenge of "low quality evidence"; see A. J. M. White Hughto and S. I. Reisner, "A Systematic Review of the Effects of Hormone Therapy on Psychological Functioning and Quality of Life in Transgender Individuals," *Transgender Health* 1, no. 1 (2016): 21–31; M. Hassan Murad et al., "Hormonal Therapy and Sex Reassignment: A Systematic Review and Meta-Analysis of Quality of Life and Psychosocial Outcomes," *Clinical Endocrinology* 72, no. 2 (2010): 214. Methodological problems often plague social science research among diverse, underrepresented populations. See K. R. Kuhlman et al., "Testing Plausible Biopsychosocial Models in Diverse Community Samples: Common Pitfalls and Strategies," *Psychoneuroendocrinology* 107 (2019): 191–200.

15. Yarhouse and Sadusky, "Complexities of Gender Identity," 116.

16. C. Dhejne et al., "Long-Term Follow-Up of Transsexual Persons Undergoing Sex Reassignment Surgery: Cohort Study in Sweden," *PLoS One* 6, no. 2 (2011): e16885.

17. Rikke Kildevaeld Simonsen et al., "Long-Term Follow-Up of Individuals Undergoing Sex Reassignment Surgery: Psychiatric Morbidity and Mortality," *Nordic Journal of Psychiatry* 70, no. 4 (2016): 241–47.

CHAPTER 12: PRONOUNS, BATHROOMS, AND SLEEPING SPACES

1. Some people use the phrase "preferred pronouns" in this conversation, but most trans* people I talk to don't like this phrase. It comes off as invalidating the depths of a person's experience, as if they woke up one day and simply preferred one pronoun over another—like preferring Pepsi over Coke. One of my trans* friends compares their pronouns to writing with their right hand and not left hand. They don't just "prefer" to write with their right hand.

2. John Piper, "He or She? How Should I Refer to Transgender Friends?" *Desiring God*, July 16, 2015, www.desiringgod.org/interviews/he-or-she-how-should-i-refer-to-transgender -friends.

3. "The Nashville Statement," A Coalition for Biblical Sexuality, https://cbmw.org/nashville -statement/.

4. Laurie Higgins, "Christians Caving to 'Trans'-Cultists' Language Rules," Illinois Family Institute, November 26, 2019, https://illinoisfamily.org/homosexuality/christians-caving -to-trans-cultists-language-rules/.

5. Personal communication.

6. Quoted in Greg Coles, "What Pronouns Should Christians Use for Transgender People?" Center for Faith, Sexuality & Gender, 1–16, www.centerforfaith.com/resources, 1–16.

7. Piper, "He or She?"

8. Geoffrey Chaucer, *The Canterbury Tales* I.664.

9. Mark Yarhouse, "Understanding the Transgender Phenomenon," *Christianity Today*, June 8, 2015, www.christianitytoday.com/ct/2015/july-august/understanding-transgender-gender -dysphoria.html.

10. Coles, "Pronouns," 12–13.

11. There's a debate about whether misgendering someone could actually lead to arrest under Bill C-16. According to one lawyer, arrest and jailtime is a possibility (Nina Dragicevic, "Canada's Gender Identity Rights Bill C-16 Explained," CBC, November 2, 2018, www.cbc.ca/cbcdocspov/m/features/canadas-gender-identity-rights-bill-c-16-explained). Here are a couple court cases that involved misgendering; to my knowledge, no one has been sent to jail yet: Morgane Oger v. Bill Whatcott, [2018] 2 BCHRT 131, www.canlii.org/en/bc /bchrt/doc/2018/2018bchrt131/2018bchrt131.html; K.W. v. School District P. and J.B., [2018] BCHRT 144, www.canlii.org/en/bc/bchrt/doc/2018/2018bchrt144/2018bchrt144.html.

12. These dictionaries include *Cambridge Dictionary* online, *Dictionary.com*, and *Merriam-Webster*.

13. Another example: Imagine meeting trans* supermodel Andreja Pejić for lunch. (Unless you checked her chromosomes, you wouldn't know she was biologically male.) Andreja has arrived early and is sitting at a table. You enter the restaurant and tell the host that your guest already has a table for you two. The host asks, "Where's your friend?" You probably wouldn't say, "He's over there at the table in the back," regardless of your feelings about pronoun use. You'd say, "She's over there at the table in the back," since the host isn't going to be looking around for a Y chromosome or a penis but for someone who looks male or female. Pronouns might be applied to how someone socially presents themselves, not necessarily to a person's biological sex in every case.

14. "they," pronoun, *Merriam-Webster*, www.merriam-webster.com/dictionary/they.

15. Thanks to my good friend Greg Coles for suggesting this idea.

16. Also, we shouldn't fool ourselves into thinking that any perfect policy or amount of supervision will make it impossible for students to have sex with each other. Those who really want to hook up with each other at summer camp will find a way. Sex-segregated sleeping arrangements aren't going to stop them. I mean, if I had a nickel for every story I've heard—or been a part of—as a teenager …

CONCLUSION: OUTRAGEOUS LOVE

1. Ann P. Haas, Philip L. Rodgers, and Jody L. Herman, *Suicide Attempts among Transgender and Gender Non-Conforming Adults: Findings of the National Transgender Discrimination Survey* (New York: American Foundation for Suicide Prevention / Los Angeles: Williams Institute, 2014), http://williamsinstitute.law.ucla.edu/wp-content/uploads/AFSP-Williams-Suicide-Report-Final.pdf.

APPENDIX: SUICIDALITY AND TRANS* PEOPLE

1. Jennifer Schreiber and Larry Culpepper, "Suicidal Ideation and Behavior in Adults," UpToDate, September 17, 2019, www.uptodate.com/contents/suicidal-ideation-and-behavior-in-adults.

2. Kim-San Lim et al., "Global Lifetime and 12-Month Prevalence of Suicidal Behavior, Deliberate Self-Harm and Non-Suicidal Self-Injury in Children and Adolescents between 1989 and 2018: A Meta-Analysis," *International Journal of Environmental Research and Public Health* 16, no. 22 (2019): 4581.

3. Lars Wichstrøm notes that nonsuicidal self-injury and suicide attempts are "only partly overlapping phenomena, and not necessarily just representing different degrees of suicidality" ("Predictors of Non-Suicidal Self-Injury Versus Attempted Suicide: Similar or Different?" *Archives of Suicide Research* 13, no. 2 [2009]: 105).

4. One recent study of adolescent cutting proposed that, far from being related to suicide attempts, such instances of self-harm "can paradoxically be understood as survival techniques," where one is deliberately "harming oneself to feel less pain" (D. Le Breton, "Understanding Skin-Cutting in Adolescence: Sacrificing a Part to Save the Whole," *Body and Society* 24, no. 1–2 [2018]: 33).

5. S. Bachmann, "Epidemiology of Suicide and the Psychiatric Perspective," *International Journal of Environmental Research and Public Health* 15, no. 7 (2018).

6. J. M. Grant et al., *Injustice at Every Turn: A Report of the National Transgender Discrimination Survey* (Washington, DC: National Center for Transgender Equality and National Gay and Lesbian Task Force, 2011), 2, www.thetaskforce.org/wp-content/uploads/2019/07/ntds_full.pdf. Other publications on trans* suicide attempt rates have used the data from this study. For example, Ann P. Haas, Philip L. Rodgers, and Jody L. Herman,

Suicide Attempts among Transgender and Gender Non-Conforming Adults: Findings of the National Transgender Discrimination Survey (New York: American Foundation for Suicide Prevention/Los Angeles: Williams Institute, 2014).

7. J. L. Herman, B. D. M. Wilson, and T. Becker, "Demographic and Health Characteristics of Transgender Adults in California: Findings from the 2015–2016 California Health Interview Survey," *Policy Brief—UCLA Center for Health Policy Research* (October 31, 2017), 5, http://healthpolicy.ucla.edu/publications/Documents/PDF/2017/transgender-policybrief -oct2017.pdf.

8. B. Wilson et al., *Characteristics and Mental Health of Gender Nonconforming Adolescents in California* (Los Angeles: UCLA Center for Health Policy Research / Williams Institute, 2017), 2–3.

9. A. Perez-Brumer et al., "Prevalence and Correlates of Suicidal Ideation Among Transgender Youth in California: Findings from a Representative, Population-Based Sample of High School Students," *Journal of the Academy of Child and Adolescent Psychiatry* 56, no. 9 (2017): 739–46.

10. M. Becker et al., "Characteristics of Children and Adolescents with Gender Dysphoria Referred to the Hamburg Gender Identity Clinic [English Translation]" *Praxis der Kinderpsychologie und Kinderpsychiatrie* 63, no. 6 (2014): 486–509; V. Holt et al., "Young People with Features of Gender Dysphoria: Demographics and Associated Difficulties," *Clinical Child Psychology and Psychiatry* 21, no. 1 (2016): 108–118; K. Khatchadourian et al, "Clinical Management of Youth with Gender Dysphoria in Vancouver," *Journal of Pediatrics* 164, no. 4 (2014): 906–11; E. Skagerberg et al., "Self-Harming Thoughts and Behaviors in a Group of Children and Adolescents with Gender Dysphoria," *International Journal of Transgenderism* 14, no. 2 (2013): 86–92; R. Kaltiala-Heino et al., "Two Years of Gender Identity Service for Minors: Overrepresentation of Natal Girls with Severe Problems in Adolescent Development," *Child Adolescent Psychiatry and Mental Health* 9 (2015): 9. All these studies are cited in M. Aitken et al., "Self-Harm and Suicidality in Children Referred for Gender Dysphoria," *Journal of the American Academy of Child and Adolescent Psychiatry* 55, no. 6 (2016): 513.

11. M. K. Nock et al., "Prevalence, Correlates, and Treatment of Lifetime Suicidal Behavior among Adolescents: Results from the National Comorbidity Survey Replication Adolescent Supplement," *JAMA Psychiatry* 70, no. 3 (2013): 303.

12. From Kevin Caruso, "Suicide Causes," suicide.org, http://suicide.org/suicide-causes.html.

13. T. A. Becerra-Culqui et al., "Mental Health of Transgender and Gender Nonconforming Youth Compared with Their Peers," *Pediatrics* 141, no. 5 (2018): e20173845; L. D. de Freitas et al., "Psychiatric Disorders in Individuals Diagnosed with Gender Dysphoria: A Systematic Review," *Psychiatry and Clinical Neurosciences* 74, no. 2 (2020): 99–104; S. L. Reisner et al., "Mental Health of Transgender Youth in Care at an Adolescent Urban Community Health Center: A Matched Retrospective Cohort Study," *Journal of Adolescent Health* 56, no. 3 (2015): 274–79; Melina Sevlever and Heino F. L. Meyer-Bahlburg, "Late-Onset Transgender Identity Development of Adolescents in Psychotherapy for Mood and

Anxiety Problems: Approach to Assessment and Treatment," *Archives of Sexual Behavior* 48, no. 7 (2019): 1993–2001.

14. Kenneth J. Zucker, "Adolescents with Gender Dysphoria: Reflections on Some Contemporary Clinical and Research Issues,"*Archives of Sexual Behavior* 48, no. 5 (2019), 1986-87.

15. These statistics are taken from Zucker's ("Adolescents with Gender Dysphoria," 1985–86) summary of data reported in N. M. de Graaf et al., "Suicidality in Adolescents Diagnosed with Gender Dysphoria: A Cross-National, Cross-Clinic Comparative Analysis," paper presented at the meeting of the European Association for Transgender Health in Rome, Italy, 2019. Zucker was one of the authors of the de Graaf et al. study.

16. Haas, Rodgers, and Herman, *Suicide Attempts among Transgender and Gender Non-Conforming Adults*, 3–4.

17. Again, the distinction between completed suicides and suicide attempts is very important. For example, in an article that refers to the tragic suicide of trans* teen Leelah Alcorn, gender-affirmative researchers Dan Karasic and Diane Ehrensaft write of "the alarmingly high suicide rates in LGBT youth" ("We Must Put an End to Gender Conversion Therapy for Kids," *Wired* [July 6, 2015], www.wired.com/2015/07/must-put-end-gender-conversion-therapy-kids/). However, studies that investigated this question have not found a higher rate of completed suicide among LGBT youth than among heterosexual youth. See A. P. Haas et al., "Suicide and Suicide Risk in Lesbian, Gay, Bisexual, and Transgender Populations: Review and Recommendations," *Journal of Homosexuality* 58, no. 1 (2011): 15–17; K. A. Clark et al., "Estimate of Lesbian, Gay, Bisexual and Transgender Youth Suicide Is Inflated," *Journal of Adolescent Health* 64, no. 6 (2019): 810.

18. Zucker, "Adolescents with Gender Dysphoria," 1986.

19. J. A. Bridge et al., "Association Between the Release of Netflix's *13 Reasons Why* and Suicide Rates in the United States: An Interrupted Time Series Analysis," *Journal of the American Academy of Child and Adolescent Psychiatry* 59, no. 2 (2020): 236–43.

20. Raymond P. Tucker et al., "The Relationship Between Suicide-Related Exposure and Personal History of Suicidal Behavior in Transgender and Gender-Diverse Veterans," *LGBT Health* 6, no. 7 (2019): 335–41; J. R. Randall, N. C. Nickel, and I. Colman, "Contagion from Peer Suicidal Behavior in a Representative Sample of American Adolescents," *Journal of Affective Disorders* 86 (2015): 219–25.

21. Keith Hawton and Kathryn Williams, "Influences of the Media on Suicide: Researchers, Policy Makers, and Media Personnel Need to Collaborate on Guidelines," *British Medical Journal* 325 (2002): 1374–75. See also J. Pirkis et al., "Media Influences on Suicidal Thoughts and Behaviors," in *International Handbook of Suicide Prevention*, 2nd ed., ed. R. C. O'Connor and J. Pirkis (Malden, MA: Wiley-Blackwell, 2016), 743–57.

22. S. Kennebeck and L. Bonin, "Suicidal Behavior in Children and Adolescents: Epidemiology and Risk Factors," UpToDate (last updated November 9, 2019), www.uptodate.com/contents

/suicidal-behavior-in-children-and-adolescents-epidemiology-and-risk-factors?search=suicidal
-behavior-in-children-and-adolescents-epidemiologyand-risk-factors&source=search
_result&selectedTitle=2~150&usage_type=default&display_rank=2. See also S. Abrutyn and
A. Mueller, "Are Suicidal Behaviors Contagious? Using Longitudinal Data to Examine Suicide
Suggestion," *American Sociological Review* 79, no. 2 (2014): 211–27; A. S. Mueller and S.
Abrutyn, "Suicidal Disclosures among Friends: Using Social Network Data to Understand
Suicide Contagion," *Journal of Health and Social Behavior* 56, no. 1 (2015): 131–48; S. C.
Collings et al., *Media Influences on Suicidal Behaviour: An Interview Study of Young People
in New Zealand* (Auckland: National Centre of Mental Health Research, Information and
Development, 2011), www.tepou.co.nz/uploads/files/resource-assets/media-influences-on
-suicidal-behaviour.pdf.

23. E. Moore, A. Wisniewski, and A. Dobs, "Endocrine Treatment of Transsexual People: A
Review of Treatment Regimens, Outcomes, and Adverse Effects," *Journal of Endocrinology
and Metabolism* 88, no. 8 (2003): 3467–73.

24. In one recent follow-up study, 25 percent of those who surgically transitioned were
"dissatisfied" with the results. L. Karpel et al., "Psychological and Sexual Well Being of 207
Transsexuals after Sex Reassignment in France [French]," *Annales Medico Psychologiques* 173
(2015): 511.

25. A number of studies have reported that transition regret appears most often among
MtF trans* persons, especially those experiencing late-onset gender dysphoria. See
M. L. Djordjevic et al., "Reversal Surgery in Regretful Male-to-Female Transsexuals
after Sex Reassignment Surgery," *Journal of Sexual Medicine* 13, no. 6 (2016): 1000–07;
R. Blanchard et al., "Prediction of Regrets in Postoperative Transsexuals," *Canadian
Journal of Psychiatry* 34, no. 1 (1989): 43–45.

26. H. Asscheman et al., "A Long-term Follow-Up Study of Mortality in Transsexuals
Receiving Treatment with Cross-Sex Hormones," *European Journal of Endocrinology* 164,
no. 4 (2011): 635–42; C. Dhejne et al., "Long-Term Follow-Up of Transsexual Persons
Undergoing Sex Reassignment Surgery: Cohort Study in Sweden," *PLoS One* 6, no. 2
(2011): e16885. The significantly higher rates of suicidal phenomena following medical
transition led Dhejne et al. to conclude that sex reassignment "may not suffice as treatment
for transsexualism, and should inspire improved psychiatric and somatic care after sex
reassignment for this patient group." While suicidal ideation appears to be higher among
MtF trans* people, the suicide attempt rate appears higher among FtM trans* people. See
N. Adams, M. Hitomi, and C. Moody, "Varied Reports of Adult Transgender Suicidality:
Synthesizing and Describing the Peer-Reviewed and Gray Literature," *Transgender Health*
2, no. 1 (2017). These higher rates of suicidal phenomena may be tied to the fact that
trans* people who have medically transitioned continue to report lower quality of life levels
compared to the general populace. See A. Kuhn et al., "Quality of Life 15 Years after Sex
Reassignment Surgery for Transsexualism," *Fertility and Sterility* 92, no. 5 (2009): 1685–89.

27. The minority stress theory was originally formulated by Ilan H. Meyer with regard to lesbian, gay, and bisexual populations; see "Prejudice, Social Stress, and Mental Health in Lesbian, Gay and Bisexual Populations: Conceptual Issues and Research Evidence," *Psychological Bulletin* 129, no. 5 (2003): 674–97. More recently, it has been applied to trans* people; see R. J. Testa et al., "Development of the Gender Minority Stress and Resilience Measure," *Psychology of Sexual Orientation and Gender Diversity* 2, no .1 (2015): 65–77.

28. It appears that depression is a key link between social rejection/ostracism and suicidality. See E. A. Tebbe and B. Moradi, "Suicide Risk in Trans Populations: An Application of Minority Stress Theory," *Journal of Counseling Psychology* 63, no. 5 (2016): 520–33.

29. Most gender-affirmative advocates attribute virtually all mental health issues and co-occurring psychopathologies to the effects of the minority stress that trans* people experience living in a transphobic culture. See, for example, M. L. Hendricks and R. J. Testa, "A Conceptual Framework for Clinical Work with Transgender and Gender Nonconforming Clients: An Adaptation of the Minority Stress Model," *Professional Psychology: Research and Practice* 43, no. 5 (2012): 460–67. One of the unfortunate effects of this tendency has been the large-scale abandonment of serious research on effective psychological interventions for those suffering from gender dysphoria. Leigh Spivey and Laura Edwards-Leeper—two leading gender-affirmative researchers—have recently admitted that there is a "dearth" of empirical data on psychological interventions and that this is "surprising," given the "elevated rates of psychological distress among transgender youth" ("Future Directions in Affirmative Psychological Interventions with Transgender Children and Adolescents," *Journal of Clinical Child and Adolescent Psychology* 48, no. 2 [2019]: 343–56 [343]). Other experts question the uncritical assumption that the minority stress theory can account for virtually all mental health issues among trans* people. See, for example, Sevlever and Meyer-Bahlburg, "Late-Onset Transgender Identity Development of Adolescents."

30. Helen's perspective is quoted at length by psychologist Lisa Marchiano in an online roundtable discussion: "Suicidality in Trans-Identified Youth and the Question of Media Ethics," October 17, 2016, 4thWaveNow, https://4thwavenow.com/2016/10/17/suicidality-in-trans-identified-youth-the-question-of-media-ethics-a-roundtable-discussion/.

31. Greg Lukianoff and Jonathan Haidt, *The Coddling of the American Mind: How Good Intentions and Bad Ideas Are Setting Up a Generation for Failure* (New York: Penguin, 2018).

32. Nassim Nicholas Taleb, *Antifragility: Things that Gain from Disorder* (New York: Random House, 2014).